Where Eagles
Speedway in Moth

Jim Henry

London League Publications Ltd

Where Eagles Dared
Speedway in Motherwell

© Jim Henry
Foreword © Bluey Scott

A CIP catalogue record for this book is available from the British Library.

Published in September 2021 by London League Publications Ltd, PO Box 65784, London NW2 9NS

ISBN: 978-1-909885-27-1

Cover design by Stephen McCarthy Graphic Design
46, Clarence Road, London N15 5BB.

Editing and layout by Peter Lush

Printed and bound in Great Britain by Ashford Colour Press Ltd, Gosport, Hants PO13 0FW

Foreword

I am pleased to be able to write a short foreword to this book which records the history of the Lanarkshire Eagles. I have fond memories of my days in Scotland, especially in my days when I raced speedway bikes for a living.

I came over from Australia at the start of the 1951 season hoping to secure a place in the Edinburgh team alongside my friend Jack Young. However, the Monarchs had their team put together and I had to move on.

As luck would have it I was given the opportunity to try out at the new league track in Motherwell. I was signed by the Lanarkshire based promotion and was put straight into the Lanarkshire Eagles team at second reserve beside fellow Aussie Noel Watson.

I struggled a bit, was dropped, then I spent weeks mostly getting a few second halves before I regained my team place in August. Thankfully I managed to impress enough to be invited back to ride for the Eagles in 1952. Again, it took a few weeks to return to the side but once I did, I proved my worth. I was a regular until the track closed at the end of 1954. Sadly, the track didn't see much action apart from a short spell in 1958.

The book records my trials and tribulations and all the bruising falls and crashes as I learned my trade and honed my skills. Despite this I did not, perhaps, fully realise how my efforts were appreciated by the fans. I was even more surprised to find that when I did stay on to finish races the local press thought I wasn't as exciting because I wasn't falling and crashing. So much for "credit where credit is due". I could say I was even more surprised when reports filtered back to me about the heritage event staged in Motherwell and that I was the rider mentioned by folks who had been Eagles fans all those years ago.

I hope you will enjoy this history of the Lanarkshire Eagles which records a time of very happy memories for me.

Bluey Scott
Queensland, Australia
April 2021

Introduction

The town of Motherwell lies in what was the County of Lanarkshire beside the River Clyde and to the south east of Glasgow. Much of Lanarkshire was underlain by of coal, blackband ironstone, ironstone and limestone and was at one time known as the Black County. It is now the administrative centre for the North Lanarkshire Council area which extends northwards from Motherwell. The population is estimated at 32,500 (2016) but sits in a much greater extended conurbation.

It was largely in a rural setting before the arrival of the railways but that was to change and in the mid-1800s Motherwell steadily became one of the major iron and steel producing centres in Scotland. It drew upon indigenous sources for many decades but became steadily more reliant on imported raw materials.

Over the years the town has merged with neighbouring Wishaw to the south east and lies close to Bellshill and New Stevenson.

It was home of the massive Ravenscraig Steel Works whose huge tower helped pick out Motherwell from the M74. The tower has gone and the area is being redeveloped for a number of uses. Dalzell (Dee el) Plate Mills are the only major steel works remaining in Motherwell.

Motorcycle speedway racing came to the UK in 1928 from its acknowledged birthplace in Australia. It was not until 1930 that in came to Motherwell. It was planned to be a practice track and was located on Airbles Road behind the Traction House, a distinctive brick building on Hamilton Road known as Paragon Speedway. It was built by Alfie Williams who group of riders known as The Blantyre Crowd. It is possible a team event featuring Glasgow and Blantyre were staged but no records of meetings there have been found.

A couple of years later, in 1932, a company called Lanarkshire Speedways built a pukka speedway track on the same site. It appears to have been the site of a disused tip. A massive ground collapse probably caused by decaying rubbish required infilling and this delayed the opening meeting until early June. Two of the four planned meetings escaped being rained off. It is known the meetings staged were open events, but little else is recorded. Towards the end of June 1932 plans were announced for a new greyhound stadium and speedway in Motherwell came to an end until 1950.

A speedway context for the Eagles era

By 1950, the economy was going a bit better but the immediate post war boom in speedway was probably starting its decline. However, at that time the impending downturn was not envisaged and a growth period was forecast for speedway in Scotland. Some even saw tracks in most of the major Scottish cities in sufficient numbers to set up a separate league. This came to nothing. Speedway was even having a mini revival in Ireland with a track in Belfast and more tracks in Dublin.

The optimism of the post-war boom still remained in 1951 and Motherwell lined up in the revised Division Two alongside Coventry, Cradley Heath, Edinburgh, Fleetwood, Glasgow Ashfield, Glasgow White City, Halifax, Leicester, Liverpool, Newcastle, Norwich, Oxford, Southampton, Stoke, Walthamstow and Yarmouth. Southampton withdrew after a few fixtures. Division One remained the same while Division Three had a change of teams including Plymouth from Division Two.

1952 saw big changes with the Third Division changing to become the Southern League. The top league added 1951 Division Two champions Norwich. Division Two saw changes losing teams so Motherwell faced Coventry, Cradley Heath, Edinburgh, Glasgow Ashfield, Glasgow White City, Leicester, Liverpool, Oxford, Poole, Stoke, and Yarmouth. Poole were the only newcomers. This was a portent of things to come. The losses were down to the falling crowds as other forms of entertainment became popular, especially television. There was also the effect of the Entertainment Tax, which drew significant funds out of the gate money.

1953 saw the Coronation of the new Queen and the advent of the second Elizabethan era. While this generated public acclaim, the rush for television sets and the Entertainment Tax continued to undermine speedway. This season saw another drop in Division Two numbers and Motherwell now faced Coventry, Edinburgh, Glasgow White City, Leicester, Liverpool, Poole, Stoke, Wolverhampton and Yarmouth. New Cross closed in June and Liverpool closed a bit later sending shock waves through the sport.

The winter of 1953–54 was not a rosy break. In 1954 the top league lost Bristol who, together with the remaining 1953 teams and most of the Southern League teams formed the new Division Two. There were only two divisions now. The lower league started out with Motherwell facing Bristol, Coventry, Edinburgh, Exeter, Glasgow White City, Ipswich, Leicester, Oxford, Plymouth, Poole, Rayleigh, Southampton, Swindon, and Wolverhampton. By mid-season, Edinburgh, Glasgow, Plymouth and Wolverhampton had closed. This left Motherwell as the lone Scottish venue. The owners also ran midget cars and the much maligned – in speedway circles – new sport of stock car racing. There is no doubt that Motherwell would have entered Division Two in 1955, but the other teams, all based south of the border, refused to countenance sending their teams north just for one meeting and effectively killed off league speedway in Scotland until 1960.

There is no doubt that Motherwell would have entered Division Two in 1955, but the other teams, all based south of the border, refused to countenance sending their teams north just for one meeting and effectively killed off league speedway in Scotland until 1960.

Jim Henry
June 2021

About the author

A fan of Edinburgh Monarchs since 1961, Jim became interested in speedway history in the 1980s. With Graham Fraser he founded *The Speedway Researcher* magazine and this spawned the website which carries, thanks to many helpful contributors, a large and ever growing record of speedway meetings in the UK since 1928. Jim compiled information for Scottish venues and has written the history of *Glasgow's Speedways 1928 to 1940* and, with Ian Moultray, written *A History of Marine Gardens Speedway*

and *Speedway in Scotland*. He moved on from track raking at Powderhall, Edinburgh to become Clerk of the Course at Powderhall, Shawfield, Armadale and Linlithgow between 1989 and 2014. A retired town planner Jim has been chair of his Local Community Council, is a volunteer at the National Mining Museum Scotland taking a special interest in Mining Memorials in Scotland and is Secretary to the WSRA Members in Scotland Committee. Jim is marred to Anne and they have two sons and four grandchildren..

Acknowledgements

Many people have helped bring this book to fruition. I sat and pulled it together deserting my long-suffering wife Anne. While I was compiling the base information, I was fortunate to be able to call up the help of fellow researchers who were gathering information of about the venues that were of interest to them. I should add the magazines were borrowed from Mike Hunter and Ian Moultray and thank for their help.

I hope the following is a comprehensive list of those who helped fill in the gaps that could not be gleaned from newspapers or the speedway press of the day.

The Scottish track information came from Mike Hunter, Ian Moultray, Derek Carruthers, John Somerville, Dennis Darling, Norrie Tait, Gordon Mitchell, Robin Goodall, Keith Gilbert, Bluey Scott, Norrie Isbister, Tom Blackwood, and Peter Colvin.

South of the border I was helped by Colin Parker, Stuart Stait-Aris and Chris Durno (Coventry), Nigel Nicklin and Roger Beaman, (Cradley Heath); Tony Lethbridge (Exeter); Mike Craven (Fleetwood); Barry Stevenson (Halifax); Roger Thorpe (Ipswich); Alan Jones and Tim Grant (Leicester); Norman Briggs (Liverpool); Barry Wallace and Phil Hood (Newcastle); Bryan Tungate, Mike Kemp, and Mike Gardner (Norwich), Glyn Shailes and Jim Gregory (Oxford); Colin Rugg (Plymouth); Gordon Day and Richard Hine (Poole); Vic Butcher (Southampton); Terry Campbell (Stoke); Rob Bamford (Swindon); Alan Bates (Walthamstow); Mark Sawbridge (Wolverhampton); Keith Farman (Yarmouth).

The foregoing list makes tough reading for me as many of those who helped me are no longer with us.

Others who have helped include Keith Corns, who helped with programme scans and other items, Graham Gleave, Nigel Bird, Les Hawkins, and Arnie Gibbons, together with collectors who helped but wished to remain anonymous.

Matt Jackson has kindly given me his bio-pictures of the men who raced for the Eagles much of which has been set aside to concentrate on their time with Motherwell.

I would also like to thank staff in The National Library of Scotland, the Mitchell Library in Glasgow and the North Lanarkshire Heritage Centre in Motherwell.

Newspaper sources include: *The Scotsman; The Edinburgh Evening News; The Edinburgh Evening Dispatch; The (Glasgow) Herald; The Daily Record; The Bulletin and Scots Pictorial; Glasgow Evening Times; Glasgow Evening News; The Glasgow Citizen; The Motherwell Times; The Wishaw Press; The Hamilton Advertiser.*

Magazine sources include: *The Speedway News; The Speedway Star; The Speedway Gazette; The Speedway World; Broadsider.*

Some of the photographs have been supplied by John Somerville from his superb and ever growing speedway photograph archive. Other photographs were supplied by Ian Moultray from the Friends of Edinburgh photograph archive. John Houston has also helped with riders' names for the teams, 1951 to 1954 inclusive. The generous supply of, and permission to use, the photographs is really appreciated because they give faces to the names of many of the Eagles riders and add that special dimension to the book."

Jim Henry
June 2021

London League Publications Ltd would like to thank the staff at Ashford Colour Press for printing the book, and Steve McCarthy for designing the cover.

Contents

Chapter 8 was written by Matt Jackson.

Abbreviations:

Ch: Challenge match
NLD2: National League Division 2
NT: National Trophy
NS: North Shield

SC: Scottish Cup
4TT: Four team tournament
LC: Lanarkshire Cup
QC: Queen's Cup

Bonus points are shown in the text as '+1' after the rider's actual score in the meeting. They are awarded to a rider who follows a team-mate home in first & second or second & third places. The riders are paid for them and they count in their individual averages, but not in a team score.

Programmes from meetings when Motherwell
visited Edinburgh and the two Glasgow teams.
(Courtesy FOES and Keith Corns)

1. 1950: Open meetings

The Lanarkshire Eagles opened for business on Friday 14 July 1950 with a challenge match against a watered-down Newcastle Diamonds League side. The first Eagles side featured three Glasgow Tigers heat leaders, Gordon McGregor, Tommy Miller and Junior Bainbridge with Newcastle assets Tommy Bateman, Don Lawson, Ernie Brecknell and Don Wilkinson and Scottish junior Jim Blyth completing the team. The promotion started out without a rider on their books, but within a few days they had signed a couple of Australians, Noel Watson and Clive Gressor. Most of the meetings featured a makeshift Eagles outfit drawing upon riders based in Scotland and others from south of the border. An assortment of riders staffed the representatives of Scotland's Black County racing against scratch and Second Division teams with a varying degree of success.

July

On 14 July the Motherwell track, The Stadium, at Milton Street, was formally opened. The honours were performed by John Mann CBE, Convener of Lanarkshire County Council. He was presented with a gold watch on behalf of the promoters by Margaret Gray, daughter of one of the directors, Alan Gray. Mr Mann was delighted to open the track and recalled how the 13 acre derelict colliery had been transformed.

Baillie Fox, deputising for Provost Crichton, added his best wishes for the new venture on behalf of Motherwell and Wishaw Town Council.

The racing action thrilled the 12,000 or so paying spectators. The makeshift home side triumphed 48–36 against Newcastle. However, pundits thought the track – 430 yards – was too big, causing processional races. Also, the dog track between the racing and spectators spoiled the fans' enjoyment and prevented close scrutiny of the racing.

Newcastle's Frank Hodgson won the first race from Gordon McGregor and Tommy Bateman. The Eagles guest rider, Glasgow Tigers' Tommy Miller, set the track record in heat three. The first attempt to run the race saw Wilf Jay tip Will Lowther's back wheel, sending both riders flying. Lowther missed one outing due to injury.

Tommy Miller scored 11 points and was the 'home' star, however Newcastle's Derick Close raced through the card unbeaten. Tommy faced Frank Hodgson in the most thrilling race of the night. Earlier 'Atomic' Tommy had thrilled the crowd by overhauling Son Mitchell. Oddly, Tommy failed to reach the second half final, when 'filled in' (blinded) with cinders and tailed off out of the race.

On 21 July, the Motherwell promotion staged its first individual meeting, which was watched by 15,000 fans. Australians Noel Watson and Clive Gressor, both signed earlier in the week, gave the Eagles two of their men in the field. Prior to joining the Eagles, Noel was an Ashfield asset and was signed on the recommendation of the Giants' star man Ken Le Breton.

Edinburgh Monarchs' Jack Young completed a faultless 15 point maximum to win the Gala Cup. Young disposed of his main challenger, Ashfield Giants' Merv Harding. After a three lap struggle chasing hard after Young, Harding's machine seemed to slow. A flat tyre had prevented Merv continuing his challenge. Some spectators thought second finisher Merv, had given up when he saw he was not gaining on the Monarch.

Newcastle's Don Wilkinson gave Young a race for a lap or so in heat 18, but a fall ended his challenge. Harding was runner-up with 14 points which included a lucky last race win when the less experienced Clive Gressor fell while ahead. Edinburgh's Harold Fairhurst hit the fence in heat 12 and fell. He pulled out of the meeting after Len Nicholson hit and wrecked his bike. The expected assault on the track record never materialised.

Highlight of the meeting was heat 19, when Eddie Lack flew from third to first on the first bend of lap four, picking off both Bob Lovell and Peter Dykes with an outside run. The Gala Cup was presented to Jack Young by fellow Australian, Glasgow Tigers' Junior Bainbridge.

The local press, having seen two meetings, commented that speedway had a big future in Lanarkshire, but closer finishing was needed if interest has to be kept going until the league series was started.

A wet day on 28 July held back the crowd to 12,000, and saw another makeshift Eagles side staffed by guests. They included Cradley Heath's Frank Young, the brother of Edinburgh star Jack. However, unlike the opening event, this side had two Motherwell men. Former Sydney bus conductor Watson fell after crossing the line at the end of heat eight, but he was not injured and won his next outing.

The North of England side featured Cradley Heath's star, midlander Alan Hunt. The racing thrilled the public, and, that is all that matters. Hunt showed his liking for The Stadium track and won all his races. He beat Derick Close in a match race which saw the two riders side-by-side for almost all the distance. It was only a late surge by Hunt that took him to the flag by a length.

The Eagles' guest Junior Bainbridge, who had driven up overnight from Plymouth thought the track needed serious attention and said that he would not ride there again until it was fixed.

August

On 4 August, the Eagles faced a side called The Rest. The fans saw the Eagles lose Clive Gressor in heat two when he crashed into fellow Eagle Noel Watson's machine which was lying on the second bend. Gressor suffered knee and wrist injuries. Noel completed a hat-trick of falls and scored only a single point from one completed outing. Clive's remaining rides were shared between Don Wilkinson and Joe Ferguson.

Wilkinson rode well, including a neat heat two effort on the corners, which made up for a poor start. In this heat Don came through from the back to beat Larry Lazarus. He became Eagles' joint top scorer with Gordon McGregor, on 11 points. Unfortunately, Don's good form, which included a win in the reserves race, came to an end in the second half trophy event. He suffered a hard fall after his bike picked up and threw him off onto the concrete starting gate area. Don managed a reassuring wave from the stretcher as he was carried off for treatment.

The loss of Clive and Noel due to falls were probably not the main cause of the Eagles' 44–39 defeat. Ernie Brecknell's nightmare evening was another big contributing factor. Normally worth double figures, Ernie had a fall and two engine failures which pegged back his score to two points.

The Eagles' fans went home happy because Gordon McGregor won the Bothwell Scratch Race. He came from the back, and picked off an opponent in each of the last two laps. Junior rider 'Buffalo Bill' Byford brought a touch of the wild-west to Motherwell when he reared at the start of the Junior Scratch and was thrown from the bike. It was noted that about 200 people were removed by the police from the bing (tip) area adjacent to The Stadium.

The following day Motherwell Juniors moved into The Stadium to use the football pitch on the centre green.

Prior to the meeting on 11 August there was a bit of controversy. Ian Hoskins, Glasgow Tigers' promoter, found out that Tommy Miller and Ken McKinlay had been booked in for a match against a full blown Cradley Heath league team. However, he allowed his men to honour the bookings, but both turned in a below par performance. More had been expected from Tommy, who had driven north from an outing at Wembley; however, his gating letting him down. Veteran leg-trailer George Newton won his opening ride for Eagles, passing Gil Craven on the last bend. Eagles' reserve Ernie Brecknell collected a reserve's maximum. He was gifted his second win in heat 13 when both Cradley riders had engine failure.

The expected lowering of the track record did not happen. Despite a fast time in heat one, the old record remained unchanged. The full-strength Heathens side was not seriously challenged by the cobbled together Eagles side and won 49–33. Heathens' Alan Hunt again showed his liking for The Stadium track, and went through the card unbeaten.

Crowds were on the up, but only those on the coal bing outside The Stadium where a view of racing could be obtained free of charge. Yet again the freeloaders were moved on by the police.

Friday 18 August saw another visiting league side, Sheffield Tars. This name was used by the Sheffield team for part of 1950, rather than their usual Tigers. Cradley Heath's Gil Craven answered a late call up to replace Newcastle's Herby King and helped the Eagles to a narrow win. The result was in doubt right to the line in heat 14. Gil gathered 10 points paid 11 for his team and Will Lowther was also paid for the 11 points he gathered.

Best race of the encounter was heat nine when Craven overtook Guy Allott, but his partner, Wilf Jay, could not quite find the horses to complete a 5–1. Top Tar was veteran Len Williams who scored 10 points. Len frequently did well on his visits to Scotland.

Noel Watson bagged five points before a heat six fall put him out of the match. He did come back to make it to the final of the Lowlands Scratch Race.

The track had been improved by the removal of the excessive material from the bends and the slicker than usual surface helped produce a bit better racing. This meeting saw the track lights in use for the first time towards the end of the second half.

On 25 August, a Glasgow based Ashfield Giants Select, missing their top Australian trio of Ken Le Breton, Merv Harding and Keith Gurtner, became the first Scottish opposition for the Eagles. They went away defeated 50–34.

The two opening heats saw fast times from Noel Watson and Don Wilkinson respectively. The track slowed a bit in the ensuing heats as Eagles edged ahead. The scores might have been a bit closer, but for the Giants Select losing Bob Lindsay to an opening ride crash in heat three when three riders hit the deck. Lindsay was adjudged to be the cause of the stoppage and excluded from the rerun. For some reason the reserves did not take the rides Bob missed out.

The Eagles had a few problems and could point to engine troubles for Ernie Brecknell. After overtaking Bruce Semmens, Ernie had been winning by a good margin, but on the last bend his engine failed. He had enough speed and a large enough lead to coast in for third spot. Noel Watson posted his first maximum, albeit a paid one. He scored 10 and two bonus points. Will Lowther was next best for Eagles with 10 points.

Semmens was the top Giant, with 11 points, and his battle with Don Wilkinson in heat four was the race of the night. The two swapped places at each bend to the flag. Geoff Godwin with eight paid nine was next best for the visitors. Another close race was the reserves race won by Jim Blyth from Niven McCreadie. Rain just before heat 10 put a damper on the meeting.

September

On 1 September Tommy Miller and Junior Bainbridge missed out on the Glasgow Tigers Select's visit. The rift between the Tigers' and Eagles' promotions must have been patched up and the two met for the first time. Rain cut the attendance and the stay-away fans missed seeing the Eagles wear their new race jackets for the first time.

The Tigers Select found the Eagles easy prey once they found the measure of the track. Then there was no holding them and the visitors won 47–37. A late surge in the last three heats flattered them a bit. The Eagles were not helped by their riders falling off. Don Lawson fell in heat two. It was initially feared that he had broken his arm, but he returned to score three in his remaining rides.

Clive Gressor was not so lucky. He went to Law Hospital after he crashed into the starting gate, sustaining wrist and leg injuries. Don Wilkinson accompanied Clive to hospital for a check-up. The crash effectively ended the Australian's speedway career in Britain. Noel Watson continued his improvement and ended up as top scorer for Eagles with nine paid 10. Next best was Ernie Brecknell on seven paid eight.

Top scorer for Tigers was Gordon McGregor, a man who starred for Motherwell in coming years. Gordon scored 11 points, losing only to Ernie Brecknell. The next best Tiger was veteran Joe Crowther on 9 paid 10. Joe moved on from Glasgow a few days later and in 1951 become an Eagle.

The following week, 8 September, saw an Edinburgh Monarchs Select become the third and last Scottish side to visit The Stadium in 1950. The meeting saw the Eagles on the end of a thumping 51–33 defeat. In front of another poor crowd, blamed on an unexciting second half, the Monarchs took the lead in heat three and forged ahead from there.

Noel Watson did not sparkle as usual. He struggled a bit, especially on the turns. After an opening heat win, he only managed to add one more point, falling in his last race. Will Lowther was his steady self, missing out on second place in heat one by a proverbial hair's breadth. Guests Ken McKinlay and Ernie Brecknell did well with seven and eight respectively, but didn't bang in home heat leader sized scores. The Eagles' second strings, Tommy Lack and Jim Blyth, also struggled a bit.

Good form was shown by the Monarchs' juniors Harold Booth, Ron Phillips and Bob Mark. Booth, who featured in an exciting heat one tussle with Lowther, was one point short of a maximum while the Phillips and Mark pairing shared 19 points. Experienced Monarch Eddie Lack also collected 11 points. The Eagles were well out of the running at the end of 14 heats.

On 15 September, the meeting should have been a bit more evenly matched than the 48–36 result suggests. The Eagles team ended their season with a defeat from a Scottish Select featuring second string riders from the other three Scottish sides. While the visiting team had no recognised heat leaders, they combined well to beat the home team.

The Eagles started well with a 5–1, but it was reversed in the next heat as Wilf Jay and Stan Beardsall took their first of three maximum heat wins. One time Glasgow Tiger, Wal Morton, managed only one point in the match, but won through to the second half final.

Noel Watson was in the wars again. He fell in heat 12 after he over-slid during his attempt to re-pass Bob Mark. In the rerun, Ray Maughan's engine failed and he had to push home for his second place. Three races finished with the relatively fast time of 83.9 seconds, but Ray Maughan was clocked at 100.4 seconds in the race where he pushed for the points.

Ron Phillips top scored for the Scottish Select with 11+1. Bob Mark added 8 paid 9. For the Eagles, Son Mitchell scored 11 points. Will Lowther did well again and scored 9+2.

The curtain came down on the short season at The Stadium on 22 September. In a pairs competition, the 'home pair' of Noel Watson and Will Lowther set the pace in their first four races when they were undefeated. They added enough in their remaining two races to lift the trophy sending home fans away happy. In the opening heat they both overtook Harold Booth then Ron Phillips to claim victory.

The trophy was presented by Tom Fraser MP, Under Secretary of State for Scotland, who was pleased to see The Stadium that had grown out of the derelict pit bing. Runners-up medals went to Gordon McGregor and Norman Lindsay of Glasgow Tigers who had started well, but then ran out of steam. In third place were Newcastle's Son Mitchell and Don Wilkinson, who had often ridden at The Stadium. Son was individual top scorer on 17 points with only Gordon McGregor showing him a rear wheel. Noel Watson, Gordon McGregor and Harold Booth all did well, each scoring 14 points.

The *1951 Stenner's Speedway Annual* commented that "Motherwell opened in mid-season with a view to team building for 1951 league status, but not much progress was made in this direction. Only signing of note was the Australian Noel Watson, but it should not be too difficult to find second strings and reserves from Bothwell Park MCC which operates a speedway of its own – entirely on amateur lines ... 1950 racing at Motherwell was on a Division Two plane with the management borrowing whom they could from clubs in that league to fill vacancies in the line-up of Lanarkshire Eagles." The *Annual* also confirmed that Motherwell, led by a board of five directors, would be riding in Division Two in 1951.

2. 1951: Joining the National League

The Lanarkshire Eagles management spent the winter trying to assemble a competitive team. They retained Noel Watson and Clive Gressor and in October 1950 had added Australian Keith Gurtner from Ashfield. At the turn of the year, they still needed five riders. While they improved the track lighting and added new facilities, the main priority was to build a team.

Motherwell joined the National League Division Two, which included the other three Scottish teams. It started the season with 17 teams, but Southampton withdrew from the league early on in the campaign. Apart from the Scottish teams, the league was mainly based in the north of England and the midlands. Walthamstow were the only team from the south of England. The Third Division was made up of teams from the south of England along with Cardiff.

By mid-February, the Glasgow veteran Joe Crowther, who had ridden before the war, was recruited. Crowther was inextricably linked with Will Lowther. After 1950 at Newcastle, Will came back north joining up again with Crowther. Wee experienced leg trailing Londoner, Danny Lee, moved to the club from Edinburgh.

The Eagles needed a heat leader and were keen to add recently married Gordon McGregor. Both Gordon and the Motherwell promoters thought the price tag of £1,200 was excessive. They went to the Speedway Control Board for arbitration and the Eagles paid a transfer fee of £850, £100 more than the original offer.

Stockport born Stan Bradbury came from Coventry and the club also acquired a young Australian, Bluey Scott. Recommended by Jack Young, Bluey, or Eric to his parents, was also friendly with Clem Mitchell. Bluey became a firm favourite of the Eagles' fans. The local press loved his do-or-die efforts that resulted in a lot of falls and crashes into the fence.

Bill Baird, a Scot, made his debut for his fourth Scottish speedway team – a feat that would never be repeated – joining the Eagles after spells with the Tigers, Monarchs and Giants. Scot Bob Lindsay from Ayrshire completed the octet. Motherwell bosses tried and failed to add American Bud Reda.

The pre-season practice was held on Tuesday 27 March. Joe Crowther sustained an injury which resulted in a poisoned thumb or septic finger depending on the reporter.

The Eagles acquired a mechanic, Luke Ramage, who had a good pedigree. He had at one time spannered for Drew McQueen and worked at White City keeping the Tigers' bikes in trim.

March

The 1951 season opened on 31 March. It was due to start at 7.45pm, but was brought forward to 7.15pm. The 7.45pm starting time presented a problem for fans getting home by public transport.

The visiting Swedish Lions team and their hosts attended a lunch in the Royal Hotel in Motherwell. Mr J Sherry extended a welcome to his guests and Mr Ringstrom, Swedish team manager, translated Mr Sherry's welcome for his team. John Robertson, a Motherwell director and Clerk of the Course, introduced his team. After lunch the Swedes went shopping in the town centre.

That evening, after an opening ceremony performed by Provost Alexander Crichton, 15,000 fans watched new Eagles signing Gordon McGregor, their acting captain, set the stage for the new season by scoring a full maximum. He also took a second of Jack Young's track record. Team mate Noel Watson slipped below the old record later in the match.

The Eagles used two riders, Merv Harding and new Australian Chum Taylor as guests. They replaced injured Joe Crowther and bike-less Will Lowther. New Australian signing Bluey Scott was introduced to the fans. A winter down under had clearly benefitted Noel Watson because he produced his best Eagles score, 11+1. Motherwell tracked nine riders. Harold Booth was an extra reserve replacing Bill Baird. After 14 heats the Eagles won 48–36. The top Swedes were Bertil Carlsson and Olle Segerstrom on 8+1, while Sune Karlsson scored eight. Karlsson, perhaps inspired by the Dalzell (pronounced Dee-ell) Highland Pipe Band, won the second half final.

April

On Friday 6 April the Eagles made their debut as a league team against Lancashire's Fleetwood Flyers in a North Shield fixture. Scant match reports advise that heat four was the thriller. Bill Baird got away at the start and was challenged by Ray Harker who in turn had track spare mounted Danny Lee on his tail. Eventually Lee, the third best Eagle with seven paid eight, overtook to join Baird in a 5–1.

The Eagles tracked Will Lowther and new Scottish find, Irvine's Bob Lindsay – sometimes also known as 'Farmer Bob'. Skipper Joe Crowther was still unfit and Keith Gurtner was on his way on the SS Mooltan. Keith wasn't expected to dock at Tilbury until 13 May. Noel Watson fell in the second half final when he lost a chain, but wasn't seriously injured. Gordon McGregor took another maximum, but had to do it the hard way, coming from the back each time.

Noel Watson, who scored 8+1, was in the wars. He over-slid leading heat three and was bumped by Hargreaves in heat 14. He then gave a show of petulance in the second half final. Reports vary, some say he flung his 'dead' machine down while other reports suggest he fell off as he moved off the track.

Fleetwood did well, despite engine problems which ruled out some riders from programmed races. Don Potter and Alf Parker both scored 11 points, both losing only to Gordon McGregor. Their next best man was Hamilton's Angus (William) McGuire on 4+1. The 46–38 score in the Eagles favour was no real surprise.

On Monday 9 April the Eagles rode in their first away fixture. Their debut was at Brough Park in Newcastle and they were on the wrong end of a 52–32 score, an easy win for Diamonds. The Eagles' heat leaders did the business, with Noel Watson outstanding, but they had little backing from a woefully long tail. Noel scored 11 points while Newcastle specialist Will Lowther added 10 and Gordon McGregor bagged nine. For the Diamonds,

Derick Close scored a full 12 point maximum while Wilf Jay and Son Mitchell gave him sound support.

Friday 13 April could have held a few fears for Eagles as they faced the Glasgow Tigers. The Eagles riders were up for this, the first official fixture at The Stadium against Scottish opponents. Fans of both teams were kept on their toes because the match was finely balanced up to the end of heat eight when Eagles' debutante, Joe Crowther, beat his former team mate Junior Bainbridge. Joe scored nine points after an opening race engine failure. McGregor also scored nine while Lee scored 8+2.

From heat nine onwards, the Eagles surged ahead and, despite a couple of setbacks, kept on course for a convincing win. Close finishes were the hallmark of this meeting which ended 46–35. Gordon McGregor's unbeaten home record ended when he fell trying to slip past Junior Bainbridge on the last lap in heat five. Fellow heat leader Watson also came to grief as he tried a pass.

Lee cracked his ankle in his second half spill which also saw Will Lowther injured. Poor Danny's engine failed and, as he slowed, Will Lowther ploughed into him. Danny spent the night in the Edinburgh area before going south.

The Tigers were without Tommy Miller. His presence would probably have made the scores a bit more interesting. The Tigers had bike problems, their machines throwing chains, which cost them a pile of points. Junior Bainbridge was top Tiger on 11 points. The Tigers' Frank Hodgson withdrew from the meeting after he sustained an unusual injury caused by a stone thrown up by a rider in front. Before the end of heat 13, the tractor came on to the track to start grading. Watson and Jim Blyth missed the obstruction and the tractor driver was ticked off by the Steward (referee).

The Tigers gained revenge on Wednesday 18 April with Tommy Miller back in their line-up. Tommy led the home charge by scoring one of his many maximums. Frank Hodgson added 8+1 while Norman Lindsay bagged seven as the Tigers side beat the Eagles 51–32.

The former Tigers in the Eagles ranks, McGregor, Crowther and Lowther, scored 24 of the total, but again the Eagles' tail dragged them to defeat. With Lee missing they brought back Bluey Scott but, because he was still finding his feet on strange tracks, he failed to score.

Watson was excluded for forcing Jack Hodgson from the track but the injustice was that Jack was also excluded for leaving the track. Adding to Noel's woes was a fall when he was well ahead.

Friday 20 April saw the Eagles sustain their first home defeat. The victorious visitors were the Ashfield Giants from Glasgow who took the North Shield points with a 45–39 win. The Giants' colourful Australian Merv Harding top scored with 10+1.

On a positive note, the Motherwell track was improving. Gordon McGregor set another new track record and picked up £5 for his efforts. Other riders bettered the old time, which was bettered or equalled four times. This indicates that the track conditions held good throughout the meeting. Gordon broke the old record three times and Noel Watson equalled the old time.

Only McGregor and Watson were in the big scoring groove with a 12-point maximum and 11 respectively. It was clear that Eagles needed a third heat leader to boost their fortunes. McGregor sent the home fans away happy with a last-to-first ride in the Rider of the Night final which saw him pick off Harding on the line. Fans were treated to a rendition of *A Gordon for Me* by well-known Scottish singer Robert Wilson.

The club's juniors were mostly local men with Slim Irvine from Troon, George Kilgour from Salsburgh and David Robertson from Carmyle in Glasgow appearing. In the second half, Robertson fell, was injured, and taken to Law Hospital.

The return between the Eagles and the Giants was on 24 April, but the Eagles got little change out of the Giants. Another poor showing saw the Giants march to a record 63–21 win. The worst thing was that the Eagles were making the gate, but couldn't keep the Saracen Park men at the back.

A consolation for the Eagles' fans was that Gordon McGregor relieved Bruce Semmens of his 'unbeaten at home' tag in heat 10. The Eagles top three were McGregor with seven points, Crowther 6+1 and Watson with five. On the downside, Stan Bradbury battered the fence in heat four causing sparks to fly. He badly injured his knee and pulled out of the meeting. Bluey Scott benefited from this misfortune by taking Stan's remaining rides.

Merv Harding and Willie Wilson both scored paid maximums with 11+1 and Bob Lovell scored 10+2. The aforementioned Bruce Semmens scored 11.

The Eagles, with a few passengers, took a narrow 42–41 win over Newcastle Diamonds in a match that went to the wire on 27 April. Crowther celebrated his 38th birthday with a maximum. He then went on to win the second half event. Maybe Joe was in a hurry to enjoy a cake made by Mrs Letham of Canderwater Farm, Coalburn. It was fortunate Joe did well because the weakened Eagles were up against it. The visitors, who were all well acquainted with the track, pushed them hard. With Bradbury out injured, the Eagles gave an outing to Malcolm Riddell.

Ray Maughan and Bill Baird crashed in heat 12 and the resulting 3–2 put the Diamonds in front. A Watson and Baird 4–2 in heat 13 put the Eagles back ahead and Joe's fellow maximum man, Gordon McGregor, won heat 14. Bluey Scott pulled out after injuring his wrist when he fell.

The next day saw the Eagles in Edinburgh. The Monarchs' 62–21 win over the Eagles saw the Monarchs become joint leaders with the Glasgow Tigers at the top of the North Shield table.

The Eagles were not as hopelessly outclassed as the score suggests and there were several exciting finishes. McGregor gave Jack Young a hard race in heat one, and Crowther, showing something like his old form, almost piped Harold Fairhurst for second place in heat two. Joe was in the closest finish of the evening in heat eight. After a great struggle, he got in front of Don Cuppleditch early in lap four, but the Monarchs' rider surged ahead on the last bend and won with little to spare. Watson scored 5+1 and impressed with his performance, while McGregor, with six points, did well. In heat 10 Baird and McGregor both came to grief when their bikes locked at a bend. Eagles had two former Meadowbank riders, Baird, and Harry Andrews who signed shortly before this match, but they only collected one point between them.

For the Monarchs, Jack Young and Don Cuppleditch both scored full maximums, while Dick Campbell scored 11+1 and Bob Mark took 10+2.

May

On Wednesday 2 May, the Eagles visited Fleetwood. The weakened visitors inflicted a third home defeat on the home side in a week, winning 44–38. The Eagles riders rode up the Fleetwood track banking to great advantage, while most of the home men stuck to a slower inside line. Eagles drew ahead in the opening heat and slowly inched ahead for a narrow win, despite being down to seven men after Lindsay hit the fence and fell in his second outing. Unusually, two, Gordon McGregor and Joe Crowther scored maximums. Apart from a first race fall, Watson would have had a full house too and he had to settle for nine points. Jeff Crawford, who followed the Eagles' example of where to ride, top scored for the Flyers with 8+2.

The trip south had been eventful with the weatherman throwing the book at them. Gordon McGregor crashed into a fence in avoiding a road roller. The damage was repaired and he set off, but had to stop again for further repair work.

Two days later, Edinburgh visited The Stadium and routed the Eagles 57–27 in a North Shield encounter. 'Journalistic licence' was taken by a magazine reporter who wrote "The Eagles had their fangs (should it not be wings?) severely clipped when they suffered their biggest home defeat of the season".

In heat eight, the Eagles tried to improve matters by switching Lindsay for Malcolm Riddell, but the steward did not allow the change. Only McGregor, who scored 11, and to a lesser extent, Watson who scored six, did anything worthwhile for the Eagles. McGregor fought out a thriller with Jack Young in the opening heat, but was handicapped by a slow bike and worked hard for his points.

For the Monarchs, Jack Young scored 12 points while Don Cuppleditch added 10. Heat four was restarted twice. In the first staging, Young took off with the tapes streaming from his neck and the steward stopped the race for safety reasons. In the second, Andrews crashed when tapes wrapped round his front wheel and it seized. Harry then shared the track spare with Crowther who had bike problems all night. Bradbury pulled out of the meeting because of an injured knee.

The following evening, 5 May, Noel Watson captained a Hamilton side which raced a Glasgow team at Hamilton Showgrounds in the annual agricultural show event.

On Wednesday 9 May, the Eagles made their National Trophy debut at Halifax. Only McGregor stood up to the Dukes as the Eagles were well and truly trussed up like a turkey to the tune of 79–29.

On cold night, the 4,000 crowd was about 6,000 down on the usual turnout, probably due to the Eagles' poor early season form. McGregor provided some opposition gathering 10+1 from six rides and Watson scored eight from six rides.

The Dukes' star Arthur Forrest scored an easy six ride maximum, while Vic Emms was paid for 18 with five second places after an opening race win.

On Friday 11 May, just before the match the Eagles were presented with their colours by three local ladies, Mrs C Stewart, her daughter Eileen and Miss Margaret Forsyth. The Stewarts had made the flag they presented while Miss Forsyth's flag had been made by Peter Reid.

In an attempt to improve the team, the Eagles management secured Bill Dalton from the closed Sheffield team. Bill had a good debut, although even he could not help secure a home and aggregate win. The fans loved his efforts to hold out Arthur Forrest in heat 12 which just failed on the line. However, Bill clearly repaid his fee with eight paid nine. The Eagles had also hoped to sign Guy Allott, but the telephone system of the day let them down.

In the meeting, the Eagles crashed out of the competition thanks to a 69–39 home defeat. Halifax won 148–68 on aggregate. After a bright start by the home men, the visitors moved ahead in heat six and just blew the Eagles away. Arthur Forrest and Vic Emms were the Dukes' best again, both scoring 15+1. Watson was the top Eagle with a score of 12+1.

McGregor had a bad night ending with eight points. Gordon's cause was not helped by a crash involving Arthur Forrest when Arthur ran into Gordon, who had slowed to bring his rearing machine under control. Despite being carried off, McGregor came back for the rest of his rides. His bike was bent so he had to use the track spare. He fell in heat 13 after touching Bill Crosland's back wheel before crashing into the fence. It was reported that he was dazed by his heat nine crash and hardly knew where he was. The rest of the side had a bit of an off night. Bill Baird crashed into the safety fence in heat 14 and ended up in Law Hospital for a few days with suspected broken ribs.

Arthur Forrest and Jack Hughes had visited the track when it was under construction in 1950. They had been visiting friends who lived in the Lanarkshire area.

On Monday 14 May, the Eagles entered the National League fray, losing 52–32 at Leicester. This was Keith Gurtner's debut for Eagles and he did it in style with an immaculate maximum. Keith had been collected at Tilbury Docks earlier in the day by John Robertson. A bigger sensation than the maximum was the news that Gurtner had collapsed soon after winning his last race. He had been ill on the boat and was totally exhausted after his efforts. Keith did not have much support but McGregor scored six and Dalton and Lowther added five each.

It wasn't to be third time lucky for Eagles when they returned to Halifax two days later. The Dukes made it three in a row against the Motherwell men with another big win, 60–24. Only Lowther returned a reasonable score, seven points, and the Eagles' only race winner was Dalton who scored five.

The Eagles' poor display a week earlier affected the crowd as it dropped to 3,000. Those who turned up saw Jack Hughes and Al Allison both bag full 12-point maximums while Vic Emms scored 9+3.

The Eagles had a night off on Friday 18 May. The promotion held a Best Pairs event featuring Scottish teams. McGregor's injured foot slowed him down and his contribution to the meeting was limited. Watson sustained a head injury in his opening ride. Stan Bradbury paired up with Will Lowther for the rest of the tournament.

The visiting pairs all did much better with Edinburgh duo of Jack Young with 15 points and Eddie Lack on six, just piping Tigers' Junior Bainbridge and Ken McKinlay and Giants' Merv Harding and Bruce Semmens by a point for the prize.

The Eagles' men's cause was not helped by poor gating, a problem that haunted the team for many meetings. Those not pleased with their performance could go to the about to be opened Calderbank, near Airdrie, training track on a Sunday afternoon to sharpen up their skills.

On Wednesday 23 May, another new competition faced the Eagles when they met Glasgow Tigers in the Scottish Cup at White City. The Eagles gave the Tigers a run for their money and the 57–51 score reflects a close encounter all the way through. It was only in the closing stages that the home team pulled away to win.

If concussion victim Watson had ridden, it is possible Eagles may have snatched a win. The two Tigers old boys, Crowther, who scored 7+3, and Lowther, on seven, did well early on, but then tailed off. Dalton was the top Eagle with 12+1 and McGregor contributed 10+1 points.

For the Tigers, Tommy Miller missed out on a maximum by one point as McGregor put one over on him. The Eagles crashed out of the Scottish Cup two days later. After their great effort at White City, the home leg proved to be a disaster. The Tigers won with comparative ease, scoring more than they had at home, winning 61–47. The aggregate score was 118–98 in the Tigers' favour.

With only McGregor, with 13+1, and Watson, on 12 points, on form, it was always going to be an uphill struggle. Yet again the Eagles made it difficult with slow starting. Tommy Miller set a new track record in heat two, a race in which he was chased by McGregor. He gave second best in one race to Watson and ran a third in his last outing.

Watson blew his motor in heat 15 when chasing Junior Bainbridge. They always say motors go best before they blow as evidenced by the fact Noel had earlier equalled the old track record.

The Tigers' Junior Bainbridge was their top scorer with 15+3 from his six rides. Tommy Miller was pegged back to 15; the two Macs, Ken McKinlay and Alf McIntosh each scored 10 points. In the second half, Newtongrange novice Stan Sprott fell and broke his collar bone.

June

On 1 June the Eagles' weakness was exposed by the lowly Liverpool Chads who secured a 50–34 win at The Stadium. There was a dry and dusty track again and this, together with the Chads' superiority, reduced the fans enjoyment. All attempts to water the track failed and they watched it dry off as soon the water landed on the granite chip surface. This prompted the Eagles' management to press on building their own water tanker.

Yet again, only McGregor and Watson with nine points each had an answer to the visitors. Even Watson had the bad luck to fall in his last outing as he led the field. Noel had provided excitement in heat seven when he raced through from the back past the team riding Chads pair.

Glasgow Ashfield's Larry Lazarus ahead of the two Eagles. (JSC)

Left: Leg trailer Danny Lee. (JSC). Right: Australian Keith Gurtner
ready for the Eagles' match at Walthamstow.

Left: Joe Crowther with Derick Close. Crowther was rejuvenated with Motherwell, having ridden Glasgow Lions (before the War) and Tigers (after the War). The team had changed its name.

Below: Motherwell 1951: Back Stan Bradbury, Bluey Scott, Scott Hall, Derick Close, Will Lowther; front: Gordon McGregor, Noel Watson, Keith Gurtner. (Both photos JSC)

15

Crowther's new bike did not perform well and he packed up after two rides, one on his bike and the other aboard the track spare. He had led heat two when the bike packed in.

The aforementioned dusty track conditions did not help the Eagles cause because, enveloped in the clouds of dust, they fell off the pace. Lee's plans for a second half ride were thwarted by the track doctor.

McGregor and Gurtner dished up some excitement in the second half final with McGregor just taking it on the line. McGregor had earlier thrilled the fans when he burst through between the Chads men. The Chads were solid throughout with diminutive Len Read best on 10+1.

The second half featured the Scottish sounding Angus McKenzie who rode briefly for Belle Vue. Poor Angus made one start, crashed on the second bend first time round and sustained a leg injury.

The Supporters expressing thanks to Glasgow paper the *Evening Citizen* for staging a good display featuring the Eagles in the window of the local branch of Burton's the Tailor.

Motherwell had an internationally honoured rider on Saturday 2 June when Noel Watson represented Overseas versus Great Britain at Stoke. At reserve he was introduced into the match in heat 13. It was not a glorious debut as he lost control, left the track, and crashed into a film crew on the inside wrecking sound equipment and injuring his arm.

Four Eagles crossed the Irish Sea to race at Chapelizod in Dublin on Wednesday 6 June. Despite the gulf in points, 48–24 favouring the home side, the racing was close and many races went to the wire. Heat nine was a humdinger as home man, Harringay's Split Waterman, and Eagle for the night Wembley's Bruce Abernethy passed and re-passed six times. Abernethy just lost it on the line as Ivor Davies came from the back to pip him. Lindsay was best Eagle with 7+1 while Dalton scored six.

On 8 June, Londoners Walthamstow came calling. In an unusual move the Eagles' management programmed McGregor and Watson as the opening pair. Gordon scored 10 and Noel scored 9+1. However, the rest of the side did the business carrying the day 47–37. The Eagles' Bluey Scott continued to impress. He picked up a second in his opening ride, but caused concern by sweeping wide round the fence rather than riding a tighter line.

Yet again, dust spoiled the racing. After three heats the match was held up to remove loose material off the bends. This didn't work and a water tanker was brought in after heat six. It took 20 minutes to complete the task. The London Wolves' top man was Harry Edwards with 11.

The Eagles fans were pleased to see McGregor return to top form on 15 June against Ashfield in the Lanarkshire Cup. He led his team to a 65–43 win. Gurtner, who scored 14+1, spoiled his possible clean sheet by stalling at the gate in heat 12. He had moaned to the meeting Steward after he came back to the pits, saying he wasn't on the grid. The Steward replied that the green light was on and he should have been ready. Scott crashed then somersaulted out of the meeting when, after a big wobble, he ploughed into the fence. Thankfully he just suffered bruising. This was his second encounter with the fence. The first time round he had just bounced clear. Fellow reserve, Bradbury, had a better night winning both his races from the back like most of his Eagles colleagues. McGregor scored 17+1 and Dalton did well on 8+2. Lee had a try out in the second half preparing for a return after his injury.

The Giants' cause was not helped by a knee injury sustained by Semmens, a specialist round The Stadium, in his opening ride. Merv Harding was top Giant with 11+1 and Willie Wilson gathered 10.

On 22 June Crowther struck form, landing his first maximum for the Eagles as they tore into the Halifax Dukes. This time, the Eagles managed to defeat the Dukes 53–31 to take the National League points. The Eagles came from the back and put up a good show of team riding. Watson made up for a poor start in his opening ride to pile up 10 points. As ever, the enigma that was McGregor had the fans perplexed as he scored only 7. Yet again, Dalton showed up well, just missing a paid maximum, scoring 9+2. Scott was in the wars when his chain broke causing him to crash heavily. Arthur Forrest top scored for the Dukes with 9+1.

Highlight of the night was the first clash between Jack Young and Tommy Miller. Their first race battle was considered to be the best seen at The Stadium. Jack won from the gate with Tommy chasing all the way. Young fell in heat two trying to pass Miller. He had to cut back on speed built up as he tried an inside pass which was blocked by Miller. Young won heat three when he came from behind, this time without mishap.

A rare visit to London on 25 June saw a 50–34 defeat by Walthamstow Wolves. The Eagles were considered by the critics to have been the best visitors of the season. Bike troubles reduced Crowther's contribution to nil and he only took one ride. Heat five was a cracker as veteran Will Lowther, who scored 6+2, pegged back Reg Reeves to shepherd team mate Watson to the flag. Gurtner scored his second away maximum, although Jim Boyd ran him close in heat nine.

Benny King and Harry Edwards both scored 10, but Benny was paid for 11. A nine heat Junior challenge match between Bothwell Bulls and Newtongrange Rockets was staged after a junior football club match between Motherwell Juniors and Bellshill Athletic on Tuesday 26 June. It is reported that the senior men did well, but the juniors had a tough time of it. The only information is the Bulls lost 35–15.

The Flyers' Jeff Crawford, who like the Eagles' Keith Gurtner, raced in blue leathers, was the home hero of the night at Fleetwood on Wednesday 27 June. His second place to team mate Wilf Jay in the last heat prevented the Eagles taking both league points. The Eagles had this one in the bag, but let it slip as the two Flyers shot off as the tapes rose to clinch a 5–1 giving them a 42–42 draw. Despite trying everything he knew; McGregor could not get past Crawford for second place to take the win.

McGregor had earlier taken advantage of Don Potter's curiosity in heat 10, slipping past as the Flyer looked back over the wrong shoulder. Gordon had scored 8+1, a total matched by Dalton. Crowther just missed out on a maximum losing out to Wilf Jay who scored nine. Home hero Jeff Crawford scored 6+2 while Norman Hargreaves and Ray Harker both scored 6+1. Looking back was against the rules and had the steward spotted it, Potter would have been excluded.

On 29 June, the Yarmouth Bloaters were lucky because the Eagles had bike problems or their 65–19 defeat at The Stadium which could have been even worse. Joe Crowther ground to a halt due to engine failure. McGregor was the only man to score a full maximum while Keith Gurtner and Bill Dalton took paid maximums by gathering 9+3.

The Bloaters were not helped by the withdrawal after one race by Reg Morgan, due to engine failure. Fred Brand scored a reasonable seven points, but the next best was Stan Page on four. The highlight was the scratch race final which was completed at the third time of asking as riders fell in the first two attempts. Gurtner won from McGregor.

Gordon's lack of ability to gate was immortalized in a fan's piece of poetry:
As Gordon leaves the starting gate – He never takes the lead;
But at the bend, with a lot at stake, He really cracks on speed;
As he skids "roon" he passes "yin", Another, and another;
When he went through the roar it grew, It's Gordon McGregor for ever.

July

Newcastle Diamonds sparkled at The Stadium on 6 July, winning 44–40. The Diamonds had been poor elsewhere home and away and this was a rare high spot in their season. The Eagles heat leaders produced the goods, but the rest of the side did not. Lee was unlucky to lose a chain when leading heat eight, but fellow reserve Bradbury did better, scoring three points.

The Eagles had a chance in the last heat, but Derick Close took the win ahead of Gurtner and McGregor after Son Mitchell, who was remembered for his singing skills in 1950, dropped out due to an engine failure. The top men for Eagles were Watson with 11 and Crowther on 10. For the visitors, Derick Close was unbeaten, scoring a full 12 point maximum.

The invincible tag, hung on the Monarchs' castle by the local *Edinburgh Evening Dispatch* the Thursday before, fell off in spectacular fashion when Lanarkshire Eagles came, saw, and won. The 48–36 league win at Old Meadowbank on 7 July was well taken and compensated for the Eagles' own home reverse the night before.

Without Don Cuppleditch, in Leicester Royal Infirmary with concussion, and Harold Fairhurst, the Monarchs' weakness at reserve was fully exposed. Were the Monarchs poor or the Eagles good? The answer is probably somewhere in between. The Monarchs' Jack Young scored another full maximum with Mark, Campbell and Lack scoring seven each. Crowther was the top Eagle with 9+2 and Gurtner scored 9+1. Watson chipped in with eight and McGregor with 7+2.

It was a Black (and White) Friday on 13 July at The Stadium. The Eagles' fans were buoyed by the performance of their men in a World Championship qualifier. The event was won by McGregor, on 14 points. He collected the £30 cheque from Mr Mawson, the *Sunday Dispatch* sports editor.

Watson took the runner-up spot with 12. Crowther added to the fans' joy by sharing third place with Monarchs' Don Cuppleditch, both scored 11 points.

Gordon had to come from the back in his opening rides, but failed to secure a clean sheet. He gave second best to Halifax's Al Allison in heat 15. Allison did, however, lose to Watson who lost to McGregor and Belle Vue's George Smith.

Left: Gordon 'The Tash' McGregor was the Eagles' first big signing. (JSC)

Below: The Motherwell track staff including Gordon Mitchell's father. (FOES)

Heat 12 saw the most action when Don Cuppleditch fell when holding second place. Watson swerved to avoid him, saving Don from serious injury.

The Eagles profited from Stoke's bad luck the next day at Sun Street to win their second away match on the trot. Stoke lost Gil Blake in heat three when he reared and fell heavily on the concrete starting grid. He ended up in the local hospital. The Eagles inflicted on the Potters their first home defeat of the season, 47–37. Gurtner returned to top scoring form with a maximum showing. Watson came back from his problems the week before, mastering the track to score 10 points while McGregor scored 9+2. The Potters' Bill Harris and namesake Ray were their best with eight points each.

On the Glasgow Fair Monday Holiday, 16 July, Eagles had three men, McGregor with 12 points, Gurtner 11+1 and Crowther 10+2, unbeaten by the American tourists. Their points laid the foundation of a 42–30 win. The Americans, based at Shelbourne Park, Dublin, started well, but gradually the Eagles got on top and pulled away. The original line-up included Manuel Trujillo, a Californian-born leg trailer who had started out before the War. He was replaced by Wimbledon's star Ernie Roccio. The side visited most tracks in the UK during their stay in Ireland. They included Lloyd Campbell, a 22-year-old from San Diego, Royal Carroll (Junior), the son of a racing father, and Johnnie ('Gumboil' or 'Crashwall') Gibson. The latter nickname was acquired after a spectacular crash when he severely injured his face, requiring plastic surgery to repair the damage.

McGregor's maximum was his fifth full house of the season, but he had to give second best to veteran Crowther in the second half. Johnnie Roccio, who had shared his first bike with his sister Helen, had some good news before the start of the meeting. The home management passed on news of the birth of his son in the USA.

Lee was injured in a second half when he looped, fell heavily on the concrete starting gate before his bike landed on top of him causing him greater damage. There was no rest for Danny when he arrived at Law Hospital. Many of the patients and staff were Eagles fans and they kept asking him for details of the meeting. Such was the concern for Danny that the promotion asked fans to phone the speedway office for information because the hospital switchboard had been inundated with calls.

There was more challenge action at The Stadium when the Eagles faced The Rest on 20 July. Cradley Heath were pencilled in as opponents, but, at the last minute, the Heathens had to pull out. The strong visiting line up won by 10 points, 47–37. Bob Mark, who scored 11, showing the home promotion what they had missed out on. The Monarchs had offered Bob to the Lanarkshire side at the start of the season, but were turned down. The Eagles got off to a bad start and never managed to catch up with the visitors. The Eagles' gating, again, let them down. Their cause was not helped by Crowther who injured his ankle after he had scored 2+2. Gurtner scored 10, but both Watson, with seven, and McGregor, 7+1, were down on their usual returns.

Heat eight featured a battle between Willie Wilson and Bob Lindsay for the minor placings. The Giants' Willie just made it at the end. Heat 13 was an epic. A false start caused a rerun in which Crowther was injured in a crash at the first bend. In the third attempt, Lindsay fell and remounted to take an unopposed third place because Ken

McKinlay was out of the event. Some felt Ken had been harshly treated because he had moved out to clear the fallen Lindsay and baulked Joe in the process.

It was back to National League action on 27 July for a match against Coventry at The Stadium which went to the wire. It took a last heat 5–1 by Gurtner and McGregor to snatch victory from the Bees, completing an unbeaten night for both riders. Gurtner had a full maximum while Gordon scored 11+1. The visitors had no real stars, but they all chipped in to keep the Eagles' fans worried about the destination of the match points. Despite the buzz everywhere else, the men in the Eagles part of the pits were supremely confident that their team would do it. Gurtner gated first and Gordon pulled in behind him, and so they chased round to the flag.

The Eagles' cause was not helped by the poor spell of form of Dalton and Lowther. Bob Lindsay was given his chance in the team proper. The Eagles' troubles, however, started in heat two when Watson fell as he had Derek Tailby in his sights.

Coventry probably counted this as one that got away. Six up by the middle of the match they were losing by two following two Motherwell 5–1s. Two Coventry 5–1s restored their narrow advantage before the start of heat 14. That last heat must have been the scunner to end all scunners for them as the Eagles took the match 43–41 and the match points. (Scunner = sickener.)

Joe Crowther travelled to Coventry for a World Championship event the following night but he could not compete due to his injury. McGregor, who scored six at Coventry in the same event as Crowther progressed to the next round while Watson scored 10 at Stoke to also progress closer to Wembley.

August

At Oxford on 2 August, a seven-man Eagles side did not have enough fire power to challenge the Cheetahs. Without Lowther, who had sent a telegram advising he was ill and unable to travel, they went down 53–31 with only Watson and Gurtner, who both scored nine points, putting up any resistance. McGregor had an off night, scoring 5+1, while the rest each scored less than Gordon. Gurtner had the consolation for Motherwell fans as he set a new Cowley track record of 66 seconds. The Cheetahs' Bill Kemp scored a paid maximum with four second places.

The Eagles seemed to be a side that bounced back quickly. The next day, they put the away defeat behind them. It was quite a feather in the Eagles' cap because they defeated table-topping Norwich Stars 46–38. The opening Stars pair, with Bob Leverenz outstanding, did the most damage, but they did not receive much support their team mates. Australian Bob scored a full maximum 12 and received good support from Phil Clarke on eight and Fred Pawson with 7+3.

On the other hand, the Eagles men scored solidly and pulled together as a team. Gurtner's good run continued with a 10 point return while McGregor added 8+2. The terrible twins of old, Crowther and Will Lowther, both scored 7+1. The Eagles pair of Gurtner and McGregor had rounded off the match with a 5–1, which was a signal for The Stadium to erupt with joy. Hats and other items flew into the air in response.

21

The team's good form spilled over to the following week and on 10 August the home fans were treated to a 55–29 win over a Stoke side that had bike problems. Scott got a late call up to replace Crowther, who was still having problems with his ankle. Bluey excelled, taking wins in both of his races in the match to score a reserve's maximum six. Bluey was described as riding with confidence and taking the bends very smoothly. His confidence was reflected in a fast time in one of his two his second half heat wins. Dalton, wearing the Eagles number one race jacket, was hoping for better returns after purchasing the Motherwell track spare and managed to get over a spell of not being fully fit.

McGregor assumed the captaincy in Crowther's absence and scored a full maximum. Lowther and Gurtner were unbeaten scoring 11+1 and 10+2 respectively. Keith rode despite feeling ill, but suffered a bout of sickness once the match was over.

The Entertainment Tax started to bite at The Stadium with those supporters using the stand having to fork out an extra three pence (1.5p) to help keep the Chancellor happy. Out of the three shillings and nine pence (approximately 18p) the tax man took one shilling and nine pence (approximately 8p).

The following evening, the Bellshill Branch of the Supporters' Club staged a dance. Tickets cost the princely sum of £0.125 or 2 shillings and six pence – half-a-crown – in old money.

The Stadium bubble was burst by the Giants from Glasgow at the next home meeting. It went to the wire. Ron Phillips split the McGregor and Gurtner pairing to give the Giants the points thanks to his hard fought second place in heat 14. Ron was carried shoulder high by his jubilant team-mates. The Eagles' 4–2 meant the score ended 43–41 in the Giants' favour. The Eagles were in with a shout until Bluey Scott dropped off when in sight of the line in heat 12. Merv Harding was hard on Bluey's heels and hit the fence, taking avoiding action. Watson was a bit out of sorts after his long haul south to compete at New Cross and Wembley in the World Championship.

The Eagles' young Australian cannot be singled out because all but McGregor, who scored 11, and Gurtner on nine points, had a bit of an off night. There was little between the two sides, but the Giants had two big scorers to the Eagles' one. Bruce Semmens was in top form yet again, scoring a maximum and setting a new track record of 75.4 in the opener. Australian Jim Courtney, better known as a long-serving Secretary of the Australian Veteran Speedway Riders' Association, made his second half debut. Unfortunately, Jim fell in his second outing and was taken to Law Hospital.

On Saturday 18 August, the Eagles made a poor away showing. They went down 59–25 at Coventry. Without McGregor, on World Championship duty at Birmingham, the visitors were too weak to bother the Bees. Stan Williams scored a full maximum 12 while Derek Tailby scored 9+2.

The only notable feature was that Glasgow blacksmith Scott Hall made his Eagles debut, scoring 1+1. Gurtner was the best Eagle on 10 points, followed by Dalton and Bradbury on four each. Watson and Scott were both a bit jaded because they had spent until 4am fixing their battered machines from the night before. The pair had to resort to the track spare because both suffered bike problems. Bluey then compounded matters by having a go at the Brandon track fence.

22

The visiting Eagles' fans probably expected a bigger defeat at Saracen Park on Tuesday 21 August. However former Giant Gurtner, 9+1, and McGregor, with 11 points, were ably assisted by Lowther on eight, and made the Giants fight for their 45–38 win.

Both sides fought hard on a rain-soaked mud bath of a track. Bruce Semmens had a torrid time with an opening race fall. Bruce had to settle for three points. Merv Harding top scored on 11, while Willie Wilson 7+1 and Cyril Cooper with seven gave him support.

Before the meeting at The Stadium on 24 August, Tommy Miller had been doubtful as to whether he could ride, but he turned out and scored his usual 12 point maximum. A solid display for the Eagles carried the day, resulting in a 46–38 win over the Glasgow Tigers in this Lanarkshire Cup event. Lowther and Gurtner top scored with 9+1 apiece, with Crowther next best on 8+1.

The up-and-down form of the Eagles prompted the management to dip into the transfer market. Fans who turned up to The Stadium on Monday 27 August had expected a new star in the team to perform on a track still wet from weekend rain.

New signing Derick Close was expected to ride for the Eagles, but the fans had to wait a wee bit longer for their £1,000 plus investment from Newcastle. Watson had spent money too, buying a new frame. It is hard to say if his seven points return made Noel feel his money had been well spent. Gurtner also had 7+2 while Crowther scored 7+1. Scott's unexpected heat 12 win, leading home Dalton, put the Eagles level. The old hands did the rest, giving Eagles a narrow 43–41 win over Leicester Hunters. The Hunters could have won it in the last heat, but McGregor and Gurtner let Len Williams go through to complete his 12 point maximum and pegged Scotsman Jock Grierson into last place.

Around this time, McGregor was invited to race in the Regent £100 Gold Casket event at White City. Gordon was drawn against Bob Mark while Ken McKinlay faced Willie Wilson. Tommy Miller, the other Scottish rider was seeded to the final of this match race event.

On another front, the Eagles management was trying to fix up a date for Gurtner to race Jack Young for his Scottish Match Race Championship.

Signed from under the noses of Edinburgh, Derick Close made his home debut for the Eagles on 31 August. Close made a winning start, but fell after an over-slide in his last outing, missing out on a maiden paid maximum for the Eagles. Derick claimed that he had been pushed over the white line by a rival causing his fall. Close was not the only one in the wars. Scott tangled with the safety fence in heat four when well ahead. He made amends by winning his last outing.

Derick Close's 8+1 helped give the Eagles a 55–29 win over the Fleetwood Flyers. The Flyers had only three out of the 14 race winners, but managed to prevent any Eagles scoring maximums. McGregor and Gurtner both scored nine, but McGregor was paid for 11 and Gurtner for 10. Lowther had a rare fall in his opening ride and was bit shaken. Don Potter was the highest Flyer with nine while veteran Wilf Jay added 8+1.

McGregor had been taking part in the Regent (Petrol Company) £100 Gold Casket competition, a match race event for Scottish born riders. He was knocked out of the competition by Edinburgh's Bob Mark who went on to be runner-up to Tommy Miller. Gordon's cause was let down by bike problems and a borrowed bike owned by Dalton's bike proved a bit flat.

September

The Eagles had three former Tigers, McGregor, Lowther and Crowther, in their ranks when they visited White City, which always made it a very combative affair. This meeting on 5 September was no different, and the Eagles showed more determination than the Tigers to clinch a 44–40 victory. To be fair, Gurtner and Close played their role defeating of Tommy Miller on 'his own midden'.

McGregor and Lowther put the Eagles in front in heat one, but the Tigers clawed back to be level by heat three. Gordon and reserve Bradbury put the Eagles ahead in heat four and they managed to keep Tigers at bay throughout. Lowther must have been smiling when he won the final heat to carry the Eagles past the winning post. Will scored 7+1 while Gordon and Derick were best with 9+1. Former Tiger, Crowther, only scored a couple of points, but they came in the vital heat 13 when he combined with Stan for a 3–3 to keep the Eagles four ahead before the last heat.

For the Tigers, Junior Bainbridge posted a full maximum 12 while Tommy Miller was pegged back to 10. The rest of the Tigers had a bit of an off night.

Oxford Cheetahs proved to be poor opposition for the Eagles at The Stadium on 7 September. The 61–23 win saw five Eagles unbeaten by a visitor. Oxford started brightly and Harry Saunders won heat one from McGregor. Heat two was a thriller as Crowther and Close were left at the gate by the Cheetahs pair, but they fought past to take a 5–1 win. Thereafter, it was one-way traffic with the Eagles men out-gating the Cheetahs and taking the flag in the remaining 12 heats. Watson led the rout with a 12 point maximum, his first of many, while Crowther on 10+2 and Derick Close on 9+3 were unbeaten by a visitor. McGregor dropped a point scoring 10+1.

For the Cheetahs, their best was Bill Kemp on 5+1. A recurrence of a leg injury caused Tommy Miller to call off from the Match Race decider against Junior Bainbridge.

The Glasgow Tigers left with their tails between their legs when the Eagles won 50–34 on 14 September. Tommy Miller was his usual immaculate self at Motherwell, but lacked support. Junior Bainbridge was next best on seven.

Crowther injured his knee in his heat four crash with Alf McIntosh and pulled out of the meeting. His rides were taken by the reserves and Dalton took full advantage to be paid for 11 points. Close only gave second best to Miller scoring 11 while Watson scored 10+1.

The Tigers' Len Nicholson was injured when he fell after heat 11 was over. Tommy Miller beat Junior Bainbridge 2–0 in their Second Division Silver Helmet Match Race and Tommy went on to win the second half final for good measure.

Revenge for the big defeat at The Stadium earlier in the year was sweet for the Eagles the following Monday when they won 43–41 at Liverpool. The match had swung both ways until heat eight when the Eagles pushed ahead. The Chads could have sneaked it, but Gurtner pulled out a race and match winning effort to hold Peter Robinson and Len Read to a 3–3, one of eight races that were drawn. Close gathered 11 while McGregor scored 10 and Gurtner eight. For the Chads, it was veteran reserve Tommy Allott who put up most resistance with 11 from four outings.

24

Local Motherwell car dealers Skellys sponsored the big individual event of the season at The Stadium. The programme hailed the event as The Skelly Trophy and Gold medal. The line up on 21 September was not quite star studded, but had seven heat leaders from the Eagles, Tigers and Monarchs. Motherwell specialist Tommy Miller won the prizes with ease. The Eagles' Close and McGregor and Edinburgh's Bob Mark all scored 12.

It was nearing the end of a poor season for the Newcastle Diamonds and the Eagles had no trouble in shattering the home side 56–28 at Brough Park on Monday 24 September. Newcastle closed down for 10 years soon after this match.

Crowther, who had not been scoring well at home, collected a paid maximum, 10+2, as did former Diamond Derick Close. The Diamonds were lucky that one-time track specialist Lowther had an off night or a record away win might have been possible. Yet another former Diamond, Gurtner did well scoring 10. Wal Morton was the top Diamond with eight; Son Mitchell on 6+1 and Don Wilkinson on 5+1 were next in line.

The report in the *Speedway News* of the Eagles and Monarchs encounter at The Stadium the following Friday, which was won 42–40 by the Edinburgh side, concentrated on the first two heats. It reported the unusual opening to this match. First, McGregor fell and then Lowther retired with machine trouble giving Monarchs a 5–0.

In the second heat, Bob Mark crashed into the fence and Dick Campbell had machine trouble to give the home side a 5–0 score. The match score stood, unusually, at 5–5. The Eagles took the lead for the first time in heat nine with a 4–2, giving them a two-points advantage. The next four races were shared and then came Edinburgh's last heat win.

World Champion Jack Young and emerging star Don Cuppleditch were the Monarchs' last heat pair and their win over Gurtner and Dalton was probably a foregone conclusion before the race started. Jack Young marked his last Motherwell appearance with a 12 point maximum while Cuppleditch scored 8+1. For the Eagles, Close scored 10+1, McGregor added eight and Crowther 7+1.

A trip to champions-elect Norwich was always going to be a tough ask. The Stars whacked the Eagles 62–22 on Saturday 29 September. Only Close with five points and McGregor with seven managed race wins. The points helped Stars to retain their title. Bob Leverenz scored a 12 point maximum. He began by setting a new track record. Bob's partner Fred Rogers scored 8+4 while Phil Clarke and Alec Hunter both scored 9+1.

October

The Eagles did well for a visiting Scottish side at the tricky Caister Road track in Great Yarmouth known locally as the 'Bloater Pond' on Tuesday 2 October. Their 49–35 defeat was a respectable effort. Fred Brand and Bob Baker stood out for the Bloaters scoring 12 and 11 respectively. The Eagles scoring list was solid without any standouts. Bradbury did well, taking one of Eagles' four race wins and scored 5+1. McGregor was the best Eagle on eight while Close scored 7+1. The report in the *Speedway News* said that "Motherwell proved attractive opponents to Yarmouth" and that "they never gave up trying" in their first visit to Caister Road.

Another narrow 43–41 home win came three days later. Visiting Cradley Heath Heathens could have bagged a draw in the last heat, but Gurtner was the Eagles' ace as he split Les Tolley and Harry Bastable to ensure the points stayed in Scotland. Gurtner had a poor night and his second place doubled his score to 4+1. Close bagged a maximum and Watson signed off his first league season with a respectable points tally before returning to Australia for the winter. The Heathens were best served by Phil Malpass on 10 with Eagles early season target, Guy Allott, paid for nine and Laurie Schofield supporting with 8+1. The *Speedway News* commented that "It was a seesaw tussle throughout and the home team were fortunate to secure the only 5–1 of the night."

In the second half, the Eagles faced Edinburgh in an experimental six-a-side match for the Lanarkshire Cup, over nine heats. Not surprisingly, the fresher Monarchs tore the Eagles apart, who by now were having all sorts of bike problems. The result was 40–13 to the visitors.

The six-a-side theme was continued on 12 October when the Eagles faced a Glasgow Select in a 15 heat experimental match and lost 48–42. The idea was that each rider had five rides, but if he wasn't going well, he could be replaced by a team mate who could ride as often as needed until they scored 12 points. Close scored 14 while Gurtner scored 12. Guest Ken McKinlay contributed 9+1. For the Glasgow Select, Tommy Miller scored 14 from five rides while Bruce Semmens notched 12, also from five rides. Extra rides were given to Willie Wilson who scored 10+1 from six rides.

The Eagles wrapped their opening league season with a 41–40 defeat at Cradley Heath on Saturday 19 October, despite having seven of the 14 race winners.

The teams exchanged 4–2s and Heathens had two 3–2s to one for Eagles in a match that did not feature a single 5–1. The Eagles went to the last heat with a chance of a win, but Les Tolley won to secure the match for Cradley. A long tail did not help either team, but home advantage just weighed in their favour. The Eagles might have gone ahead late on, but Bradbury knocked off Allott in heat 11 and was excluded. The Eagles had a chance to draw level in the second last heat, but Allott suffered bike problems and Scott fell and failed to finish. This left the Eagles one point down going into the last heat. Lee rode for the Eagles and failed to score in what was probably his last speedway race.

The rising Heathens star Harry Bastable was the best Heathen with 10 while Les Tolley scored 9+1. For the Eagles, Close and Gurtner both scored 11, while Dalton got eight.

Motherwell finished seventh in the 16 team National League Division Two with 16 wins and a draw from 30 matches. They were 15 points behind champions Norwich, but just three behind Edinburgh who finished third. They finished a point ahead of Ashfield and four clear of Glasgow White City. Southampton had dropped out of the league after completing seven fixtures, not involving Motherwell. McGregor finished as top scorer for Motherwell on 239, eight clear of Gurtner on 231. Twelve riders rode for the Eagles in league meetings.

Stenner's 1952 Speedway Annual said that "Motherwell finished the season a very sound team and command a high rating for a new team. Racing at Milton Street was good and the crowds satisfactory. The Eagles won more matches than they lost, and captured for themselves an enthusiastic following from the area." In their Division Two rider rankings, Derick Close was placed seventh.

26

3. 1952: Consolidation

For 1952, the National League Second Division had 12 teams, compared to 17 in 1951. Poole and Oxford had been promoted from the Third Division, which itself had been replaced by the Southern League. The 1951 Division Two Champions, Norwich, had been promoted to the First Division. Teams that did not run from the 1951 Division Two included Newcastle, Fleetwood, Halifax and Walthamstow. Only Poole was south of the English midlands.

March

Winter speculation that Bluey Scott might move on to Edinburgh proved unfounded because he turned out for Eagles in their opening fixture at Ashfield on Tuesday 25 March. It was probably a good thing the first event only needed four men because the Eagles had Noel Watson and Keith Gurtner en route back from Australia. As it was, the Eagles foursome finished third. The Tigers won with 31, Ashfield Blues had 28, the Eagles gathered 19, one ahead of Ashfield Reds. Bluey was injured in a heat eight incident and pulled out of the meeting.

One of the few reports to hand for the fixture at The Stadium on Friday 28 March is in the Edinburgh Monarchs programme. It noted that Monarchs opened their season with a Lanarkshire Trophy match at Motherwell losing 48–36. The report's author thought that it wasn't a thrilling meeting and felt the weather was too cold for the racing to be appreciated. The Monarchs' Harold Fairhurst said he had never felt so cold racing before and thought that a rider would have needed to be out in every race to get warm.

Johnny Green, injured two nights before at White City when he wanted to see what the other side of the fence was like, surprised his team mates with a vigorous show despite his ankle injury and gathered nine points.

Needless to say, the Eagles had, in Derick Close, their match winner and they were bolstered by two guests: the Tigers' Ken McKinlay and the Giants' Larry Lazarus. Another report noted Bluey Scott's progress as he went round well clear of the fence that he had so loved to tangle with in 1951. Bluey, who had wintered in Scotland working in a steel yard, even managed two race wins.

Derick Close scored a maximum for the Eagles, but he had a stern test in heat 10 when Bob Mark and he raced much of the way neck-and-neck. Bob got revenge in the second half trophy heat, but Derick had the last laugh, winning the final.

The Eagles had three men missing. Bill Dalton was still in South Africa because of a return boat ticket mix-up while Noel Watson and Keith Gurtner were still on the high seas.

April

Transfer listed Will Lowther came back into the short-handed Eagles side that, on Friday 4 April, was still awaiting its Australians. The Speedway Control Board turned down appeals for a deferral of the match against Liverpool Chads and the match at Stoke the following evening. Will was joined by Scott Hall. As it was the Eagles top two of Close and McGregor both scored 11 and their team won 50–33 for what was to be an almost unbroken run until mid-August. The Chads' Peter Robinson started with a duck, then went on unbeaten to stop the home riders, Close and McGregor, from recording maximums.

Despite their pleas, the fixture at Stoke took place and the Eagles faced the Potters at Sun Street Stadium on 5 April down on strength. More trouble came because Bob Lindsay and Joe Crowther were involved in a car crash on the way to The Stadium and arrived at about 7.15pm. Joe's bike was wrecked in this off-track incident and he had to use the track spare. However, delayed shock affected his on-track performance in this 47–34 defeat. Joe had three rides and failed to score. Bob's bike survived the crash and he battled on.

Bike-less Joe Crowther was left out as Australians Gurtner and Watson made it back for their 1952 season debuts at The Stadium on 11 April. Gordon McGregor stood in as captain for Joe and scored a paid maximum. Gurtner impressed with a dashing score of 10 points and he continued on his winning ways in the second half final. Watson started with a duck, then rattled in a couple of wins. A solid show by the Eagles gave them a 49–35 victory and the league points. Stoke had no one outstanding and they won their only heat when Close had bike failure in heat five. Ken Adams was best Potter on eight and this included a race win over Derick Close. John Fitzpatrick was the Potters' only other race winner.

Friday 18 April saw East Anglians Yarmouth arrive at The Stadium on league business. The shorthanded Bloaters borrowed Glasgow juniors Niven McCreadie and Jack 'Red' Monteith to fill the reserve berths. Both scored a couple of points. This was better than three of the Bloaters regulars. Yet again, the Bloaters – Fred Brand apart – showed their dislike of Scottish tracks as the Eagles smoked them out to the tune of 62–22.

Young Australian Lindsay Nixon made his first appearance in the second half with a winning debut. He beat local novice Niven McCreadie, Edinburgh's Jock Scott and another local lad, Jim Russell. Lindsay stayed until the middle of July before moving south to try out for a team place there.

On Friday 25 April, birthday boy Joe Crowther was on a new bike and back in the team to face league newcomers Poole Pirates. Unfortunately, Joe failed to extend his series of birthday maximums recorded from 1949 to 1951. However, his contribution of eight points from three rides in the reserve berth was a telling one. Missing from the Eagles line-up was Stan Bradbury who, to say the least, was not pleased about it. However, he was soon back in favour and staked his place for a long run.

Poole were in with a chance up to the last heat which became a battle between Close and Brian 'The Nipper' Crutcher. The race was won by the more experienced Eagles' man after Crutcher had led for a couple of laps. With McGregor accounting for Ken Middleditch in a tussle for third place, the points stayed with Motherwell in this narrow 44–40 victory. Crutcher had spark plug trouble in an earlier heat which caused his bike to fail just before the line, allowing Watson past. In the last heat Ken Middleditch used a borrowed machine due to problems with his own mount. Crutcher headed for Glasgow after the match to catch a sleeper south rather than travel by road.

Around this time the press carried an advert for knitted sweaters for discerning fans of the Tigers, Giants and Eagles. The item, in the team colours, had the team name above a drawing of a motor cycle and was priced at 9/6 (or 47.5p).

May

Coventry Bees buzzed into Motherwell on 2 May, but were swatted 50–34. McGregor bagged a paid maximum with sound backing from Close, Watson and Gurtner. Watson was on for a paid maximum when his bike packed up in his last race. The Bees pulled away in the opening heats and it took the Eagles to heat nine to reign them in and get their beaks ahead. When they did, they soared on to a great win.

For the Bees, Stan Williams's bike problems kept his returns down and Johnny Reason's fall in the last heat left him with broken ribs. Les Hewitt was also in the wars. He crashed in his opening ride and was carried off, He spiritedly returned for a couple of more outings before pulling out of the meeting.

The return fixture at Coventry took place on 3 May. Light rain made an already wet track surface well-nigh impossible to race on. Most of the races were decided on the first and second bends and Coventry had the edge in most instances. The Eagles' Keith Gurtner was the star of the meeting with a full maximum, but, despite support from Close, the Eagles could not ground the Bees. The Eagles had the majority of race winners, but lacked second-string support. The Bees had a sting in their tail and won 45–39.

The riders from both teams deserved a medal each for riding in this meeting, but the fans were the losers because the entertainment value was very limited. Gurtner's pass of Charlie New in heat five stood out, when defeat had looked a distinct possibility for the Australian.

The Eagles travelled to Oxford on Thursday 8 May. It was a close contest and little separated the two sides. It was no surprise that the two teams went into the last heat level at 39–39. With a draw on the cards for much of the last heat, McGregor came from the back when Ron Wilson went wide on the third lap to take third place. This swayed the result in the Eagles' favour. The 43–41 result was the Eagles' first away win of the season. Derick Close was magnificent on the very tricky rain-soaked track. His outside overtake of Harry Saunders in heat 10 was hailed as an amazing piece of track craft.

Bike problems for Watson and Gurtner cost the Eagles victory in the home match against Glasgow Tigers on 9 May. Gurtner, who had travelled over for the season accompanied by a church minister, could have done with divine inspiration for this one. Watson also had bike problems and these problems contributed to the Eagles downfall.

The Tigers had three heat leaders in Miller, McKinlay and Bainbridge to the Eagles' two. Gordon McGregor's maximum score did not have the backing from the rest of his team. The Tigers led from heat four and had the match in the bag at the end of heat 13. The last heat Eagles' 4–2 made the score – 44–40 – just a little bit more respectable.

Close had an up-and-down meeting. He finished his league races behind his Scottish Match Race Championship opponent Tommy Miller. However, in the second half he returned the compliment.

The other Glasgow based team, Ashfield Giants, had been the bane of the Eagles' life in 1951. However, on their showing on Saturday 10 May, they were a pushover. The wet track conditions of mud-bath proportions suited the visitors from Motherwell more than the Giants and the Eagles ran out comfortable 51–32 winners. Such was the margin of the Eagles' superiority that they had 10 of the 14 heat winners. Close won all his races from the gate. The Eagles could have made the margin of victory larger had Watson's bike performed properly. It did not stop, but did not deliver competitive power and he trailed in last in two heats. An away win had been forecast by some pundits, but the margin of victory for the Eagles surprised them.

The Glasgow Tigers were let off the hook on 14 May because the Eagles' riders suffered machine problems which pegged them back at vital times. McGregor lost three certain points when his engine stopped in heat six, and machine troubles affected other riders. There were other problems for the Eagles. For example, in another heat Close suffered some confusion over the flag displayed and shut off a lap early, thereby losing his first place. The net result was that the close fought match went the way of the Tigers, 43–41.

The bike problems paled into insignificance as Keith Gurtner broke a bone in his hand in a second half crash into the fence. This injury was compounded by him being hit by the following Jack Hodgson. The next day he realised that his leg hurt. Keith was diagnosed as also having a broken bone in his ankle.

Without the injured Gurtner, the Eagles pulled off a good 51–33 win at home to Oxford on Friday 16 May. The Eagles gave Scott Hall an opportunity in the team and he chipped in with two points. Bluey Scott celebrated his birthday about now and, while he did not score many points, he did have about 20 birthday presents from fans.

The power house of Close, Watson and McGregor each grabbed a paid maximum. They all used the outside line on the bends to their advantage, passing opponents when they missed the start. Oxford did well up to heat 10 and were only two points adrift. However, yet again, the opposition just crumpled at the end of the meeting. The last four heats went 5–1 to the Eagles suggesting, wrongly, the Cheetahs had been poor opposition.

Danny Lee, who had not ridden at all in 1952, announced his retirement and Motherwell also released Bob Lindsay by agreeing to his transfer request.

Gurtner came back from injury at The Stadium on 23 May, but pulled out of the National Trophy first leg meeting against Coventry after his engine failed in heat six. He was carrying hand and ankle injuries from a few weeks before. He had modified the handlebars of his machine to allow him to ride. He had originally hoped the medics could modify his plaster (or stookie) but that wasn't possible. Stan Bradbury stepped into Gurtner's remaining rides and compensated for the missing Australian.

Close was in great form. He won five of his rides and followed home team-mate Watson, who was having a bit of an off night due to bike problems, in the other one. Close nearly set a new track record, but had to be content with matching the existing one.

Coventry started without heat leader Johnny Reason and John Wright moved into the side. They did well to hold Eagles to a 61–47 score and had set themselves a reasonable target for the return the following evening.

The Bees produced a solid display at Brandon to clip the Eagles' wings in the second leg. With a 71–35 win, the Coventry side secured an aggregate score of 118–97 to go into the next round. Close was best Eagle on 12, but Watson and McGregor failed to match him. Crowther failed to score and was replaced after a couple rides. With the tie lost, the Eagles lost Bradbury too. He was unlucky to find the fallen Derek Tailby in his path and crashed in an attempt to avoid the stricken rider. Why Derek was still trying to race is not clear because he had fallen earlier in the race and been lapped before remounting.

The Eagles managed one race winner – Noel Watson – at Poole on Monday 26 May. He was the best Eagle on seven points and the Pirates ended up as 62–22 winners to take the league points. Close was the next best on six and the rest contributed little. The Wimborne Road track was quite slick and suited the home team much more than the visitors. The Poole riders had the luxury of indulging in a spot of team riding and Ken Middleditch gathered three bonus points on his way to a paid maximum. Brian Crutcher, on the other hand, compiled his maximum on his own.

The end of May, Friday 30 to be precise, saw Keith Gurtner make his second attempt to get over his recent injury. This time it worked. It was vitally important that the Eagles put one over on Edinburgh. Keith was in heat 10 which was, to say the least, incident packed. The Monarchs' Bob Mark failed to make the distance due to bike problems.

Left: The tidy style of Gordon McGregor. Right: Stan Bradbury,
who rode for one and a half seasons for the Eagles. (Both photos JSC)

Left: Will Lowther who ended his long speedway career at Motherwell (JSC);
right: a Motherwell programme (Courtesy FOES).

For the Eagles, Watson was leading the heat when he fell and Dick Campbell performed heroics to jump his bike over the Australian. In the process, Campbell wrenched his knee and retired from the race and the meeting. The only one taking the flag was Gurtner.

Harold Fairhurst, scored a rare away maximum while colleague Bob Mark had the unusual distinction of taking four starts and having engine failure in all four. Bob's last engine failure happened in heat 14 when he and Don Cuppleditch could have swung the match in the Monarchs' favour. As it was the lanky Englishman, known as The Candy Kid, won from the two Eagles. The net result of all this was that the Eagles shaded the match with a narrow 41–40 win. At this time, a rider had to complete a race to win points. In later times the Monarchs would have had points credited to Campbell and this would have given them a draw.

With the Giants away from home on Saturday 31 May, the Tigers and the Eagles entertained the stay-at-home fans. Even with three second half regulars, the Tigers were more than a match for the almost full-strength Eagles who gave an outing to Australian second-halfer Lindsay Nixon. Nixon had tagged along with Gurtner and rode regularly in second halves at Motherwell before he moved south to try his hand at Southern League Wolverhampton. The Eagles lost 50–34 and Derick Close lost the Scottish Match Race Championship to holder Tommy Miller.

June

At Leicester on Monday 2 June the Eagles were without Crowther, injured in a crash at Aldershot where he was riding in the opening rounds of the 1952 World Championship a couple of days earlier. Scott and Gurtner had also competed in the meeting scoring one and eight respectively. Neither progressed to the next round.

The Eagles also missed fellow invalid Watson, who had been injured the previous Friday at The Stadium. They drafted in the still transfer listed Bradbury and Lindsay, another rider who was unhappy at the club. Bradbury moved into the number three race jacket which allowed them to retain Scott Hall at reserve. Only a solid display by McGregor, and, to a lesser extent, by Close, saved Eagles from a whitewash (or track coloured wash?) on a very wet Leicester track. A last heat 5–1 for the McGregor and Close pairing made the score, 52–32, a bit more respectable.

Tuesday 3 June saw the Eagles at the home of Yarmouth Bloaters. On a track so often a bogey for Scottish teams, the Eagles performed reasonably well without really threatening to take the league points. Fred Brand and Bob Baker rattled in full maximums in this 49–35 home win.

Close managed a single race win in his nine point return. This came in the rerun of heat seven after being the victim of a coming together with Terry Courtnell who was excluded. Gurtner, McGregor and old hand Lowther, who had a good night, were the only other Eagles to take the chequered flag for the visitors.

Back home on Friday 6 June, the Eagles faced Cradley Heath Heathens on league business. Watson was back, but bike troubles reduced him to a single second place. He was well placed each time his bike stopped. On a more positive note, Close recorded a full maximum for the Eagles who won 48–36.

Bluey Scott, the harum-scarum Australian of 1951, was back in the thriller mould again. In heat 10 Bluey encountered problems on one of the bends and fell off his borrowed bike. He came to a halt, but the bike had a mind of its own in those pre 'cut-out' days. It set off

32

in the direction it had come from. Needless to say, the oncoming riders were somewhat alarmed and scattered in all directions to avoid the riderless machine.

The Eagles' bike problems continued on Saturday 7 June in the return match at Cradley. This time they hit both Close and Watson. Both borrowed Bluey Scott's machine at one time or another to complete the match. The Eagles had an early advantage, but let it slip allowing the Heathens back in to win 47–37. Had McGregor received a bit more support things might have turned out differently.

Fellow Friday night track Leicester visited Motherwell on Monday 9 June as the current league leaders. Despite trying hard, the Hunters never really threatened the home side who ran out winners 48–36. McGregor scored a maximum and Close was paid for the lot. Leicester were lucky Gurtner was still carrying his injury and his score of six reflects this.

Lionel Benson and Les Beaumont were the best visitors with nine points each, although Lionel was paid a bonus point after shepherding Joe Bowkis round in one of his races. Leicester eventually finished third in the league, so it was a good result for the Eagles.

Friday 13 June, and for the who saw this as a bad omen the visit of the Glasgow Tigers on Lanarkshire Cup business could have had the fans wondering what was going to happen. With track specialist Tommy Miller in town, it was a case of seeing who could lower his colours. As it was nobody did. Tommy scored a maximum. He started out by beating Harold Fairhurst in his Scottish Match Race Championship decider. Tommy rounded off the night with a clean sweep in the second half.

The match went to a last heat decider which saw the Eagles win 44–40 thanks to a McGregor and Gurtner advantage over Don Wilkinson and Alf McIntosh. The Eagles had a heat leader and strong second-string riding at numbers two and six to cover the eventuality of a last heat decider. After heat three, the Tigers had a very healthy eight-point lead and that is often a sign that the visitors have settled in. The Tigers stretched the lead to 10 points by the end of heat six, but the Eagles held their nerve and clawed back a 5–1 before conceding two more 4–2 reverses. It was not until heat 10 that the Eagles gathered themselves to rattle in two 5–1s and a 4–2 to set the stage for the McGregor and Gurtner's match winning 5–1.

There were very few heats that did not have a thrill in the meeting at Edinburgh's Old Meadowbank the next night. Heat six proved to be an unfortunate one for the Monarchs' Harold Fairhurst because, after he had managed to hold off Close for most of the race, he hit a bump at the last bend making him go just a little bit too wide. The Motherwell man immediately seized his chance to cut through and gain a narrow win and, with Gurtner in third place, the Eagles recorded their first heat success.

The Eagles' two outstanding men were Close, who dropped a single point to Bob Mark, and McGregor on eight while Bob Lindsay, a last-minute inclusion at reserve, had four rides and collected five points. Bradbury's seven points haul is also worthy of mention. The Eagles collected only one other heat advantage in this 46–38 league defeat.

Back to Friday night action and Stoke Potters visited The Stadium on 20 June. The visitors were described by some pundits as being woefully weak. They finished in 10th place in the 12 team Second Division. McGregor, who scored 10+1, was a point shy of joining his team mates Close and Watson on the maximum trail. The three heat leaders laid firm foundations for Eagles' 54–30 victory. The Potters' young Londoner Reg Fearman stopped Gordon when he became one of only two Stoke heat winners.

Following a rain-off on Saturday 21 June at Saracen, the Giants and Eagles had to wait until Friday 27 June for their next dose of speedway action. As it was, new Giants' signings from Fleetwood, Wilf Jay and Norman Hargreaves, repaid Norrie Isbister's faith in them by scoring vital points that helped give the visitors a 61–46 win in this Scottish Cup first round first leg fixture.

After a spell of good form, McGregor had an off night and the rest of the team could not carry him as a virtual passenger. He was not the only one who had trouble against the Giants. Only Bluey Scott had a good meeting, but that was before engine trouble pulled him up. The *Speedway News* commented that "With the exception of Close, who scored 16 points, Eagles never reached the high standard of their recent meetings and never looked like reducing the half-way deficit of 10 points."

The Eagles were always behind with only Close up to his scoring capabilities; the visitors were never seriously challenged. Bruce Semmens and Willie Wilson were the top Giants. Bruce, who was a qualified pilot and owned his own plane, flew to 15+2 while Willie 'The Wasp' gathered 13+1.

July

In America folks on this 4 July were celebrating Independence Day. In Motherwell, the Eagles fans celebrated a home 49–35 league win over Cradley Heath. The Heathens included new signing Geoff Bennett who had joined them from Birmingham, but he failed to hit the heights. A crowd of 12,000 saw the Eagles get back on the winning track. Les Tolley, promoted from the reserve berth, was the best Heathen with nine. Tolley continued his run in the second half winning the Final with little to spare from Close, Gurtner and fellow Heathen, Phil Malpass.

The Eagles' win can be put down to double figures from Close and Watson plus eight apiece from McGregor and Gurtner. Close settled for a paid maximum as he nursed home Hall in heat six.

Jim Tolley starred in the Heathens' good win over the Eagles, who had all their riders, except Derick Close, off song, on Saturday 5 July. These two featured in the race of the night when the home man just held off Close, who also featured in a thrilling final heat. Harry Bastable just took it on the last bend and held a narrow advantage to the flag. Jim Tolley's brother Les, riding at first reserve, scored 10+1 for a happy night in the Tolley household. What the score might have been had the normally reliable Fred Perkins managed to turn in a point is anyone's guess. As it was Heathens won by a good margin of 51–33.

Close scored 9+1 while Watson had three second places and an engine failure, gathering six. Lowther and Gurtner both scored 5+1.

It was a near thing at Old Meadowbank on Wednesday 9 July. Sadly, for the Eagles, it was the Monarchs' heat leader Dick Campbell's first maximum of 1952 that paved the way for a narrow home victory.

After a first heat crash, McGregor, who was still in a spell of poor form, was excluded for stopping the race. A surprise for the Eagles came in heat four when the Monarchs' reserve, Harry Darling, rode round the field to win in 69 seconds, beating Bradbury and Gurtner.

The Eagles had a last heat chance of taking a draw, but McGregor could not pass Cuppleditch to grab the vital point and this match, billed as an Edinburgh Cup fixture, went to Monarchs 43–41.

Tommy Miller was reported as being £110 richer from his two successful World

Championship rounds at White City and then at Motherwell on Friday 11 July. Tommy regularly cleaned up at The Stadium and this was no exception. Some Eagles followers in the huge crowd were no great fans of the Blantyre man and somewhat unsportingly booed and catcalled, not that Tommy was bothered too much. On the track, Tommy had problems in heat seven when out-gated by Wembley's Eric Williams, but Tommy passed him on the last lap by taking a tighter inside line to win the race.

The quality of the field was such that nine riders scored double figures. Runner-up was Swede Dan Forsberg on 12 while four riders, Close, Henry Long, Geoff Mardon and Ken Middleditch all claimed joint third place. The Eagles' other flag bearer, McGregor, had yet another poor meeting and was out of the hunt after a couple of races. The meeting featured Wimbledon's American Ernie Roccio who was, sadly, killed in a track crash at West Ham a week or so after this meeting.

In the return leg of the Scottish Cup tie on Saturday 12 July, the Eagles scored more at Saracen Park than they had done at home. The Giants relished the prospect of progressing to an all-Glasgow final with a 120–94 aggregate score and a 59–48 win on the night. Former Giant Gurtner and Derick Close were the best for the visitors, but the Giants were up for it and the Eagles were out. Motherwell did lead for a short spell, but it did not last.

The top Giant was veteran Wilf Jay with 14 and another former Newcastle man, Close, was the top Eagle on 12. Again, the Eagles suffered from out of sorts heat leaders in a match where the last six heats were started using a flag following a starting gate failure.

As the score says, there was little daylight between the Eagles and the Tigers at the end of 14 heats at The Stadium on 18 July. The result was 43–41 in the Tigers' favour. They were eight points up after three heats, but the Eagles pulled back level by heat nine. It stayed level until heat 13 when the Tigers got a couple of points ahead again. The Tigers had Tommy Miller in the last heat and he held off Close and McGregor to give the Tigers the win. Tommy Miller started his maximum by setting a new track record in heat one. The wee man was motoring as he took two seconds off the previous mark.

Close, who so often carried the Eagles, had bike troubles which pegged back his score and Lowther, who normally rode well above himself when he faced the Tigers, didn't score from the first reserve berth.

After defeat by the Tigers the week before, Glasgow's other team, the Giants, came to the steel making town. They also took the league points back down the River Clyde on a night when the starting gate malfunctioned again and races were started using a flag. This resulted in a few unsatisfactory starts. This time the margin was a bit greater and the Giants won 45–39 on 25 July. Apart from Close, who had to do things the hard way coming from the back each time, and, to a lesser extent, Gurtner, the Eagles riders were just not at the races.

The Giants had no individual star and their win was down to a solid effort from everyone. Bruce Semmens was at the centre of some controversy when his robust style of riding caused the local fans to become very animated.

Watson lost in his second race due to a flat tyre, but his other three races only yielded five points and McGregor was only two points better.

The Eagles completed their run of defeats against their fellow Scottish teams with a 45–39 defeat at Old Meadowbank on 26 July. It is ironic that they scored as many in Edinburgh as they had on their home circuit the night before. Yet again Close and Gurtner rose to the occasion but, with the others not delivering, they were second best to the Monarchs.

The scores were level for the first seven heats, but once they fell behind it looked as though the Eagles were on the slippery slope. Not so. They came back to a couple of points adrift going in to the last heat, but the Monarchs duo of Dick Campbell and Don Cuppleditch combined to ensure the score pleased the home fans.

August

Friday 1 August saw the first ever drawn match at The Stadium. The Edinburgh side took an early lead in the first heat and held on to it until the very last heat when an Eagles' 4–2 managed to salvage a draw. The Monarchs' faithful in the crowd probably expected better because up to that point, Don Cuppleditch and Bob Mark had only dropped a single point each, Close had been beaten twice and McGregor was off song yet again with only four points. As it turned out, they managed to score the vital 4–2 and, many thought that had McGregor a bit more straight-line speed. A 5–1 and a match win would have been a distinct possibility.

Watson and Cuppleditch tied for fastest second in the second half event. Watson won the coin toss to decide who would make it to the final.

It was a red-letter day for 15-year-old Nessie Stark who won the *Motherwell Times* Lucky Lady competition. Not only did she win new clothes and a meal at a swish hotel, she was the guest of the Motherwell Speedway Directors for the meeting and met her hero, Derick Close.

Stan Bradbury was still seeking a move and was interesting Wolverhampton. Unfortunately, the £250 price tag was considered to be too great. He appealed to the Speedway Control Board to reduce it.

What a change for the Eagles when McGregor and Watson were in the groove. On Friday 8 August, the Eagles' big three did the business, but Gurtner was way off form with a miserable four points. The rough track surface caused by a heavy downpour before the match made conditions a bit tricky and maybe did not help his cause.

The Chads from Liverpool did not have any big guns to match the Eagles and went down 51–33 after taking a surprise opening heat lead. However, to be fair to the visitors, Peter Robinson, Harry Welch and Don Potter all made a fight of it.

Yet another Scottish team bit the dust at Great Yarmouth on Tuesday 12 August. The tricky Caister Road circuit saw the Eagles crash to a 62–22 defeat by the Bloaters' men who were becoming masters of their own racing strip. Short in stature, but big on points, Johnny Chamberlain chose this meeting to top score for the seasiders for the first time. The 20-year-old Australian took 11 points from his four rides. For the Eagles, Close scored half his side's total and the rest were very poor. Surprisingly, only reserve Peter Harris, known in Scotland as 'Gundy', was unbeaten by a visitor. The long haul back to their homes must have been a real drag for any traveling Eagles fans.

The Eagles sprung back from the defeat at Yarmouth to beat the struggling Oxford Cheetahs on their Cowley strip on Thursday 14 August. The Second bottom Cheetahs, who finished the season bottom of the table, had the best of it up to heat 10 but could not keep up their momentum in the last four heats. Close scored a maximum and was ably supported by Gurtner on 10+1. The match went to heat 14 when Close, backed by McGregor took the vital 5–1 to win the match 43–41, leaving the home fans disappointed.

To ensure everyone had a fair chance of making the last 16, 32 riders fought out a series of qualifiers for places in the Scottish Riders' Championship. It was the Edinburgh duo of Campbell and Cuppleditch plus the Giant's Semmens who made it to the podium at

The Stadium on Friday 15 August. The next places were filled by Gurtner who tied with Giants' Ron Phillips. A broken chain for Close and a fall for Watson spoiled their podium place aspirations. Wilf Jay crashed in heat two and Jim Blyth was injured avoiding him. With no reserves a few races featured three riders only.

Missing Keith Gurtner, who was on international duty for Australia at New Cross on Wednesday 20 August, the Eagles put up a fair show at White City. The Tigers were without the injured heat leader duo of Tommy Miller and Junior Bainbridge, so the Eagles were probably not as down on power as the home side. Bradbury was also missing from the Eagles line-up. Lindsay and Niven McCreadie at reserve could not replace the missing duo, and scored a single point between them. The Eagles actually had eight race winners in the 14 heats in this 45–39 defeat, but the Tigers effectively limited the damage in most races to 3–3s.

Bluey Scott sparkled in the match with Oxford Cheetahs at The Stadium on 22 August and was looking like a maximum man. Unfortunately, in his last ride he met up with Jim Boyd who had other ideas and separated Bluey from Watson and from his paid maximum. The young red-headed Australian settled for third place and a bumper pay night. Maybe it was nerves, but his last race gate was not so good as the others. Scott Hall also had a good night with seven points after an opening race fall.

The meeting saw a good return for McGregor who took a paid maximum while an opening race fall robbed Watson of a chance of double figures. Jim Gregory was best of the Cheetahs octet scoring seven.

Close did not need to make the start to compile his maximum at Brandon against Coventry the following evening. In every race he had to come from the back to win. In heat nine, he gated last and left it until the last bend before passing Vic Emms to take the flag. The only other Eagle to shine at Coventry on Saturday 23 August was McGregor who chipped in with 10. With 22 between Close and McGregor, the rest of the Motherwell based sextet only managed eight points between them in this 48–30 defeat. Of the eight, threequarters were scored by Scott who started brightly with a race win over Johnny Reason and Stan Williams, but could only add another three points.

The Eagles were the third Scottish team to go under to the Chads in reasonably quick succession when they visited Stanley Stadium in Liverpool. On 25 August, the Eagles had been in front a few times but they could not get back on even terms after heat 10 when the Chads nudged in front by a couple of points.

Six Eagles scored points, but the reserves, veteran Lowther and youngster Lindsay, failed to contribute and that was the telling factor. Close scored yet another maximum on the big pacey track but without that vital backing at the lower end of the team, the Eagles just missed out. There was a possibility that Eagles could have snatched a win had they managed at least a 4–2 in the last heat, but Chads had Peter Robinson in that heat and he produced the match winning ride just at the right time.

Scottish teams had troubles at Yarmouth but, equally, the Bloaters had troubles in Scotland to even things up. With Close, McGregor and Watson on form, with Close scoring another maximum, the Bloaters were always in line for a rough time of it. With Lowther bouncing back to form with seven points and Lindsay chipping in with three, the home men soon piled up 55 points to the visitors' 29. Johnny Chamberlain was the sole Bloaters' race winner on Friday 29 August. This was Keith Gurtner's last outing for the Eagles. He was unhappy at Motherwell and was transferred to Edinburgh before the next match.

Derick Close's qualification for the World Final came to the attention of Tom Morgan in the *Speedway News*. After looking at Close's high scores in league racing, he outlined that "Bringing it all down to cold figures, Derick scored 113 of 120 possible league points in exactly a month; and in between times he found opportunity to reach the last stage of the World Championship Final, among other things. If Derick is not careful, he will be outshining Tommy Miller as Scotland's best; and − whisper it quietly − he may even be chosen for England." He continued: "Close has beaten some of the top-rung speedway boys and on one occasion at Wimbledon defeated Tommy Price when the Wembley man was reigning champion ... he got an England jersey at Birmingham last year and now that he has reached the final above test men Eric French, Eric Williams, Cyril Brine and Tommy Miller, perhaps the selectors will have another look at him."

September

Brian Crutcher apart the main body of the England side visiting on Friday 5 September were First Division riders. The match was watched by the Duke of Hamilton and he was presented with a gift by Sheila Robertson, promoter John Y Robertson's daughter. The Scotland side, which contained five native and three 'adopted' sons repulsed the Auld Enemy, who included a couple of Welshmen, by a narrow margin. Taking account of the quality of the opposition, which included a former World Champion Freddie Williams, this was an outstanding win for the team representing Scotland.

Tommy Miller was pegged back to second by Eddie Rigg in his fourth ride depriving him of his maximum and Close had three uncompleted rides due to engine failures before he strung together an unbeaten three outings to score nine. Watson, Don Cuppleditch and Willie Wilson were replaced after hitting problems. Bob Mark sparkled with 6+3 in his three outings, yet again showing his liking for The Stadium. The win by the Scotland side gave them the series rubber by three matches to two and an estimated 45,000, a Scottish speedway record crowd, must have gone home delighted.

Close put defeat by Tommy Miller in the Scottish Match Race Championship behind him to give the Eagles his best attention in the league fixture at Saracen Park on Tuesday 9 September. Close scored a maximum, but without that vital support, the Eagles could not wrest the two points from the Giants. Meeting reports indicate this was a closely contested match with great racing, reflected in the 43−41 score. Top Giant was Willie Wilson with 10+1 with Larry Lazarus on 10, while Eagles McGregor chipped in 7+1.

This fixture, on Friday 12 September, was the Eagles' first match without Keith Gurtner. It was a debut night for former Monarch Johnny Green. The deal was a transfer for both riders, not a rider swap as might appear the case on first inspection. The Eagles were also without Close, who was on test match duty for England at Harringay, and had an uphill struggle on their hands.

The Giants took full advantage of the weakened Eagles to win by a reasonable margin and take the points thanks to a 44−39 win. The men in black and white were not helped by a miserable night for Watson, who was well capable of scoring more than the two he did. Noel's poor return was thanks to bike problems which arose when he was in scoring positions. Back in the top six, Lowther had a miserable night scoring just one point. An exclusion for Green and a fall for Hall, in the last heat, cost points. Thankfully Scott's fall did not matter as the match was effectively lost and an Eagles 5−0 would have only taken the draw. Green's exclusion was for breaking the tapes and Cyril Cooper raced off with the tapes wrapped round his neck. The race was stopped to remove the offending tapes.

The Stoke Potters line up at Sun Street on Saturday 13 September was strong enough, despite no one scoring double figures, to see off the Eagles by a convincing 50–33 margin. Close scored a full maximum and Watson was only beaten by Gil Blake, but that was only 23 points, which was 20 points shy of a winning total. Between six of them the rest managed 10 points and, of those, Lowther contributed five. McGregor had a miserable night with a couple of lasts, a fall and a single third place. Not the kind of return expected of a heat leader.

The Eagles needed a reliable third heat leader. Often, like at this meeting, two men would go great guns, but two top men winning seven races without support cannot win matches.

The Eagles visited the south coast and at Poole on Monday 15 September, they faced the strong Pirates octet who were edging towards their first Second Division championship. Motor trouble for Close reduced his contribution to four, but with the rest of the team scoring in dribs and drabs it did not make much difference. The Eagles had a single race winner in Watson who won heat two. Scott was third after Crutcher dropped out with engine trouble and this was the visitors' only heat advantage. At the end of 14 heats, Poole had taken a clear 60–24 win which maintained the Pirates on track for the league title.

On Thursday 18 September, Derick Close became the third Scottish based Second Division rider to appear in the World Final at Wembley Stadium. Derick scored only four points, but he did better than established First Division men Cyril Roger and Ron How to become the 14th best rider in the World.

The Eagles visited Leicester's Blackbird Road, on what was normally a home fixture night, on Friday 19 September. They made a better show of it, but still lacked the top end fire power to worry the home side. The Eagles' management could be faulted for not giving Lowther at least one more outing at the expense of Hall who had a hard night. However, in those days it wasn't seen as good form to use a reserve unless it was absolutely necessary and team men were not pulled out just because their form was not that great. Yet again it was Close who worried the opposition, but he could not stop Len Williams scoring a maximum in the Hunters 48–36 win.

Back at The Stadium in Motherwell on the same night, the home fans had the option to have their fix of Castrol R, the oil used in speedway engines. It was a fixture filler which gave the juniors and novices a chance to strut their stuff. Glasgow Tigers' Australian Bob Sharp won the meeting with ease, but very few of those riding had any team experience and he was the favourite from the outset. The Giants' John Paul was runner-up and unattached Tammy Woods from Bathgate and Jim Russell were joint third.

Despite being on their way to the League championship, the Pirates faltered at Motherwell on 26 September. Close and Watson both scored maximums and the rest of the team rallied round to secure a win. Green had a bad start in the first heat. He reared as the tapes rose and lost control, ending up on the centre green. McGregor had bike problems in the same race; his bike cut out before restarting to allow him to claim third spot. Poole had their noses in front for a fair part of the match, but the Eagles levelled by heat nine. The Eagles pushed ahead in heat 12 and the next few heats set the stage for a last heat decider. After a poor night from McGregor up to that point, the terracing pundits must have been bracing themselves for defeat because he was programmed to appear in the last, vital, heat. The pundits were wrong and he rose to the occasion in the race to lead home Ken Middleditch and Bill Holden to win the heat and the meeting for his team. His three points contributed to winning the match 43–41.

39

October

The match at The Stadium versus Coventry on Friday 3 October was unusual. Neither side scored a 5–1. The heat advantages were all 4–2s and there were few bonus points. In all, ten 4–2s and four 3–3s were recorded. The home team were never ahead.

The Eagles had bad luck when Lindsay's bike fell silent in heat 13 when he had third place in the bag. It started again, but then he was at the back and out of the points. McGregor, who was having another poor night, came good yet again to win the last race to ensure the league points were shared with a 42–42 draw. Had Hall managed to pass one of the Coventry pair, he would have given Eagles a win.

Derek Tailby was commended by the meeting Steward for his quick fire lay down when McGregor fell off a short way in front of the Bee.

The local car dealers Skellys sponsored the big individual meeting on Friday 10 October and saw it go to an extra heat to decide the destination of their trophy. Close, McKinlay and Cuppleditch lined up for the final and the lanky Monarch won the race and the pot from Ken McKinlay with home favourite Close last. Cuppleditch did the business from the tapes and led easily to the flag. Tommy Miller, who had looked a likely winner, blew it in heat 20 when he came third behind Cuppleditch and McKinlay. Tommy was already a point down after defeat by Close.

Wet treacherous conditions gave home advantage on Monday 13 October. McGregor scored his first maximum for some time and Close also added one to his record. Green was missing with flu, and Niven McCreadie rode at reserve.

Despite the state of the track, there were only a couple of fallers, Scott and Watson. The problem was that they both did it in the same race which gifted Leicester a 5–1. This meeting brought down the home curtain on the Eagles' second full league season and fans must have been happy with a 49–35 win. For the Hunters, Len Williams was best on 7+1.

A month or so ago, the Eagles had given the Chads a scare. This time, at the big Liverpool track on Monday 20 October, the home team raced to an easy win and, Close apart, had things their own way. Close finished his league season with yet another full house. Unfortunately, the next best Eagle was Hall with four points, so it was no surprise that the Eagles lost 59–25. Harry Welch and Don Potter both scored 11 for the Chads.

In the league, the Eagles finished eighth with 40 points from their 44 meetings. They were the lowest of the Scottish teams, who finished fifth, sixth, seventh and eighth in the 12-team league. Poole won the title comfortably from Coventry. In the *Stenner's 1953 Annual* rider rankings for the Second Division, Derick Close finished second to Tommy Miller, and ahead of Brian Crutcher.

The review of Motherwell's season in *Stenner's* said that the team's tail was "over-long" and that the management had failed to strengthen it. The writer, Len Simpson, said that "While Motherwell's Wembley finalist proved himself a star of the Division, his colleagues, with the exception of McGregor, Gurtner and Watson, just weren't quite good enough to make an impression on the opposition, although let no one say they failed to do their best. Their limitations, however, told their own tale."

He added that "The Eagles had a bad time when they went point-hunting south of the border, although in common with most Scottish teams they were always capable of winning on other circuits in their own country." However, he concluded that "If they can retain their leading riders and add a couple of young up-and-comings to the books they might stir the top end of the league up this year [1953]."

4. 1953: Just three teams in Scotland

Work started in late February on preparing the track. Trials were staged on 19 March in readiness for the opening fixture on 27 March, which was to be a Best Pairs tournament. Bluey Scott was the man who impressed as he showed a turn of speed on the bends.

Motherwell were still in the Second Division. The league started with 10 teams, two less than the previous season, but Liverpool dropped out halfway through the season. Scotland had lost a team as well. Ashfield had withdrawn from the league, so there were only three Scottish teams. Apart from the Scottish teams, four were from the midlands, one from East Anglia, and one was from the south coast.

The new line up-under Tom Reid was now captained by Gordon McGregor and included former Ashfield men Ron Phillips and Jimmy Tannock. The Giants' mascot Jimmy Cramb, and Johnny Duffy, the Giants' backroom mechanical man also arrived and Ron Philips bought his young fuel and oil man Pat Horsfield. Will Lowther was given a free transfer which effectively ended his lengthy career. Johnny Green's planned move to Sheffield didn't happen and he settled for another year at Motherwell. Ian Hoskins, writing in the *Speedway News*, said that "... the signing of Ron Phillips, Bill Dalton, Johnny Green and Jimmy Tannock should strengthen their tail, especially away from home."

The Eagles tried to sign South African Vern McWilliams, who had been spotted by Bill Dalton, but injury ruled him out. The Motherwell management looked for a new rider to boost their fortunes. Moves to sign former Giant Merv Harding from New Cross and Harry Welch from Liverpool failed. Both stayed put, but Welch moved to Glasgow Tigers when Liverpool closed.

Noel Watson, originally thought to be staying in Australia, had a poor opening meeting on Friday 27 March. An engine failure and a disqualification (exclusion) reduced his score. He had barely been three days in the country, having been collected from Tilbury and driven north by Bluey Scott.

The meeting highlight was the race between Derick Close, back for his third season, and Tommy Miller. Tommy, using the White City track spare, led for a while but slowed as he drove wide into the bend at the start of the last lap. Close took his chance to drive through on the inside by which time Tommy had powered up and was chasing him. Close fell on the last bend and Miller piled into the track fence to avoid him. Despite pushing bikes, both failed finish in time. Track conditions were blamed as the cause of the two men's falls. It had cut up as the evening progressed.

Miller had one other scare when Phillips led for a spell, but Miller passed him, demonstrating his skills were not just gating. Phillips, signed in early March, did well in his other rides and Ashfield boss Norrie Isbister felt he had let the rider move for too low a fee. The Best Pair was the Tigers' Miller and Larry Lazarus who were way out ahead of the Eagles pairings of McGregor & Tannock, and Close & Hall; each a star and junior who finished joint runners up.

April

With the new signings Phillips and Tannock, the Eagles defeated Coventry Bees 53–31 on 3 April. More had been expected of the Bees, winners at Glasgow White City two days earlier, but they never settled and were described as a lacklustre lot. Watson and Close formed the main strike force, both scoring maximums, ably assisted by McGregor and Phillips. Close demonstrated team riding in heat three when he shielded Bluey Scott from Derek Hewitt for almost the full four laps before going on to win the race. In most of the other races, the Eagles had the drop on the Bees from the tapes. Watson attributed his new found speed to Johnny Duffy's work on his bike.

The Bees apparently found it hard to cope with the track banking which seemed to help riders who could gate. Their best man was Johnny Reason on 10 who gave the maximum men a close run for their money and spoiled Phillips' night in his other outings. This early season form was not continued – Coventry went on to win the league, while Motherwell finished sixth.

In an effort to foster Scottish talent John Paul, Gordon Mitchell, Ron Houston, Stuart Irvine and Jack 'Red' Monteith were introduced to the second halves.

Another promising Eagles display came on Monday 6 April at Leicester, but they ended two points shy of a win. The Eagles led until heat 13 when a 5–1 put the Hunters in front. Len Williams kept his team ahead with a win over Close, who had been unbeaten up to that point. Heat 13 had been rerun with only one Eagle as Green tumbled out first time round. McGregor was back on form, and dropped his only point to Alf Parker.

For much of the meeting at Motherwell on 10 April, the Monarchs were faster out the gate than the Eagles who found it hard to overtake. The match seesawed throughout, but many considered the Monarchs to be worthy winners. The visitors had bad luck in the opening two heats as first Dick Campbell was excluded for breaking the tapes, then Eddie Lack suffered an engine failure in the second heat. Close scored his second home maximum. Former Eagle Bob Lindsay rode for the Monarchs, but failed to score. The most spectacular race was heat six when Eagles' Phillips outmanoeuvred Harold Fairhurst.

McGregor, had an off night, made a poor start and could not catch the others. His problems were compounded by breaking a chain and his frame later in the meeting. Phillips had bike problems too, breaking a fork leg. Green and Watson also had bike troubles and even the young mascot Cramb suffered as well. The Eagles' home record went east as Edinburgh, reported as looking a bit uneasy, picked up the league points with a 45–39 win.

At Brandon, the Bees and Eagles slugged it out and the lead changed hands five times before the Coventry made the sting to win 43–41 on Saturday 11 April. The Bees probably would have had a more comfortable win if Reg Duval's equipment had been more reliable. He suffered two engine failures out of four starts. The Eagles' Scott blew a motor and completed the match on the track spare.

Les Hewitt was the Bees' star with a maximum which needed a win from the back in his last race to complete. Charlie New was, however, the hero with the crowd, winning the last heat from Watson and Scott to clinch victory for the Bees. The *Speedway News* said it was "a magnificent night's speedway" and "an exciting encounter."

The Eagles had to bear a broadside of points scoring on the south coast from the Poole team on Monday 13 April. The Pirates won all the match heats bar one, which was won by Close. Ken Middleditch, Brian Crutcher and Terry Small were all unbeaten for Poole and Close spoiled the maximum chances of the remaining five Poole men. With three Eagles on a duck – no points for those not familiar with this turn of phrase – it is no wonder that Poole's Pirates managed to win this league match 63–21 to pocket the points.

Back at The Stadium on 17 April, Stoke were level with the Eagles up to the start of heat five, but gradually lost ground thereafter to finish 28 points adrift in a match that ended 56–28. Yet again, it was a Close full house and he went through the card unbeaten, including the second half. His partner Scott followed him home three times, missing out on his paid maximum in his last outing.

The most exciting action was generated by Phillips and the visitors' Ken Adams. Their races were close run affairs and the home team's efforts pleased the 20,000 crowd. Green featured in an unusual finish in heat six. His bike failed almost on the line and he pushed it over to grab second place.

Stoke's national serviceman, Reg Fearman, had dashed from his Army barracks in North Wales and was well rewarded with 7+2. He featured in the exciting heat six giving the Eagles pair a hard time. The Potters' Alan Hailstone had a torrid night, including a fall in heat nine after hitting an 'oily' part of the track.

The Eagles first visit to Wolverhampton's Monmore Green on Monday 20 April saw Close stamp his authority on the meeting by scoring a full 12 point maximum, but still end up on the losing side. Despite the Eagles making the starts, the *Speedway News* reported that "... the home team generally found a way through." The home team, known then as the Wasps, featured many of the riders who had raced for Cradley Heath in 1952. Only Jim Tolley seriously troubled Derick in heat 12. Jim was joint top Wasp with Harry Bastable and Brian Shepherd, all three scoring nine points.

McGregor took two races to weigh up the track, then won two races. He had been holding second place in his second outing, but home reserve Brian Braithwaite used his track knowledge to overtake him. Despite gating faster than the home men, the Eagles lost their way to the flag and the Wasps fans were pleased with their 49–35 win.

The tight bends, of the Yarmouth track, which had recently been altered, did not suit the Eagles. It was a track that rarely saw good Scottish performances. So, on Tuesday 21 April Eagles took a bit of a pasting as the Bloaters rammed home ten 5–1 scores. It could have been more had Peter 'Gundy' Harris, the Yarmouth reserve, not had bike problems. Such was the superiority of the Bloaters men that McGregor was the only other Eagle to win a race and that was all he scored.

Even Derick Close found it hard going and, while chasing Fred Brand, a gap appeared and Close went for it. Unfortunately, the gap closed before he had a chance to use it and he crashed on the straight. This mishap reduced his score for the night to eight. Next best men were Watson and Phillips on four each. Even allowing for Derick dropping points, the rest of his team-mates had an off night too. The Bloaters won by a convincing 61–23.

On 24 April, at The Stadium the Wasps were two points up going into the last heat, but the Eagles' heat-leaders, Close and McGregor, combined to score a vital 5–1. The *Speedway News* said that they "careered round the track in a last do or die effort and succeeded in collecting five points." This result gave the Eagles a win and the league points with a narrow 42–40 score. Eagles had intended to track Dalton, but he failed to arrive.

Heat one had started with Watson being excluded for unfair riding, an action which cost Jim Tolley a race point. Watson was then excluded from heat five for breaking the tapes, but many fans thought he was not to blame. He was also excluded in a later outing for boring out his opponent. Boring meant a rider driving inside an opponent moving them, unfairly, off their riding line. Green and Phillips both dropped points due to engine problems. Close missed out on a full maximum, but was paid for one. McGregor also lost his maximum, pipped by Ivor Davies on the line in heat nine.

Eric Irons and Brian Shepherd were the best Wasps with seven each. Despite a solid showing on the Wasps score chart, the general opinion was that the score flattered them as the Eagles' 'luck' – or lack of it – pegged them back.

Left: Ron Phillips, who joined Motherwell from Glasgow Ashfield.
Right: Bill Dalton, who had two spells at Motherwell. (Both photos JSC)

Motherwell 1953: Back: Noel Watson, Bluey Scott, Scott Hall, Derick Close;
Front: Ron Phillips, Jimmy Tannock, Gordon McGregor, Johnny Green. (JSC)

Left: Guy Allott, who had a short spell with the Eagles.
Right: Jimmy Tannock, who rode for the Eagles in 1953 and 1954. (Both JSC)

A

Motherwell speedway supporters dance. (JSC)

May

On May Day, 1 May, at The Stadium, Poole Pirates were calling for help using the well-known distress signal as they sunk 49–35 in this league encounter. The defending league champions left The Stadium empty handed, but showed their potential throughout this fixture. However, it was the Eagles' team-riding prowess that won them the day. Brian Crutcher was shut out into third place by Close and Scott in his opening outing and in the last heat Close and McGregor concluded the match with another 5–1.

The Eagles at last brought in Dalton, who was handicapped by the effects of flu, replacing Tannock at reserve, but he only chipped in with one point. Close, who kept his record of being unbeaten by a visitor, was given sound backing by McGregor and Phillips. In heat 13 Scott was holding onto second place, but suffered a flat tyre which relegated him to third.

More had been expected from Brian Crutcher, but he was restricted by the Eagles heat leaders to six from four rides. This was one of his last meetings for Poole before he was signed by the Wembley Lions. The best Pirate was Terry Small with 8+2. For the Eagles, Close was unbeaten by a Pirate scoring 11+1. McGregor dropped two points first time out, but ended his evening with 10+1 while Phillips scored 10. McGregor went on to complete a second half clean sweep.

Veteran Joe Crowther started the comeback trail with a winning outing in the second half. He beat Hall, Tannock and Poole's Allan Kidd.

Bike troubles pegged back the Eagles men often when they were well placed, letting Leicester off the hook a shade during this May Monday Holiday on 4 May. The Motherwell management had hoped to brighten things up with a leg of the Scottish Match Race Championship between Close and Tommy Miller, but it clashed with Great Britain versus Overseas at Liverpool.

Close's unbeaten record went in heat three, when his bike gave up the ghost at the starting gate. The bike also packed in in his last outing reducing his score to six. In heat seven, Close chased Len Williams and tried to pass round the outside, but was baulked. Williams tried the same tactic in the next lap, but Close changed line and nipped past him on the inside.

Thankfully, the rest of the team rose to the occasion and what the score might have been is open to speculation as Watson was leading heat 12 when he came to a halt. Phillips was the top Eagle with a full maximum 12 and McGregor scored 7+1.

For the visitors, reserve Roy Browning was top scorer with nine points, including two wins when he replaced his fellow team men, but despite this the Hunters still went down 50–34. Harwood Pike was not too popular as he clashed with Hall in heat four. The Eagles' rider ended up with an injured shoulder which ruled him out for the night.

About this time there was a minor spat between Motherwell's Tom Reid and Ashfield's Norrie Isbister over who would stage the Ken Le Breton Trophy meeting. It seems that the Giants' fan club Stobhill Branch had approached Reid, when it looked like Norrie's team might not run at Saracen Park in 1953. Eventually, it all blew out and Norrie Isbister, who had complained to the Speedway Control Board, staged the event at Ken's spiritual home in Glasgow. Le Breton had ridden for Ashfield before being killed in a track accident in Sydney in January 1951.

Tommy Miller showed his mastery of the Eagles' Milton Street Stadium, racing to a maximum 12 points on 8 May as his share of the Tigers 40, which was four shy of the Eagles' total. The Eagles thus retained the Lanarkshire Cup. Miller gave warning that he was likely to retain his Scottish Match Race Championship. His challenger, Derick Close, was considered to be over-excited when he faced Miller, resulting in a few small, but vital, errors.

In the match the Eagles were in front throughout, but the Tigers ran them close on a few occasions before having to accept being second best. Miller lacked the support needed to take a win from Eagles, even though the Tigers had more race winners. Ken McKinlay caught the eye as he took Close and Scott from the back in heat three, the first of his three victories. He blotted his copybook when he fell on a slippery spot of the track while trying to pass McGregor, ruining a maximum. The 40-year-old Joe Crowther re-signed for Motherwell after a great display at the training session the previous Monday. He made a brief, but pointless return at reserve. The best Eagles were McGregor and Phillips with 10.

Guy Allott had a try out in the second half, but was bored out by the Tigers' Bob Sharp, who was excluded for his action. Guy went on to win the Stadium Scurry and generally gave a favourable impression. However, it would be a few months before he joined Eagles. In the same second half, Green impressed the home fans by winning his heat from Miller in a tapes to flag effort.

The Eagles travelled overnight by train to Swindon for the Saturday 9 May National Trophy first leg at the Abbey Stadium in Blunsdon. The Southern League Swindon Robins showed the Eagles the way round, winning 62–46, but no one could beat Close who scored a six-ride 18 points maximum. Ian Williams ran him close a couple of times, but could not beat him. With McGregor the only other Eagle on form, scoring 12+2, the home men ended with a 16 point advantage for the second leg. The Robins were helped by Watson wrecking the frame of his bike in his heat six crash which effectively reduced his return to two points.

For the Robins, Bob Wells was top scorer with 12+1, while Ian Williams, a Swindon legend and the brother of Wembley's Freddie and Eric, scored 11 from six rides that included a couple of pointless outings due to falls.

The Glasgow Tigers gave Eagles another dusting to the tune of 59–25 on an ultra-dry White City track on Wednesday 13 May. The dry spell before this match meant that the track needed watering during the evening. This was rendered ineffective by a strong drying wind that blew all the time. The meeting was attended by the Scotland team selectors, but it was felt the match was too one-sided to gauge the form of the potential team members.

Two race winners in 14 heats does not normally provide the goods for a victory. One win was entered in the score chart of McGregor who collected seven points. The other was logged against Phillips, who top scored for Eagles with eight. Watson had fitted a new frame, but the injury he had picked up at Swindon caused him to pull out of the meeting after two last places. His efforts did not to impress the selection committee. Close injured himself fighting to control his mount at the start of his opening ride. It proved a handicap which reduced his return to five.

For the Tigers, Tommy Miller had his usual maximum, but an unexpected paid maximum came from Alf McIntosh on 11+1. Alf followed Tommy home in heat 14.

Swindon Robins became the first Southern League team to visit Scotland on 15 May. They were blasted out of the National Trophy as the Eagles piled up race points to win the tie 124–92 on aggregate, thanks to their 78–30 win. Team work was of the essence as the Eagles' riders were paid for 13 bonus points between them compared to Swindon's three. Pundits considered the Robins were outclassed, but not outfought.

Watson was excluded from heat one for tape breaking. Many thought the tapes had broken of their own accord. He also had an engine failure in heat 12 which restricted him to seven points. Phillips could have lost out as Watson's bike slowed, but he rode wide, picked up the pace, and passed the two Robins men to win and ended with 12+3. McGregor and Close inflicted the damage on the Robins recording paid maximums. McGregor scored 17+1 while Close scored 16+2.

Close lost to Tommy Miller in the Scottish Match Race heats. Miller flew from the gate in the first to win by quarter of a lap. Close's best chance of defeating Miller came in race two when he led from the gate, but he over-slid to let Miller past for the deciding second win.

Jackie Hughes chose the Eagles' visit to the Potteries on Saturday 16 May to come good for Stoke. His maximum included two wins from the back over Close. His team-mates also did well as the Eagles slumped to a big defeat. Don Potter, with a surname similar to his team's name, supported with 11 while Ken Adams scored 10+1. The Stoke octet combined to win 59–22.

Watson and Close each scored seven which was bad enough, but the rest of the scoresheet made dismal reading because no other rider scored better than 2+1. Heat two of this Potters versus Eagles encounter was unusual. Three riders fell without remounting to finish leaving Potter to win unchallenged.

The threat of rain restricted the crowd at Liverpool on Monday 18 May. Those who turned up went away happy because the Eagles failed to get to grips with the big track and the Chads triumphed. The crowd could also be satisfied that they had their money's worth. Racing was reported as being excellent. Close thrilled the fans in heat three as he fought past the home men and scored a paid maximum, 11+1. He only had good support from McGregor with 10. Yet again, a big gap opened between the top two and the rest. Best of the rest was Green on 4+1.

Heat six was race of the night when the Chads' Bill Griffiths tried all he knew to pass Close, without success. Griffiths used a mixture of foot forward and leg trailing in his spirited efforts. However, a couple of heats later, his efforts earned him a win from the back. He passed Dalton and Green in quick succession. This was Dalton's last outing for the Eagles – he failed to score in this 51–33 defeat. Liverpool veteran Tommy Allott returned, but only managed two points.

Peter Robinson, a largely unsung star of this era, was the best Chad on 10+1 while the energetic Griffiths piled up 10. However, Liverpool closed later in the season and withdrew from the league, so this result was declared void.

On 22 May, back at The Stadium, Watson showed remarkable courage at home laying down his bike to avoid the fallen Monarch, Bob Mark. Unfortunately, his reward was a trip to the ambulance room, the result of concussion sustained saving Mark. Mark, who had been battling with McGregor before hitting the fence, was excluded from the heat. Hall took Watson's place in the rerun and picked up a paid win because Dick Campbell's bike problems prevented him from finishing. The Eagles were handicapped from the off, but the reserve duo of Hall and Tannock did score some points in their extra outings to make up for the missing Australian. In heat four, Hall and Phillips had been on for a 5–1 when Phillips's bike packed in and he baulked Hall.

When the match was over, the Eagles had beaten their east coast rivals for the first time in 1953. This match featured the first ever dead heat at The Stadium in heat 11. Don Cuppleditch had led for most of the race with Close trying everything bar riding along the top of the fence to get past. A last bend burst allowed Close to level things on the line. Cuppleditch had lost out to McGregor earlier in the meeting, otherwise it could have unusually featured two unbeaten riders, one on either side. Close had an 11.5 point unbeaten total.

The fun wasn't over as Mark and McGregor had a real coming together in heat 14. They were so close that sparks literally flew when they touched. Mark was unlucky as McGregor shaded it on the line and completed a paid maximum 11+1. The Eagles won 48.5–34.5.

On Monday 25 May, the Eagles failed to beat Poole, now without star Brain Crutcher, who had transferred to Wembley, but the 62–46 defeat provided hope for the second leg in this National Trophy tie. The *Speedway News* said that Poole "… will have to do considerably better to make their way into the fourth round … it appeared very much as if Motherwell would win on aggregate," Once more, Close excelled with 16, but only Phillips gave him anything like solid support scoring 11+1.

The canny Scots were impressed with the Poole one penny for a bike scheme. This raised funds to pay for the track spare. For those readers who can't remember the track spare, it was often a real heap of scrap frequently cannibalised for urgent spare parts during a meeting.

Ken Middleditch was the top Pirate with 16+1, losing out to Watson when he took his only race win. Allan Kidd was next best with 10 while the other six scored solidly piling up the bonus points in yet another Poole team performance.

Johnny Green was the star in the second leg tie at The Stadium on 29 May. The crowd was reduced due to grey skies and cold weather. Green collected 17+1 which was a vital contribution to the Eagles' progress to the next round. His improved form could, perhaps, be put down to a new machine. The Pirates stood solid to the end of heat four, but the floodgates opened with a Watson and Green 5–1. Thereafter, Poole Pirates were washed out 73–35, 119–97 on aggregate.

Close gave Green sound backing with 15+1, but the match was won by the solid showing from McGregor, 11+3, Watson, 11+2 and Phillips on 10. Tannock on 5+1 and Hall on 4+1 were sound reserves. Scott had a miserable night with two engine failures.

Poole's best was Ken Middleditch with 10+1, but the normally solid Pirates were all at sea. This meeting also featured a Junior League Match against Glasgow, which finished 6–6 after the two heats.

June

With Tommy Miller in the field, he was inevitably the favourite to claim the Skelly Trophy, staged as a special Coronation Day event on Tuesday 2 June. Miller won the pot and Leicester's Len Williams was runner-up after a last heat decider. Miller and Williams started the race with 12 points each and the Blantyre man won. An Eagle was third, but not, as would have been predicted, Close; rather it was Phillips who scored 12. Close, only scored four points because his machine failed three times and the bike problems continued when he borrowed Dick Campbell's bike.

Holder Don Cuppleditch ended down the field on nine. Ken McKinlay was unlucky. He collected an eyeful of shale and retired from heat 16. His first three race wins and another point from the last heat behind Miller and Williams gave him 10 for joint fourth place with fellow Tiger Junior Bainbridge. Watson and McGregor were equal on nine, well out of the rostrum places.

When Tommy was presented with the Trophy by Billy Skelly, some Motherwell fans let the sport down by booing and shouting abuse. Rightly, it was considered to be a show of poor sportsmanship and sheer bad manners. Some justified their actions suggesting that Miller was a dirty rider which was an unjust assessment. It was probably based on a single incident when he was a bit hard on an Eagle. There was no second half speedway action, but the kids were allowed to race their tricycles round the track to end this British celebration day.

Three days later, yet again the Tigers came to Motherwell, raced, and won. The Eagles' tail end was well and truly plucked and the Tigers and their strength in depth supported maximum men, Miller and McKinlay. Inconsistent tailenders let the Eagles down again. Close scored an acceptable 10. More was expected from McGregor and Watson who scored 8+2 and 8+1 respectively. Hall, Tannock and Scott, who only scored 1+1 between them, were blamed for this defeat.

The local press, was very hard on Hall and Tannock at reserve, but gave Bluey Scott a pat on the back for his scoreless effort because he had done well earlier in the season.

Most heats finished 3–3, and it was five 4–2s to the Tigers against two 5–1s for the Eagles that swung it the Tigers' way. At the end of heat 13, the score was level at 39–39, but the Tigers' Miller and Peter Dykes took a 4–2 from McGregor and Hall to win 43–41.

Yarmouth Bloaters' number one, Fred Brand, and, to a lesser extent, the crowd-pleasing Australian Johnny Chamberlain, were the star visitors on 12 June with nine and seven points respectively. However, even they had no answer to the Eagles' fire power. With three men scoring well and support from the second strings and reserves, the Motherwell men smoked the Bloaters 54– 30.

Heat nine was rerun, but the crowd was not best pleased because it ended a great duel between Watson and Johnny Chamberlain with the Bloater in the lead. Ronnie Genz fell while well adrift but, despite track staff removing him quite quickly, the Steward stopped the race. In rerun Watson won after another struggle with his fellow Australian. Genz had previously been excluded for tape breaking in heat six.

Close, aboard a new bike, was flying, until it ground to a halt in his opening ride. However, the offending machine then performed well, carrying its owner to nine points. The top Eagle was Phillips with a paid maximum 11+1 while Watson scored 10+1. McGregor gave sound support with 7+2.

The Eagles never really worried the men in blue and gold from Edinburgh on Saturday 13 June except for the first few yards of each race. Despite trapping well, the Eagles could not keep on the pace for the rest of the race and lost the match 53–31 before a disappointingly low crowd. McGregor had another off night while Phillips had two ducks before banging in two wins. Close was troubled by machine problems which pegged him back to seven points. The top Eagle was Watson on eight.

The Monarchs' Don Cuppleditch was their best rider with 11. He lost out to white line hugging Close in his second outing in heat six. Cuppleditch nearly lost to Watson in heat 10, but Watson drifted wide letting Cuppleditch through. Harold Fairhurst scored 9+2 while Dick Campbell with 8+3 gave solid support. The ever-colourful Jimmy Cox, was overhauled by impressive former Monarch Green and Tannock in heat eight.

It wasn't until heat eight at The Stadium on Friday 19 June that a Potters man managed to beat an Eagle. Don Potter displaced Hall for second place to break Eagles' stranglehold run of 5–1 heat wins. As it was, the Eagles top five riders were unbeaten by a visitor and Scott waited until the last heat before he was beaten by a Stoke man. To be fair, Stoke lost Ken Adams, the only Potter who failed to score, in a heat one fall which hindered their cause. Adams fell while leading after entering the bend awkwardly and hitting the fence. Watson laid down his bike and went sprawling over the track while McGregor sailed on to take the flag. The race was rerun after a delay to allow track watering and this time Watson won from McGregor.

Green made a bit of personal history because he completed his maiden full maximum, chipping in with 12 of the Eagles' 67. Close also ended with a full maximum while Watson scored 11+1. McGregor had 10+2 and Phillips ended with 9+3. Stoke's 17 was a poor reply, their best two riders were Jackie Hughes on five and Don Potter on four.

For the first time for some years, the Tigers' Tommy Miller did not make it to the rostrum in the contest for places in the Scottish Riders' Championship at The Stadium on 26 June. The Eagles' stars Close and Green tied for the top spot with 13 and Phillips was one point behind. Green got the better of Close while Phillips beat Green. Meeting favourite Miller met Phillips and Green in the same heat and had to settle for third place.

The Eagles duo effectively team rode Tommy out, although it was an individual meeting. He then had to admit second best to Close and even Hall tried to get into the act leading Miller for a couple of laps before being passed. This was a double treat for fans because the promotion handed out Coronation souvenirs prior to the match. Heavy rain shortly before the scheduled start made the meeting doubtful as the track was wet and heavy.

One of the celebration trophies competed for by the Division Two teams in 1953 was the Queens Cup. In the early stages it was a single tie event which gave home teams an advantage. However, the Eagles won the Queens Cup opening tie at Brandon Stadium against the Coventry Bees on Saturday 27 June. The Eagles led from the end of heat two only to see the Bees draw level. The Eagles eased ahead in heat six and kept it that way to win 57–51. A late burst of scoring by Bees made the score look respectable, but it was the Eagles all the way.

This was a great result for the Eagles because Coventry went on to win the league. In addition to a place in the next round, the Eagles also had the satisfaction of leaving with McGregor and Close as joint track record holders. The former set his time in heat one when he came from the back to beat home stars Charlie New and Vic Emms clocking 68.4 seconds. Close matched his time in heat two and like McGregor had to do it the hard way from the back. Just to prove it was no fluke, McGregor was 0.4 seconds outside his new record in heat three.

The foundation for the Eagles' win was laid by McGregor's 16 point return, but he lost out on his full maximum in his last race. Close scored 12 paid 13, his total pegged back by a last heat exclusion, while Green exactly matched his skipper's total.

For the Bees, the opening pairing of Vic Emms and Charlie New were their best riders, scoring 10+4 and 11+2 respectively.

July

The Eagles faced First Division London-based Harringay Racers, at home on 3 July, and gave a very good account of themselves. In front of the biggest crowd of the year, they won the first leg of this National Trophy tie 63–45. Such was the confidence of the home riders that they frequently came from the back to claim the points.

The Eagles' top four produced the goods and, had the support been a bit better, they might have taken a bigger lead to London for the second leg. Only Split Waterman lived up to his reputation for the Racers and even he had a couple of third places. His opening race win was courtesy of Watson drifting too wide on the turn. Split demonstrated a fantastic degree of bike control as he blocked a number of attempted overtakes by the home men.

Watson also eased off in the run off to the line in one race, and paid the price, dropping a place.

Both Close and Phillips top scored with 16+1 and both had been unbeaten until the nominated heat 18 when they could not get the better of Waterman. Green settled for 11+1 while McGregor scored 10+3.

The best Racer was Waterman, a real character of speedway in this era, who scored 14+1. Next best Racer was reserve Alan Quinn on seven while former World Finalist Jack Biggs scored six.

The Racers shattered the Eagles at Harringay the next day with a great 85–23 display to take the tie 130–86 on aggregate. A wet track, often described as big plus for the Eagles at The Stadium, was not helpful at Harringay. It was also very rough and did not help the Eagles. The Racers were so far in front that they used reserves in the last race against the Eagles top two of Watson and Close. Alan Quinn hit Close's back wheel as he dived in for an almost non-existent gap and the pair crashed heavily. Close suffered a serious head injury which ended his season and Quinn had a suspected broken collarbone. The Eagles were allowed to replace Close with McGregor in the last heat even though he was not a reserve.

All in all, it was a black day for the Eagles. Watson and Close were their best scorers with six points each. Harringay's best man was Jeff Lloyd on 15 from five races while Jack Biggs and Ken Walsh both scored 13+2. Unusually, Split Waterman scored 5 bonus points in his paid 15 total.

In the absence of Derick Close, home interest in the World Championship Qualifying Round at The Stadium on 10 July focused on Gordon McGregor. However, he did not make the cut. Birmingham's Ron Mountford dropped a few points but still did enough, 12 points, to take the winners' £30 cheque. Runners-up were the Swedes Dan Forsberg and Stig Pramberg, who gave the meeting an international flavour, on 11 each while Graham Warren and Ron Clarke tied on 10.

Edinburgh's Don Cuppleditch looked a likely winner early on, but was let down by his bike. He was leading heat 13, after a big struggle with Pramberg, when the bike failed. In heat 20 his bike packed up on the way to the tapes and another machine also failed while he was leading. Don had to settle for nine points for his night's work.

Phillips stepped in to heat 20 to replace injured Bill Holden and won the race from Merv Neil and Billy Bales. In heat 15, Bill Holden had swerved to avoid Graham Warren's back wheel and fallen. He staggered to the centre where he collapsed and his injuries ruled him out for the night. The other action noteworthy was Bales' fall as he slugged it out with Reg Reeves in heat 14. Charlie May had appeared in place of Jack Geran, and scored a respectable nine points.

Noel Watson had qualified from the National Round with 12 points, but was knocked out of the International Round with seven points. He was four points short of the lowest qualifiers who had 11 from their two meetings.

Motherwell had hoped to sign Sweden's Rune Sormander, but were refused permission. The Motherwell promotion was disappointed and their concerns were echoed by their secretary, Miss Woods, who was not impressed by the Speedway Control Board's penchant for restricting foreign riders to the top Division. According to the *Speedway Gazette*, Tom Reid had also contacted the Cardiff promotion, whose team had closed down, about any available riders.

The team was shuffled. Tannock was promoted to the team to replace Close while Jock Pryde was brought in as reserve against Wolverhampton Wasps at The Stadium on 17 July.

Pryde did not let anyone down and scored a couple of points. He was reported to have been a bit phased when Derek Braithwaite fell in front of him in heat eight. However, he cleverly avoided Braithwaite and a shaken Pryde finished the race.

It was noted that Wasps used a management technique previously adopted by Cradley Heath in using a good reserve to replace a team man who was struggling, but it still did not stop them going down 50–34 to the Eagles. Scott displayed excellent form with 10 points for the home side. Obviously, in these days there was a bit of etiquette in the use of the reserves, which made the Wasps' actions, with Eric Irons replacing Ivor Davies twice, notable.

Watson was the Eagles top man with 10+1, but Scott was ahead of Phillips on nine and McGregor scored 7+4. Paired with Watson, McGregor acted as the tail gunner to shepherd the Australian home. For the Wasps, Tolley and Eric Irons top scored with 10 and nine respectively. Harry Bastable, who was expected to do well, fell in his opening ride and never really got going for the rest of the night.

It was reported in the *Speedway News* that Derick Close had been released from the Royal Northern Hospital in London after a 10 day stay. However, he was not expected to ride again in 1953.

The Eagles joined with fellow league sides to help Norrie Isbister's attempt to keep Ashfield speedway alive. To this end Phillips rejoined Ashfield for the night on Tuesday 21 July at Saracen Park as his Eagles team mates topped a four-team tournament. The Lanarkshire Eagles foursome of Noel Watson – nine points, Gordon McGregor – nine points, Johnny Green – six points and Scott Hall – five points, totalled 29 points to win the event from Glasgow Tigers on 24, Edinburgh Monarchs on 20 and an Ashfield Giants team which trailed in last on 11. The track was in poor condition due to heavy rain and the riders were not keen, but they rode to keep faith with Norrie.

Jimmy Tannock retained his team spot as new signing from Wolverhampton, Guy Allott, was slotted in at reserve for his debut against the Tigers at Motherwell on 24 July. The incessant rain made the track tricky and it was touch-and-go whether the meeting would start. Falls, and engine failures mostly caused by water in the electrics, were commonplace. Contemporary reports described the event as farcical, likening the track to a mud-bath. The riders skidded round the waterlogged bends and all of them ended up covered in mud. Race times were eight to nine seconds longer than usual.

In heat one, Tommy Miller stalled at the start and was baulked by Noel Watson. He restarted, but could not catch McGregor, the Tigers' Bob Sharp and Watson. In heat 12, both Don Wilkinson and Arthur Malm fell. Wilkinson remounted just before he was lapped, and continued to claim third place.

The Eagles were six points adrift at the end of heat 10, but grabbed a couple of 5–1s to go two up. They held on for a couple of 3–3s in the last two heats, taking the match 43–41.

Watson pulled out after two rides and it was McGregor on 10+1, Hall on 8+1 and Scott with 7+1 who were the best for a solid Eagles side. For the Tigers, Tommy Miller was restricted to three wins while Peter Dykes on 8+1 and Wilkinson on eight were the top three Tigers. The Tigers' Junior Bainbridge missed the meeting.

Billed as Eagles versus Tigers the fixture at Saracen Park on Tuesday 28 July was another opportunity for the Glasgow speedway public north of the Clyde to show Norrie Isbister that they wanted Ashfield afloat. Unfortunately, wet weather caused the abandonment of this challenge match after 10 heats. The good news for the Eagles' fans was that they were miles ahead of the Tigers; the score at the end was 38–22. Track announcer Don Cumming, a Canadian who obviously had a sense of humour, played *Singing in the Rain* to the fans.

Phillips revelled on his old track, scoring 10. Restricted to three rides, McGregor picked up 6+2 while Watson added six points. The reserves, Hall and Allott, were unbeaten with three and 2+1 respectively from their only ride. For the Tigers, Tommy Miller had nine points while Junior Bainbridge scored five, also from three rides.

The third round of the Queen's Cup was a tough tie for Eagles – Poole Pirates. However, they managed to beat the south coast men at Motherwell 55–53 on 31 July to progress to the next round. Hall was promoted into the team and Tannock dropped to reserve.

It was hard going against the tough Pirates side and it took Watson and Phillips to combine for a 4–2 to give them victory in last heat. Watson had been a tower of strength and his last heat win completed a rare 18 point maximum. He kept the fans enthralled by his fence scraping and all action charges down the straights. Phillips had a poor birthday, but could celebrate after a heat 18 third place clinched it for the Eagles, after he had three engine failures caused by magneto problems.

Green scored 13+2 from five rides with passion, while McGregor was bit more subdued on 9+1. Not surprisingly, Green was the Eagles original choice to partner Watson in the nominated heat, but on his way to the tapes, his bike developed a fault. It was clear the problem could not be solved within the two-minute allowance, so Phillips was substituted. Even then it was touch-and-go because Ron's machine was reluctant to start. This all gave the Eagles fans a few heart stopping moments. Watson and Phillips gated clear of the Pirates, but Terry Small got past at bend four to go second, and Ron spent the rest of the race keeping Glasgow born Pirate Johnny Thomson at the back.

Scott started with a win and was then rode too wide to be effective in the rest of his outings. Small, who had wound it on to split the Eagles in heat 18 scored 11+1 while Allan Kidd, Ken Middleditch and Jimmy Squibb all added seven each and were paid for 10, 9 and 8 respectively.

The loss of Close was still a big problem and the promotion failed to resolve it immediately. To be fair, they did try to strengthen the side. They contacted the Control Board about riders from tracks that had closed, and they even looked at possible foreign riders, all without success. It had been no secret that the Eagles wanted Peter Robinson and Bill Griffiths. They were now Speedway Control Board assets following the closure of Liverpool, but nether arrived in Lanarkshire.

August

There was a great start for the Eagles at Old Meadowbank on Saturday 1 August, but it all went downhill from there on. The Monarchs forged ahead in heat three and took a 55–28 win. Rain came down after heat six and the track conditions are reflected in the heat times. Hall, Scott and Green all tumbled during the meeting. In heat nine, Johnny's fall cost Bob Mark a point as he laid down his machine to avoid the stricken Eagle. In these days, if a rider did not finish, he did not get the point. Making matters worse, Phillips's bike troubles continued and he only scored two points from his completed races. Watson was the best Eagle with seven, while his partner, McGregor, was next best on 6+1.

The Candy Kid, Don Cuppleditch, was the top Monarch on 11+1 while Harold Fairhurst was next best on 10+1. Dick Campbell was unbeaten by an Eagle after his opening race last place.

The Eagles were away so the meeting at The Stadium on 7 August featured the up-and-coming lads. It was a tight contest with fans expecting a few of them to demolish the fence on a number of occasions. Nobody did hit the fence and only one rider was injured. Despite hurting himself in his first ride, Jock Pryde tried another outing before calling it a day. He went to hospital for an X-ray on his injured left leg.

Stuart Irvine almost had his name on the trophy, but messed up his last ride. He missed the gate because his bike stalled, but he overhauled Jock Scott before trying to pass namesake Slim for that vital second place. Unfortunately, he over-slid and fell in the attempt, leaving the door open for the Tigers' Arthur Malm to clinch the trophy.

Jack Jones, who scored a single point, is probably better known as 'Igor Barnov', a name he adopted attempting to pick up rides in the early 1960s. At one track Igor (Jack) was in a speedway manager's office when who should enter, but Gordon Mitchell, who also rode in this meeting in 1953. Thankfully, 'Igor' managed to convince Gordon not to give the game away. Arthur, who had himself fallen in his opening ride, had been lucky that Harry Darling had failed to complete the course, thus gifting him a point. The Tigers' young Australian took his chances and won the last race to take the title with 13 points. Three riders tied for second spot, Gordon Mitchell, Jim Russell and Stuart Irvine. There were a few good races, notably heat 13. The first three crossed the line with a bike length separating them.

The Eagles were at Leicester, on 7 August and the meeting turned out to be a bit of a damp squib. Green and McGregor laid a good foundation, scoring 10 each, but the rest failed to build on this and the Hunters won 46–38. The Eagles' fortunes were not helped as they did not take along a team manager and heat eight started without a replacement for Tannock who had been excluded under the two-minute rule. Hall was injured when he hit the fence. He was bruised and shaken.

For the Hunters, Len Williams top scored with a full maximum and Dennis Parker added nine points. Lionel Watling received extra rides replacing Ivor Brown, then a good novice rider who would blossom into a big star of the early 1960s Provincial League. He had been promoted to wear the number one race jacket.

Scott Hall's injury ruled him out of the meeting at Stoke on Saturday 8 August. Without being able to call on a replacement in time, the Eagles raced with just seven men. The team did reasonably well but could not prevent the Potters winning 46–38.

Watson missed out on a maximum when his engine failed while leading heat 10. This pegged him back to nine points. McGregor and Green did well, scoring 9+1 and 11 respectively, but the tail failed to wag.

Ron Peace rowed with the Potters management before the match and did not ride, but it did not affect the result. Don Potter was best for the home side with eight while Jack Hughes and Ray Harris both scored 7+1.

Brave Scott Hall gave it a go at Poole on Monday 10 August, but he was not fit enough to contribute any points. The Eagles nearly lost the services of Phillips who was lucky to survive a heat two incident. Clipping Jimmy Squibb's rear wheel, he lost control for a short spell, but recovered his composure and passed Squibb for second place. Phillips collected eight points, one less than top again Green who scored nine.

McGregor amazed the locals by coming from behind to beat the star Poole pairing of Ken Middleditch and Tony Lewis in the opening heat, but that was his only contribution. The Pirates, with a 58–26 win, took revenge on the Eagles for knocking them out of the National Trophy and the Queen's Cup.

For the Pirates, Terry Small was a big scorer with a full maximum, while Middleditch scored 10+1. Bill Holden added 9+2, while Jimmy Squibb scored nine. The *Speedway News* said that Motherwell were "finding the 'going' on away tracks particularly hard without Derick Close."

Back in Scotland, Scott Hall gave it a go without any luck at White City, Glasgow on Wednesday 12 August. The Glorious Twelfth was how the Tigers' fans would have viewed the fixture because their team once again gave the Eagles the once over. What the Eagles fans said of their team's poor performance is anybody's business. This was another match that underlined just how much the Eagles missed Derick Close. McGregor did well at his old home, scoring 10, but could not best Tommy Miller. Green with eight points settled for being the second-best Eagle. Despite their best efforts, the Eagles lost 52.5–31.5.

It was a pretty uneventful night. The main talking point was the dead heat in heat two between Peter Dykes and Phillips who gathered all of 4.5. The latter had made a slow start but had passed the Tigers duo of Ken McKinlay and Peter Dykes early on. The Tigers gave chase and it was Dykes who pressed on regardless to catch Phillips on the line.

Needless to say, Tommy Miller scored another full maximum while Junior Bainbridge scored 11 with a second place behind McGregor. Dykes collected 9.5.

The big event of the year at The Stadium on 14 August was a test match, and the BBC television cameras were there to show Scotland what speedway was all about. The BBC used three cameras to capture the second half action in this test match between Scotland and England.

Heat five was the highlight. England's Eddie Rigg and Green – representing Scotland – collided just after the line with Green coming off worst. He did get up and walk back to the pits, but took time to get back into the groove. In the next race, Tommy Miller's bike packed up, and he baulked Ken McKinlay. Ken, however, rose to the challenge and re-passed Ron Mountford to win the race. Two bike failures cut Tommy's return to 12 while McKinlay scored 11+3. Phillips was top 'Scot' with 14. He scored 12 from his opening four rides, then tailed off to third place in his next two outings.

England included Welshman Eric Williams in their side – there were not enough Welsh riders to field a team – and the visitors featured seven First Division regulars. Eddie Rigg scored 12+1 while Ron Mountford scored 12. The Second Division lads showed the top flight men how to fly round the Eagles' nest. Scotland's 62–46 win was their third that year and effectively gave them the series.

Back in league action, it was a tight affair on the Motherwell circuit on 21 August, but the reshuffled Eagles, including new signing Cyril Cooper, shaded it 43–41 with three heat wins to Poole Pirates' two. A short, sharp, shower towards the end of the match gave the Eagles the edge because the deciding last three heats were raced on a rain-soaked greasy surface. The race times at the end of the meeting were 10 seconds faster than the opening heat.

Things looked as if they were going Poole's way because they led by two points after heat 12 when Green had engine failure and Scott almost lost second place. He had bounced off the fence in true Bluey fashion.

Heat 13 was the turning point as Cooper, who scored a reserve's maximum six, combined with Scott to take the vital 5–1, giving the Eagles a lead going into the last heat. Buster Brown's fall, when he was lying second, was just the luck the Eagles needed. The new man, a reserve, inspired Hall and he rode the fence to win a race shepherded home by team mate Phillips.

In the last race Green had engine failure for the second time that night while McGregor led the field. His win secured the victory and took him onto 10+1. Green was down to a poor for him four points. Watson was still struggling and he gathered only 4+1.

Yet again, Terry Small was the best Pirate as he sailed to another 12-point maximum. Bill Holden scored nine, as did Tony Lewis. The normally potent Pirates opening of Lewis and Ken Middleditch did not carry all before them. Ken had an off night, and scored 5+1.

The Steward inspected the track after heat 14 and pronounced it fit for the second half. The race times question the wisdom of that decision.

The wet weather moved east the next day and brought the meeting at Old Meadowbank to a halt after two heats with the score at 8–4 to the Monarchs in a Scottish Cup semi-final. The Edinburgh public gave Frank Varey the bird for calling the meeting off, but it was the Steward who made the decision. There is a story that while 6,000 paid to get in, 9,000 readmission slips were handed out. A hasty decision was made to rerun the event on the following Monday.

Despite their defeat, the Eagles limited damage to a mere six point deficit, 57–51 on Monday 24 August. Phillips and Green both had a poor night, scoring 4+1 and five respectively at their old track. However, Watson and Scott made up for them. Watson bounced back to form with 14 points from six rides while Bluey rose to the heights to score 10+2 including a couple of wins over Bob Mark. McGregor's seven point haul was nothing to write home about.

The Monarchs' Don Cuppleditch scored an untroubled 18 point maximum while Dick Campbell on 10+2 and Bob Mark on 10 backed him to the hilt.

The local press reported a poor turn out on Friday 28 August for an unusual fixture filler. The Eagles were not involved and their fans could watch Edinburgh Monarchs and Glasgow Tigers slug it out in the Coronation Cup.

The Monarchs' programme reported that their team held their own up to heat 13, then fell away badly to let the Tigers sweep to victory. The Monarchs received their usual sound service from Don Cuppleditch, who was well backed by the other heat leaders.

For the Tigers, who won the fixture 61–47, Tommy Miller scored a maximum, and young reserve Doug Templeton, scored seven from a reserve berth and also impressed.

In the *Speedway News*, Ian Hoskins reported that Derick Close was doing well at his home in Brough and was "making satisfactory progress."

Any Eagles fans who wanted to watch their own team would have had to travel to Wolverhampton on that night. The Monmore Green track was wet, resulting in poor quality racing. Bike problems let down Scott and Phillips, but it is pure speculation as to whether this affected the outcome. Scott had been well paced twice when his motor went silent in three out of his four outings. He had a two points return. Phillips was pegged back to 2+1. Green was the best Eagle with nine while McGregor scored 8+2.

For the record, Derek Braithwaite scored his first maximum in this 48–36 win for the Wasps. He had to overcome Cyril Cooper in his last outing to do it. Ivor Davies scored 10 for the Wasps while Eric Irons and Jim Tolley were paid for 10, scoring nine and eight race points respectively.

The Eagles then travelled a short distance east to face Coventry Bees at Brandon on the following evening. Once again, they showed their liking for this venue. Another miserable wet night favoured the Eagles riders who could take advantage of good gating. A halt to racing after heat seven cast doubts over the fate of the meeting, but, without any falls, the meeting continued and Eagles ran out comfortable 46–38 winners.

Watson scored a sound 11 and was well supported by Phillips on 9+1. Solid displays by Green with 7+3 and McGregor on 6+2 gave the visitors that wee bit of an edge, but they could count themselves fortunate that the Bees' Johnny Reason failed to score.

The Bees improved in the second half of the match, but a surprise or shock, depending on your point of view, 5–1 by Scott and Hall over Vic Emms and Jack Wright put the visitors within three points of victory. The Eagles team rode in the last two heats to share the heat points and secure their away win against the champions-elect.

Best Bee was Les Hewitt on 9 paid 10 while Reg Duval and Charlie New scored 7 each. Reason pulled out of the match after one race as he considered the track to be dangerous for him. This, together with 4 paid 5 from normally solid Vic Emms, did the Bees cause no good whatsoever.

September

Graveyard of Scottish hopes, Caister Road in Great Yarmouth, saw the Eagles gutted on Tuesday 1 September. The Bloaters had four men on maximums, two full and two paid, while Terry Courtnell took a reserve's maximum with 5+1. Hall impressed, riding hard to split Bob Baker and Danny Dunton in heat eight. Sadly, it wasn't much in overall terms as Eagles went down 61–23. Scott was joint second top scorer with McGregor on four. The top Eagle did not do that much better. Green was best with five in this poor away performance. All in all, a night to forget for the men from steel town in Scotland's Black Country.

For the smoking Bloaters, it was a bumper pay night. Fred Brand and Bob Baker took full 12 point maximums and Reg Reeves, known affectionately as 'The Laughing Cavalier' at one time in his career, scored 11+1. Roy Bowers was also unbeaten by an Eagle with 8+4.

Cooper's home unbeaten league run continued at The Stadium against Coventry on 4 September and this time he scored a full four ride maximum after promotion to the top six. He completed the night winning the two rides he had in the second half to collect the Lanark Supporters' Club Trophy.

Watson and McGregor were unbeaten taking three 5–1s, then winning their last rides with other partners. McGregor's 10+2 maximum was in doubt during heat nine, but he came from the back to do the business. Coventry, who were billed as potential league champions before the event, had three men, Jack Wright, Stan Williams and Tommy Anderson, fail to score, so it is not surprising to find they lost 57–27. To be fair to Wright, he had fallen awkwardly in heat one which did not help him. Reason with 7+1 and Les Hewitt on seven were the best Bees.

Heat 12 was the talking point at The Stadium on Monday 7 September as the Eagles raced to a good 53–30 win over the Leicester Hunters. Watson broke the tapes and for some reason the other three took his exclusion light to be a stop signal. Lionel Watling pulled off the track and the others slowed. They were, however, waved on and Jack Mountford and Tannock made a race of it. Lionel Watling was excluded for leaving the track. He had rejoined the race unaware of the Steward's decision.

The Eagles' Allott, who scored 7+2, caught the eye. In heat seven, his cut back to pass Dennis Parker was praiseworthy. McGregor and Phillips were the top Eagles with 11+1, while Green and Watson were a bit more subdued on eight and 4+1 respectively.

The Hunter's Len Williams again showed his liking for the Scottish air, scoring 10 points. Next best were Charlie Barsby and Jack Mountford on four points each.

In the second half, Len Williams broke the tapes and Cyril Cooper raced on, until the race was stopped, with a length of tape trailing from his neck.

Phillips' bike problems did not help the Eagles cause because it kept his contribution down to one when double figures had been expected at The Stadium on 11 September against

Edinburgh. The match was the first leg of the Queen's Cup semi-final. In heat two Phillips came from third to second, but Bob Mark caught up with him. They had a coming together and Phillips was pushed into the fence and third place. The *Wishaw Press* suggested if this had been a certain, un-named, Glasgow rider, he would have been excluded.

Green, who scored seven points, crashed in his last race. He touched Cooper's bike and swerved wide before crashing into the fence. The fence suffered a fair bit of damage because he ripped out a fair length of it. Johnny was flung along the track, but he took the steam out of the fall by rolling along. It looked serious, but he walked away after a few minutes.

Watson bounced back to form with 14 points from six rides, but McGregor was limited to 9+2 as the Eagles riders struggled to find that elusive match winning consistency. The Monarchs left Motherwell with a good 58–50 win, laying the foundations for an aggregate victory. Don Cuppleditch had another good night in Motherwell with 16 while South African Monarch Roy Bester had a series of wins and thirds to gather 12. Dick Campbell was paid for 12, but his total included a bonus point.

The aggregate score in the Queen's Cup tie ended 121–95 to the Monarchs the next day, but it was not without a fighting Eagles display in Edinburgh. They hung on to the home side until the end of heat 14 when the roof fell in on them. Phillips was injured in heat 15, but managed to finish the race. This was the start of a run of Monarchs 5–1 heat wins which completed the downing of the Eagles. Ron was injured in a very unusual way – he was hit by pieces of flying tyre as the rubber cover of his rear wheel flew to bits.

Watson was down on points again. This time he only managed five. McGregor and Green both scored double his return, but Green was paid a bonus for following his partner home in heat five. Second reserve Hall, often an unsung member of the team scored seven from four outings.

For the Monarchs, Don Cuppleditch scored 17 from six rides, his maximum spoiled by McGregor in the opening race. Dick Campbell scored 12+2 while veteran leg-trailer Wilf Jay chipped in with seven. Jay might have had more had heat 11 not been stopped. He was leading, but Allott fell and Phillips bagged the win in the rerun.

Although nobody knew it at the time, the Eagles' next meeting was Noel Watson's last for the team. He scored an immaculate 12 point maximum to help his team to a 62–22 victory over Yarmouth Bloaters on 18 September. He then set off to his home in Australia. News arrived in Motherwell in November reporting his death in a racing accident.

Cooper scored another home maximum 12 and stopped Watson's unbeaten run in the meeting, putting him out of the second half competition. Phillips and McGregor were also unbeaten by a Bloater as they gathered 11+1 and 8+4 respectively.

Terry Courtnell, a rider who lost his life in a horrific road accident in South Africa in 1956, was the top Bloater with eight points. So poor was the opposition that the local reporters suggested that the Eagles were reduced to racing against each other to provide the crowd with some excitement. Green also gave the crowd a 'thrill', riding into the fence full tilt in heat two, but even this did not prevent him riding unbeaten in the rest of his outings.

The second half produced a cracker of a race as Phillips and McGregor chased a place in the final. Injured Eagles hero Derick Close was a visitor and was given a warm welcome.

It was a good 112–104 aggregate win as the Eagles, missing two heat-leaders, blew away the Monarchs' challenge in a Scottish Cup tie at The Stadium on 25 September. This avenged the Queen's Cup defeat and set up an Eagles versus Glasgow Tigers final. The visitors had held on until heat 13, but then Eagles moved up a gear to finish with a flourish. Three 5–1s and a 4–2 were enough to win match 61–47 and take the tie.

The start of a race at the Motherwell Stadium. (JSC)

Left: Cyril Cooper, in a Coventry race jacket. He rode for several clubs, including Motherwell.
Right: Noel Watson. The 1953 campaign was his last with Motherwell – he was killed in a track
accident in Sydney in November 1953. (Both photos JSC)

Cooper and Phillips, the top scoring duo, combined in the last heat to put the icing on the cake with a well taken 5–1. Cooper closed with 14+1, while Phillips scored 13. Their cause was helped by Dick Campbell making a hash of the start as his bike reared.

Earlier Cooper and the Monarchs' Don Cuppleditch had served up a good race with Cuppleditch taking advantage of Cooper drifting wide on the last bend to flash past to the flag. The next best scorers for the Eagles were McGregor on 7+2 and Scott on 7+1.

For the Monarchs, it was the trio of Cuppleditch with 16, Campbell on 12+2, and Roy Bester with 10 who provided the main opposition.

October

McGregor and Green were blamed for the poor showing which saw the Eagles end the season at The Stadium on 2 October with a defeat. Their contribution was 5+3 and 4+1 respectively. The Tigers' 58–50 win put the visitors on line for their Scottish Cup victory. The Eagles could have snatched a draw in the last heat, but with Tommy Miller and Junior Bainbridge the nominated Tigers, Allott and Phillips, the Eagles' top duo up to that point, were never in it. Miller and Bainbridge swept to a 5–1. Phillips's last place meant that he did not add to his 11 point total, while Allott's third boosted him to nine. Tommy Miller completed an easy 18 point maximum while Bainbridge was one adrift from a paid six ride maximum, settling for 15+2. Ken McKinlay, the Tigers' rising star, scored 11+2 from five rides.

The Eagles lost the Scottish Cup 123–93 on aggregate. They went down 65–43 at White City on Wednesday 7 October. It could have been a lot more had Bainbridge's bike performed as it should have. He settled for a mere four points, well below his capability. Miller completed yet another 18 point maximum while Ken McKinlay was paid for the lot with 16+2.

Allott had a lucky escape in heat six when he crashed into the fence. He was pitched 10 yards and had to be assisted from the track. He came out for a couple of more rides and despite nearly repeating his heat six tumble, gathered a single point and bonus to boost his score to 3+1. Philips was the only Eagle to come out of the two legs with any credit and his 11+1 in this leg was a reasonable return. Cooper, often a spirited visitor to White City, scored 6+1 while McGregor and Green failed to sparkle contributing 4+3 and three respectively.

The Eagles finished sixth out of the nine teams that finished the season in the National League Division Two. They had 30 league points from their 32 matches, and were four behind Glasgow White City and one behind Edinburgh. McGregor was their top points scorer, followed by Phillips and Green.

In the riders rankings in the *1954 Stenner's Annual*, Derick Close was second behind Tommy Miller, and Gordon McGregor was 11th. Len Simpson's season review noted that Motherwell had moved quickly to recruit Cooper and Allott after Close's injury. He added that Phillips "turned up trumps," and that the moves "enabled the Lanarkshire side to keep punching to good purpose. Scotland's youngest track had as sound a team as anyone." He pointed out that Motherwell had never been beaten by an English team at The Stadium. Had the Monarchs and Tigers not won at Motherwell, the Eagles would have been the highest placed Scottish team.

While the season may have been successful for Motherwell, it had not been a good one for the sport overall. The closure of one of the London first division teams, New Cross, halfway through the season was a warning that all was not well. The growth of television, and the ongoing problem of the punitive Entertainment Tax meant that the sport faced difficulties. In 1954, there were only two National League divisions.

Left: Tenacious former Japanese Prisoner of War Larry Lazarus, who gave the Eagles' heat leaders solid support. (JSC)

Right: Johnny Green who joined the Eagles in an exchange deal with the Edinburgh Monarchs in 1952. (JSC)

5. 1954: Just one

Tragedy struck during the winter when, in Australia, Noel Watson, the original Eagle, was fatally injured in a track crash at Sydney Sports Ground on 6 November 1953. Noel had been leading a race when he developed a high speed wobble and fell. As he fell he brought down Alan Wall. Sadly, Noel was hit by another rider sustaining a fractured skull and he died three days later on Monday 9 November. At one time a Sydney bus conductor, he had come over to Britain to join Glasgow Ashfield, but did not make much headway. The opening of Motherwell in mid-1950 gave him the opportunity and he took it with both hands. There is no doubt that Noel was one of the most popular riders in black and white. Before the opening match in 1954 a minute's silence was observed in Noel's memory.

This was another bad year for speedway. The National League First Division ran with eight teams, compared to 10 at the start of 1953. New Cross had closed in 1953 and Bristol decided to compete in the Second Division. At the start of 1953, there were 19 teams in the Second Division and the Southern League. Two dropped out during the season – Liverpool and Cardiff – but only 15 were expected to run in 1954. However, Glasgow White City and Wolverhampton withdrew before riding a league meeting. Edinburgh dropped out after riding four league meetings, and Plymouth also quit after two league meetings. The Second Division was left with 11 teams, who rode against each once home and away. So Scottish speedway had gone from four teams in 1952 to just one by the end of 1954.

March

Despite staging practice sessions at Milton Street on 25 and 26 March wrangles over pay rates delayed the start of the season and it was mid-April before events got underway at most tracks, including Motherwell.

April

The Eagles added Tommy Miller and returnee Derick Close to their team and parted with Jimmy Tannock and Guy Allott. Former Eagles racer Joe Crowther was appointed as mechanic and coach to the side. The ever-popular Bluey Scott came back for his fourth season, while Johnny Green and Ron Phillips were also in the line-up alongside Cyril Cooper and Scott Hall. Later on, Larry Lazarus and Doug Templeton joined the Eagles and Miller moved on to Coventry.

When the racing started on 16 April, it was a red letter day for Coventry reserve Jim Lightfoot. He scored a career first 12 point maximum which helped the visiting Bees to a narrow 43–41 win. The youngster was helped along the way by team-mate Vic Emms who scored 8+1, but that did not detract from his efforts. The Bees had another maximum man in Charlie New who went on to clean up the second half.

The Eagles' McGregor had a miserable opener to the season with a fall, two thirds and a last place and 2+2 was all he gathered. A deal had been brokered which would have seen him go to Leicester, but with Glasgow's subsequent closure, Ken McKinlay went instead. A cash sale was not on the Eagles' agenda and a rider swap was the only acceptable option. New signing Tommy Miller, riding a new frame pioneered at the Glasgow and Motherwell practice sessions, started with an engine failure. This must have disappointed Joe Crowther, the former Eagles skipper and one time Tiger. Tommy's own bike failed to start, so he had to use the track spare and this pegged him back to 7+1.

Close eased himself back into the racing mode as he made his comeback from the horrendous injury he had received at Harringay in 1953. He was not fully match fit and just did not have the speed to salvage the last heat. Also, team-mate McGregor was slow off the mark and never managed to pass Johnny Reason. Close settled for five points, but at least he was back in action and would improve as the season progressed. It was alleged in the speedway press that Derick had arranged a secret trial at Motherwell, however he failed to turn up and did not attend the afternoon and under lights sessions. With the three heat leaders not producing big scores, it was the middle order and the tail that help the Eagles put up a spirited display against the Bees. The starting gate broke down at heat eight, so the races after that were started using the green light.

An 8,000 crowd watched as the Monarchs struggled against the Eagles at Old Meadowbank on Saturday 17 April. The home team took an early lead, but with only four heats to go one point separated the sides. Despite the efforts of Miller, who scored eight, and Close, the closing races saw Edinburgh hold on and they finished as narrow 43–40 winners.

The Eagles were also well served by Green who scored nine. Close improved during the meeting and finished with six points. The most consistent riders for the visitors were the reserves, Cooper and Hall, who scored four and 3+1 respectively. They were far superior to their Edinburgh counterparts. The turning point was considered to be heat 11, when Edinburgh picked up a 5–1 over Green, who had ridden unbeaten up to that point, and Phillips. The Monarchs' best rider was paid maximum man Dick Campbell with 11+1, while Bob Mark contributed 10+1.

What did the Motherwell management say to the Eagles' riders over the weekend? Whatever it was, it certainly transformed the team's efforts. They secured a superb 49–35 victory over the Hunters on Monday 19 April in a North Shield match at Leicester. Miller flew to a full maximum 12 and his partner Scott raced to an impressive paid maximum 9+3. Three times Scott was out with Miller and three times they took maximum points. Cooper's efforts from reserve were worthy of mention. His seven points made up for Phillips' off night. He only managed a second place in three starts.

For the Hunters, it was Alf Parker who gave the most exciting display when in heat eight he surged round from the back, passing Hall then passing again to win by a narrow margin over Phillips. However, Parker only managed 4+1 and the top Hunter was Reg Fearman on nine points.

This meeting at Motherwell on 23 April was the last time the rival teams would meet. This night was the end of an era for the Tigers. The result was 58–25, in the Eagles favour, and it was expunged from the records. The Tigers had ridden some matches in the North Shield, but this was their last fixture apart from a couple of challenge matches.

Ken McKinlay apart, the Tigers were no match for the Eagles. He was involved the best race of the night, heat five, when he was overtaken by Miller and Green who passed either side at the same time. McKinlay had broken his frame in his first outing and rode the track spare in heat five. He was back on his own frame, which had been welded, in heat nine to record a win over Phillips.

After the meeting his move to Leicester for £1,000 was signed and sealed, as was the Tigers' closure. This effectively ruled out a move south for McGregor.

The Tigers riders must have been demoralised as their impending closure was one of the worst kept secrets in speedway. McKinlay on nine points and Bob Sharp on seven were the only Tigers to register a good return, but the others rode to the best of their ability in the circumstances.

For the home side Miller scored a maximum 12 over his former team-mates and Close scored 10+1. Phillips added 10 while McGregor contributed 6+1.

The Eagles wanted a 30 point winning margin against Rayleigh in the National Trophy. However, they could only manage a 20 point win, 64–44, at The Stadium on 30 April. Rain played havoc with this fixture. It left the track greasy and possibly dangerous. It also kept away some potential supporters. The wet track was a bit of a leveller, but in the early heats the Rockets settled first. The Eagles had to come back from six points down at the end of heat five. Track conditions contributed to Scott's two falls, but Bluey mastered the track to win heat 11 when he had the fans transfixed as he overcooked it and corrected his error to compete four laps.

Miller dropped points as he tried to shield McGregor from Maury McDermott. He also dropped points when his bike packed in after a lap in the last race. He ended up with 13. Close was the top Eagle with 14+2 while McGregor chipped in with 11+2. Green, who scored 10+2, was excluded from heat 10 for dangerous riding. He bumped into Tom O'Conner, moving him over which was seen by the Steward as boring. Cooper's bike failed in heat nine, which caused him to drop back to third, but it restarted, allowing him to finish. Les McGillivray was the top Rocket with 10+1, while Tom O'Conner scored 8+3 and McDermott collected eight.

May

In the National Trophy second leg, after 36 heats, the aggregate score was Rayleigh 109 Motherwell 107. The Eagles started at The Weir on Saturday 1 May with a 20 point advantage and widened that by four points after the opening heat. However, after heat three the Rockets whittled the aggregate scorers back to the original margin, and by the end of heat 15, they were two up on aggregate.

The home team, which won on the night 65–43, had better service from their second strings and reserves. It is questionable if, even with the services of Green, who was injured in his second last programmed race, the Eagles could have shaded it. Green ended up with black eyes and a bump on his nose for his troubles. Tommy Miller showed his undoubted class which confirmed the value of his £1,800 transfer fee with an untroubled 18 point maximum. Phillips was next best on 8+1 while Bluey Scott contributed 6+1.

Gerry Jackson, who had done little the night before, proved to be the best Rocket with 12 while Kiwi Peter Clark also got over a poor night in Scotland to register 11+3.

Ipswich made their first visit to Scotland on 7 May and lost 55–29. The top two Tigers of 1953 were on opposing sides and it was Junior Bainbridge who came out tops when they met in heat one and again in heat five. A last chance for Miller to put one over on Bainbridge was expected in the second half final. However, this did not happen because Bainbridge could not get past McGregor in his heat. Tommy Miller had to settle for 10 points.

Bainbridge's maximum chances went in his last heat when Phillips out-gated and outraced him and completed his maximum. The Ipswich Australian collected 11 points. Bainbridge was way ahead of his team mates; the next two best were Bert Edwards on six and Len Silver on four. Ipswich reserve, John Lawrie, was injured in heat four when he collided with the fence.

65

Left: Tommy Miller, one of the top Scottish post-war riders, who rode for the Eagles in 1954 before moving mid-season to Coventry. (JSC)

Below: The 1954 Motherwell Eagles: back: Joe Crowther, Tommy Miller, Gordon McGregor, Tom Reid (manager) Derek Close, Bluey Scott; front: Larry Lazarus, Ron Phillips, Johnny Green, Cyril Cooper. (JSC)

Ipswich had Nobby Stock in their party and he was called up for the meeting at Edinburgh the following night.

Not for the first time, the starting gate broke down and races had to be started using the green light. Miller's improved form was put down to Joe Crowther, the team mechanic who had, just prior to this match found and repaired a split in the frame of Tommy's machine.

Larry Lazarus joined the Eagles from the Tigers on Thursday 13 May in time to travel to Ipswich with his new side. He started well with a reserve's paid maximum. The Eagles were also boosted by the return from injury of Green and they stormed to a fantastic 52–32 win on their first visit to Foxhall Heath.

Larry and his fellow Eagles cast their spell on the Witches and won almost as they pleased. Only Junior Bainbridge rode to form. He managed three of the five Ipswich race wins. He scored 11 points and next best were Bert Edwards on eight and Sid Clarke on six; former Tiger Bob Sharp scored 5+1.

There were no Eagles maximums, but they scored well throughout their line-up. Miller equalled Bainbridge on 11, as did Close, while Phillips took the role of third heat leader on seven.

With the Eagles away on 14 May, the home fans had the chance to see the juniors in action at The Stadium in the Scottish Junior Championship. Experienced Scott Hall, who had been displaced from the team line-up when Lazarus arrived, won after going through the card unbeaten. His main opponent, Doug Templeton, was beaten in heat three and his other main rival, Jimmy Tannock, was defeated in heat 17 as Hall clinched the trophy. Templeton finished second and Tannock took third spot. A big section the crowd were rooting for Arthur Malm, but the young former Tigers Australian had a poor night after falling in his opening ride.

The high-flying Eagles maintained their super form with Miller and Close racing to a full and paid maximum respectively at Wolverhampton in a North Shield match on the same night. As at Ipswich the night before, the Wasps fielded new men, but it was all to no avail as the Eagles flew to a 56–28 win. McGregor with 8+2 and Ron Phillips on 7+1 compounded the Wasps misery. The track did not help the home men and the visitors' quality bike control on a very wet surface paid very handsome dividends.

The Wasps did not have any recognised heat leaders on a par with the Eagles top two of Miller and Close and paid the penalty. Les Tolley was the top Wasp with 7+1 while Eric Irons scored 5+1. Former Tiger Vern McWilliams scored five points.

Again, the meeting was expunged from the records because the Wolverhampton promotion failed before they could complete their North Shield fixtures and make the return trip to Motherwell.

While McGregor had an off night at Brandon on Saturday 15 May, Cyril Cooper rose to the occasion and produced a match-winning 10 from the reserve berth as the 43–40 win avenged the opening night defeat by the Bees at The Stadium. McGregor had two last places before falling in his third outing. This led to him pulling out of the match. The Bees were considered to be understrength, but to be fair, the Eagles were on a high from two away wins on the trot which boosted their confidence.

The Eagles had a bit of luck in heat 13 when Phillips bumped Vic Emms and Vic's partner Jackie Hughes was baulked. The resulting 5–1 put the Eagles in pole position for the last heat decider which was a 3–3 draw after Jim Lightfoot was excluded at the first time of asking.

Miller matched Cooper with 10 points, while Phillips on 8+1 and Close on eight provided sound backing. Vic Emms was on for a maximum until heat 13 and had to settle for nine points. Johnny Reason with seven and Jackie Hughes on 5+1 were the next best for a poor Bees side.

The home fans were given a chance to see their rampaging team as they blew away the Leicester Hunters 66–18 at The Stadium on Monday 17 May. Ken McKinlay opened with a win, beating former team-mate Miller. This was the only heat won by a visitor. Miller turned the tables on McKinlay in heat five. If it had not been for McKinlay, a whitewash was on the cards. As it was, he had a nasty fall in heat 12 when, chasing Phillips, he over-slid before hitting the fence twice, then falling. Thankfully, he got up and walked from the track. McKinlay collected seven points and the next best Hunter was Dennis Gray on four, ahead of Charlie Barsby on three.

For the Eagles, Close and Green recorded paid maximums with 11+1 and 10+2 respectively. Miller collected 10+1 while Scott collected 9+2.

In heat two of the scratch races, Green fell and Reg Fearman had to lay down his bike to avoid him. Fearman remounted to finish and receive a commendation from the Steward for his action.

First Division opposition did not daunt the high-flying Eagles. A big crowd enjoyed watching their heroes give the Wimbledon Dons the once-over by 20 points on 21 May in a challenge match. Miller had to give second best to Ronnie Moore and Geoff Mardon, but in return he stopped both of them from gaining maximums. This was no mean feat as Wimbledon were the current Division One top team.

Surprisingly, Close had an off night. He only scored four and it was Phillips on 12+2 and Green on 11+1 who backed up Miller, who gathered 16. There were solid displays from McGregor and Scott. The Dons' Dom Perry and Cyril Maidment had been held up in London traffic in the morning, so both flew up to Scotland to Glasgow's airport, which was then at Renfrew. It must have been an expensive trip for the pair who only scored three points between them.

There were almost fireworks in heat 10 when Scott and Perry had a coming together as they jousted for third place. Scott managed to create a gap and stayed ahead of the Irishman to take the point. The Eagles' 64–44 win was a measure of how well they were capable of doing against top flight teams when they were all on song.

The Wolverhampton Wasps had folded at the beginning of the week and both Edinburgh and Motherwell tried to secure replacement opposition for their weekend fixtures. The initial proposals were that Exeter or Southampton would fill the breach. Poole's name entered the frame, but they refused as a couple of their riders could not get leave from National Service with the Army to ride. Tom Reid and Frank Varey both complained to the Speedway Control Board, which was funded by a 1.5 percent gate levy, that teams should be required to visit and rider non-availability should not be an issue.

The postponement is reputed to have cost Motherwell £400. Typical costs for a meeting were quoted as advertising £50, and the same amount for rider insurance. Riders were paid £1.20 a point and £1 a start plus traveling expenses of about 2p a mile.

June

The Lanarkshire Eagles collected the North Shield points on 4 June to give them victory in this competition. The meeting was watched by their biggest crowd of the season. The crowd size had much to do with the weather, but a local derby in Scotland was always a crowd puller. The Monarchs won only one heat, but racing did not suffer as a consequence. Many of the thrills were provided by the South African, Roy Bester, who was never far behind the Eagles' leading men.

Miller capped the only maximum score by winning the trophy event in the second half. Phillips lost only to Cuppleditch and finished with 10+1, while Close, Scott and McGregor all scored seven, although the first two added bonus points to their pay packets.

This was Bob Fletcher's debut for the Monarchs and he scored 4+1. Bob moved to Motherwell later in the season after Edinburgh closed. The former Coventry rider was on Belle Vue's books. Another debutante was Alf McIntosh, the former Glasgow Tiger who scored 2+1. The Monarchs had three men on seven points, Dick Campbell, who had machine problems with a slipping clutch, Don Cuppleditch and Roy Bester. Bob Fletcher and Alf McIntosh scored six between them, the same as the man the Monarchs had really wanted, former Tiger Larry Lazarus.

The 55–29 margin may have been larger, but for Green's engine failure in heat 10 which happened when he was well in the lead.

Edinburgh's Dick Campbell swept to a full maximum which gave him the Skelly Trophy at The Stadium on 11 June. The Motherwell promotion were looking for the first Eagles' victory in this competition, but it came to nothing. Campbell beat Tommy Miller in heat 16 which left onlookers thinking that Miller did not put up much of a fight. Close, who couldn't halt the Kiwi in his last race, had dropped points to team-mate Miller in heat 10 after Miller had come through from the back.

Junior Bainbridge, Cyril Cooper and Bob Sharp did well, considering that they had been in a road crash on their way north. The van they had been traveling in had somersaulted after leaving the road.

Green was excluded from heat 19 for cutting across Scott Hall after passing him. Yet again, the starting gate malfunctioned during the night.

There was another big win for the Eagles at home on 18 June. This was thanks to a solid showing from the whole team which gave them a 62–22 win against Rayleigh. Bluey Scott was excluded from heat one after he had completed the race. He had hit the fence a couple of times and left the track to ride on the centre green on his way round. However, he went onto complete his night undefeated by a visitor with 7+2 in his next three rides. Close was back to top form with a full maximum, his first since his comeback, while Miller scored 11+1. Green was another back to form as he scored 11.

Rayleigh Rockets had only one race winner, Peter Clarke, who had to wait until heat 12 to avoid a whitewash of race winners. Peter scored eight with Maury McDermott and Gerry Jackson both scoring four points as the next best Rockets. On the strength of the National Trophy showing, much more was expected of the Essex men. Les McGillivray had fans with their hearts in their mouths as he nearly went under the wheels of an opponent in heat 13. Scott Hall went one better than Bluey Scott in the second half as he tore down a length of fence. Hall had used a bit too much throttle in the wrong place and the bike threw him off before continuing on to damage the fence.

After a series of big home wins the opposition on 25 June, the Poole Pirates, made the Eagles fight for a 44–40 victory. It took the home side until heat seven to get in front, but Poole were far from finished. The Pirates nosed ahead again and it was only in heat 13 that the home riders began to feel they could win. A last heat 4–2 clinched it.

69

Heavy rain started falling by heat nine and this helped the Eagles yet again. Close revelled in the wet to win heat 13. Green, Miller and Close all abandoned their normal line round the inside edge and rode much wider than normal. Phillips was the top Eagle with a full maximum while Close bagged 10 points and Miller had to settle for seven. Miller was unlucky in the opening heat as Bluey Scott's bike seized while team-riding with the red headed Australian. In the confusion, Allan Kidd shot past to claim second spot.

The Pirates were well served by Bill Holden who scored 8+1, Ken Middleditch with 7+2 and Jimmy Squibb on six. Poole's Vern McWilliams injured a hand in his heat four fall and wrecked his bike in the process.

The strain may have got to the Eagles' manager, John Y. Robertson, as he took ill after the meeting. Yet again the starting gate broke down and flag starts were used this time. A proposed fastest lap contest was not staged in the second half because the track was not in a fit condition.

July

The Falcons from Exeter made their league debut in Scotland and fell prey to their feathered adversaries as Miller, with a maximum 12, and Close, 11+1, again formed the spearhead on 2 July. Yet again Green, with nine and Phillips, 8+2, gave excellent backing. The opening heat tussle between Miller and Geran was the Falcons' best effort of the night. The visitors, more used to their long pacy County Ground track, found the tighter confines of Milton Street a bit hard to handle.

McGregor's recent poor form saw him drop to the reserves for the first time since he started out in the sport with the Glasgow Tigers. He scored a third place then suffered an engine failure.

After going close so often, the Eagles finally produced every race winner in this 58–26 win and the Falcons men had to be contented with second and third places for their money. Cooper scored a reserve's maximum six points and qualified for the second half final where he gave Miller a stiff challenge.

A World finalist in 1952, Derick Close picked up the cheque for £30 in the World Championship qualifying meeting which was dominated by the Eagles men at The Stadium on 9 July. Close scored 14 while Tommy Miller scored 13. Joint third place went to Green and Edinburgh's Dick Campbell. Green did the hard job in heat seven, but failed to capitalise on beating Close and Miller by losing to Cooper and Edinburgh's Bob Fletcher in heat 15. Green on 12 and Phillips on 11 did well, but Gordon McGregor on five and Bluey Scott, together with Cyril Cooper on eight, did not really shine.

About this time Green asked for a transfer claiming that the Motherwell promotion had refused to pay traveling expenses.

The big disappointment of the night at Oxford on Thursday 15 July was the poor score returned by Tommy Miller. He managed only two third places. Had he scored his usual maximum, the Eagles could well have won this one. As it was, he fell in the first heat, bringing down Scott while Bob McFarlane laid down to avoid the Eagles pair. Close battled for 11 dropping his only point in to Ronnie Genz who held him back for the whole race. He also had a battle in his last heat as Peter Robinson gave him a race of it all the way to the flag. Reports suggested that Miller was riding as though he wasn't really interested – maybe not surprising as he was seeking a move away from Motherwell.

Johnny Green with six and Bluey Scott with 5+1 were the best in the Eagles side which scored 33 in response to Oxford's 51. The Cheetahs had three men on 11 and their total matched the entire Eagles return. They were Peter Robinson, Ronnie Genz, and Fred Curtis, formerly known as 'Kid' Curtis.

There was no two wheel racing at The Stadium in Motherwell on Friday 16 July because the Eagles were away to Bristol. The home fans had the option of watching the new sport of stock car racing. At Bristol, heat one caused some discussion as Scott hit the fence to avoid a fallen Dick Bradley. Bradley remounted and completed the race and took the one point on offer. However, Bradley made sure Scott was paid for the point which everyone considered he deserved. In the end Bristol ran out easy winners 59–22. The Bulldogs were well served by Jack Unstead on 11, Billy Hole on 10+1 while Geoff Pymar scored a 9+3 paid maximum .

Miller was back in the groove with 11 from four rides, but he did not have much by way of support. Larry Lazarus failed to score and the best of the others was Gordon McGregor with 4+1. The Eagles were not helped by the greasy state of the Knowle track which was always a daunting place for visitors, no matter what the condition of the track was.

The Eagles were on track for a big defeat when rain brought play to a close after 11 heats at The Abbey Stadium, Blunsdon, home track of the Swindon Robins, the next day. At the time the meeting was abandoned the Robins were cruising for a big win as the score stood at 49–17 in their favour.

Only Cooper had won a race, his only points of the night, while Scott matched him picking up a third place in each of his three outings. Miller, Close and Lazarus each scored one point.

For the home side, Ian Williams was unbeaten with nine, while Bert Roger, George White, and Ron Swaine all scored 7+2 before the shutters were brought down.

Despite the match not being completed, Swindon were awarded the match points as the visitors were in no position to win when it was stopped. The Swindon promotion were not happy that the Eagles had made it clear they did not want to ride. Norman Parker, the Robins manager is reputed to have threatened to ride himself, an action which is supposed to have shamed the Eagles men into starting the match.

Monday 19 July, Glasgow Fair Monday, saw Miller down on his usual return, scoring seven, perhaps due to an impending announcement about his future at The Stadium. However, he and the rest of the team did enough to take the league points on offer with a sound 50–34 win over the visiting Bristol Bulldogs.

Chris Boss was warmly applauded when he deliberately over-slid his bike to avoid the fallen Phillips in heat eight. Phillips had reared while chasing Chum Taylor but, after controlling the rearing bike, lost it again after getting the front wheel down.

Jack Unstead was carried off after his heat seven fall, but returned to take his next ride and a second half outing. Dick Bradley was the best Bulldog with 10 and Johnny Hole next best with eight. Green picked off a few opponents on the last bend, but a couple of times he looked a wee bit on the desperate side. He was beaten this way in heat 10 and Hole just missed out on passing Scott in the last heat. Scott survived a first race fall to post 8+1 while Close was top scorer with 10.

The Eagles' first ever rain off since they opened in 1950 deprived the fans of seeing the then league leaders Swindon Robins on 23 July. This was ironic because the Eagles had raced at Swindon in the wet a few days before.

The 12,000 crowd who turned up to watch the Scotland versus England test match on 30 July booed Tommy Miller in what was his last meeting as a Lanarkshire Eagle. According to

71

him, his request to move was motivated by the failure of the promotion to deliver on promises made when he signed.

Alan Hunt was not popular with his Division Two opponents who felt he rode a bit hard. Hunt was excluded from heat six for skittling Scott. Ron Mountford came off worst though, because he ploughed into Scott's bike and landed on the centre green, almost at the feet of chief guest, the Duke of Hamilton. Mountford missed the rerun and another two races.

Phillips' return was reduced to five because he was filled in in his first race and had sore eyes for the rest of the meeting. Close was top scorer for Scotland with 17 while Scott and Green were next best on seven points each.

Split Waterman, the larger-than-life speedway star, and Alan Hunt top scored for England with 14 points each while Arthur Wright and Peter Craven added 11 each to the rampant Anglo's total.

Poor returns from Miller and former Monarch, now Belle Vue Ace, Don Cuppleditch plus a few others meant that Scotland suffered a 61–47 defeat at the hands of the Auld Enemy.

August

If the Eagles fans had wanted speedway action in the first weekend of August in 1954, they would have had to have made the trip to Coventry on Saturday 7 August to watch their team. The Friday night was occupied by a stock car meeting which was won by former Eagle Stan Bradbury.

Tommy Miller was at Coventry. However, he was making his Bees debut and scored a maximum against his old team mates in the Bees 57–27 League win.

It was the intention of the Motherwell promotion to replace Tommy with a heat leader, but it didn't happen. Instead, the Eagles promoted Doug Templeton from the second half to fill the gap created in the tail of the side. While Close scored nine, he had little support and the next best were McGregor on 4+1 and Cyril Cooper on four points. Charlie New joined Tommy on maximum points while Jim Lightfoot scored 7+1.

On Monday 9 August at Poole Stadium, Vern McWilliams, now a Pirate, faced the Eagles for the third time. Each time Vern had faced the Eagles he had been with a different team. After closures at Glasgow and Wolverhampton, he had found a more durable base. The weakened Eagles, headed by Close, who scored 9+1, were no match for the Pirates and they slumped to a 51–33 defeat. Phillips scored 7.5 while the man he dead heated with, Ken Middleditch, scored 8.5. Eagle's Cooper, was next best with 4.5.

This match is unusual in that it featured two dead heats. Cyril Cooper and Norman Strachan – always pronounced Strawn in Poole – tied in heat eight and, as mentioned above, Ken Middleditch and Ron Phillips did likewise in heat 14.

The Bannister Court bowl in Southampton suited Scott down to the ground the next day. He just wound it on and kept at it. It was effective because he bagged his win in joint best time of the night. He went on to ride for the Saints in 1955.

The Eagles were having an off night and between them they only collected 30 to Southampton Saints' 54. Scott was joint to scorer with Close on 6+1. Gordon McGregor scored six. The best for Southampton was one time Stoke Potter, Londoner Johnny Fitzpatrick, who scored a full 12 point maximum. He had sound backing from Ernie Rawlins on 11+1 and Merv Hannam on nine.

The first home meeting without Tommy Miller was on 13 August and he wasn't missed as the Eagles tore Oxford Cheetahs apart to register a 58–26 win. Green was crowded out at the start in his first two outings, but recovered to score in his last two. One press report considered that he was the victim of dangerous riding, but the Steward did not appear to agree. After heat five, Green was seen to let Peter Robinson know that he was not too pleased by his tactics which had seen the Eagle run very close to the fence as he was moved over. Green had the choice, shut off or fall off.

Scott came from the back in heat 11 to grab a second place. To achieve this, he had to take on the team riding talents of Frank Johnson and Bill Thatcher.

Payback time for Southampton Saints came on 20 August as Eagles cuffed them 63–21 in Motherwell. Bluey Scott's season ended in his opening ride when he caught his throttle on the safety fence which resulted in a very hard fall. He had been going for the line with Brian McKeown at the end of the race. The crash wrecked man and machine, the frame of the machine ended in two bits. Bluey did not blame anyone but himself.

Templeton and Lazarus, who scored an 11+1 paid maximum, took full advantage of their extra rides to pile up the points. Derick Close was reported have joined the 'want aways', but stayed and chipped in a fair contribution to this easy home win.

A man short, the Eagles, without Bluey Scott, had to borrow local rider Eric Ebbs to make up the team at Rayleigh the next day. Eric put his local experience to good use to pick up three points as Eagles were given the 'rocket' by the home side. The Eagles had been pre-match favourites to beat the bottom of the table team, but the men from the Weir raised their efforts and won 49–35.

The Eagles signed Bob Fletcher, who had been with Edinburgh until their closure in July, to fill the gap. He did not make an impressive debut as the Eagles lost 55–29 at Ipswich on 26 August, but he did better than three others who failed to bag a point between them. Tich Read, or to give him his correct name George Snailum, chipped in a couple, but it was Eagles former Scottish based rivals Bainbridge, Sharp and Campbell who were the weavers of the Witches charms.

Close stopped Bainbridge's unbeaten run, but he could not stop Campbell's march to a maximum. Close scored nine while Phillips chipped in eight and McGregor scored six. The *Speedway News* reported that "It was an exciting night's racing watched by 12,500 people."

The midget car meeting staged on 27 August featured former speedway rider Eric Liddell who teamed up with Tom Forster, David Hughes, Jimmy Reid, Andy Dodds and Alex Wylie to form the Glasgow team. The winning Lanarkshire side featured a former rider in the shape of Niven McCreadie with teammates Wilf Davies, George Ellis, Jimmy Laing and Jimmy Smith. A couple of the Glasgow team had raced the 'doodle bugs' at White City in 1937.

It was former Monarch Roy Bester's night as he topped the Hunters' score chart with a 12 point maximum at Leicester on the same night. Jock Grierson was on his way to a paid maximum when his bike let him down in heat 12, so he had to settle for nine points. Fellow Scot Ken McKinlay continued his falling off record against the Eagles. He went down in heat one but he, like Dennis Gray, scored 8+1 and the Hunters still cuffed the Eagles 54–30. The *Speedway News* said that the Eagles "put up quite a good show."

Close apart, Eagles had no one to match the home men. Nevertheless, the Eagles' efforts were considered to be acceptable as the Hunters regularly ran up big scores at Blackbird Road. Templeton and Lazarus were credited with a lot of effort for scant reward. Close scored nine with Phillips and McGregor on five each.

Another unimpressive display on the road followed. This time at Exeter's County Ground on Monday 30 August. The Eagles had failed to replace Tommy Miller and get cover for Bluey Scott, and this was shown in the run of poor away results. Reserve Lazarus settled well, but wasn't given a chance to add to his total of five from two reserve rides when his mates were floundering. Close, Phillips and McGregor could only score one more than him. This time the Falcons won 57–27. It was an impressive display by the home men.

There was a sea change in the second half and the Eagles swept the board. Maybe the Falcons were happy with their winnings in the match. Goog Hoskin and Jack Hart both were unbeaten by an Eagles rider as they gathered 11+1.

September

At home the weakened Eagles still could hold their own. A wet track helped them yet again. This time on 3 September, the Eagles beat Swindon Robins 49–35.

McGregor's return to form, with 10+1, was most timely and, together with maximum man Close, they inspired Eagles to victory. The top two received sound support from Phillips and Cooper who scored 8+1 and 7+1 respectively. For the Robins, Ron Swaine was best with nine while George White scored 7+1 and Ian Williams took 6+1.

The meeting at The Stadium scheduled for 10 September against Ipswich Witches was rained off. The Eagles luck with the weather continued into the next week and, after a bright start against Leicester on Monday 13 September, rain started after heat six. Such was the intensity of the rain that it brought the match to an end after heat nine was halted because Ken McKinlay fell. The writing was on the wall as Lazarus fell on the treacherous surface in heat seven.

Leicester had just gone into the lead after McGregor had dropped out of heat eight with bike failure. Whether the wet conditions contributed to McGregor's engine failure is not known.

Were the Eagles let off the hook? Without Close, who had been injured at Belle Vue, they were certainly up against it. The match was closed with Leicester Hunters winning 25–23. At the time of abandonment Green and Cooper were unbeaten having scored six each while visitors Len Williams and Reg Fearman both had five. The match was not rerun, so Leicester took the league points.

Heat one of the second half of the meeting against Coventry on 17 September was a bit of a pantomime. Green took the lead when Charlie New's bike packed up. Johnny Reason also had engine failure and that left Green and arch enemy of the Motherwell fans, Tommy Miller. Miller then fell to leave Green an easy and popular winner. Miller took second spot after remounting. New and Reason managed to get their bikes going again and rejoined the race, but after New had taken what he thought was third spot, the Steward announced there was no third place because both riders had been lapped.

Earlier in the meeting, in heat 10, an unusual incident had happened when Miller had shut off at the end of the third lap. Cooper and McGregor did the same, but Vic Emms kept going to the flag hotly pursued by the others who realised what had happened and throttled back up to complete four laps. At the end of 14 heats, the Eagles had 44 points to Coventry's 40 and the league points.

For the Eagles, who were yet again without Close, it was Phillips, Lazarus and McGregor who shared top spot in the score chart as they each scored eight. For the Bees, Tommy Miller scored 10 and Charlie New claimed 8+1.

Unusually for the time, Reason and Lightfoot were reported to have flown north to Glasgow, but even more unusual is that they travelled via Belfast. They had missed their train at Birmingham station, and the route was the only way to arrive in time for the meeting.

The Alan Gray Memorial Trophy midget car meeting on Friday 24 September featured 12 racers and was won by Jimmy Reid of Glasgow from former Monarch and Giant Eric Liddell. Reid picked up a 100 Guinea (£105) prize. No speedway for the fans this week. There was concern in speedway at this time that stock cars were another 'problem' for the sport which was already struggling. It is interesting to note that the two sports existed together at Motherwell.

October

The second attempt to race the Ipswich Witches on 1 October also fell victim to rain. The Witches came back a week later and, although they did not know it, this meeting was to be the end of an era for speedway at The Stadium.

The Eagles bowed out with a 45–39 win, but it was former Monarch Dick Campbell who left his mark on the meeting with six clear wins. In the match, he scored a full 12 point maximum. He was supported by Bert Edwards on 10, but the rest of the team, Junior Bainbridge included, could manage no better than 4+1. Bluey Scott made a comeback, but crashed with Johnny Chamberlain in what looked an alarming prang. Neither was injured, but Scott was excluded. Close also came back and top scored with 9+1. Next best were Cooper on 8+1 with Phillips and McGregor on 7+1. This was the third attempt to race Ipswich, the two previous rain-offs had cost the promotion £500.

Despite the intention to run in 1955, the story is that the English sides were not prepared to travel for a single fixture in Scotland and, as a result, the Motherwell promotion gave up the fight to stage speedway at Milton Street. Jock Watt in the *Speedway News* on 1 September mentioned rumours that Motherwell would not finish the season, which were not true.

In 1955, speedway had seven teams in the top flight, and nine finished the season in the Second Division, Bristol and Weymouth both dropped out mid-season. The league looked like the Southern League of a couple of years earlier. The most northern teams were Coventry and Leicester. League speedway did not return to Scotland until 1960, when the launch of the Provincial League included the Edinburgh Monarchs.

George Hunter, who rode in the Motherwell
meetings in 1958 and 1972. (JSC)

6. 1958: A short season

Speedway was in dire straits in 1958 when Ian Hoskins organised a handful of meetings at Motherwell. The National League was down to one division with 10 teams. Just Wimbledon were left from the five London tracks of the 1940s and early 1950s. Belle Vue were the only team in the north of England. There was a Junior League of four teams, and the Southern Area League ran at a handful of venues at the weekend.

May

After a winter of practice sessions and trials, including a full-blown session on Sunday 13 April which was filmed by the local Scottish Independent Television station, STV, the Eagles, or to be more exact, the Golden Eagles, were back on 16 May. Doug Templeton and Jimmy Tannock, who had graced the race strip before as Eagles, were back in black and white for the opening challenge fixture against the Belle Vue Babes. Ian Hoskins promoted the meeting. The Eagles were dubbed 'the no-chance team' by some pundits. However, this makeshift team won convincingly, 50–27, in the new format 13 heat match.

It was newcomer George Hunter who caught the eye. He showed what supporters could expect in the future as he won races from the gate. This became a Hunter trade mark in the years ahead. He was joint top scorer with 11+1. George had a great race with Graham Beattie as the pair slugged it out for the four laps.

Willie Templeton scored 10+2; his brother Doug scored 9+3, while Fred Greenwell scored seven points. Tannock had a horror fall and was lucky that the following riders missed him. His helmet came off in the crash, but despite his stretcher ride he was up and about before the meeting was over. For the Belle Vue Babes, their best rider was Jack Kitchen with eight, while Graham Beattie scored seven.

Mike Parker and Ron Lea gave a midget car demonstration after the bikes had finished.

Doug Templeton scored the first full Golden Eagles maximum of the new era on 30 May. He saw off challenges from Coventry Select men Brian Meredith and Colin 'Joe' Gooddy in the match. Brian got his own back in the second half when he beat Doug in the heat before going on to win the final.

Doug's brother Willie had a night to forget. He wrecked his bike in his opening heat. Willie had ridden the white line in lap one, but next time round he found Alan Pearce in the way and the net result was a coming together and both cartwheeling up the track.

Doug established a new track record for the era in heat one. George Hunter scored 7+1. Middlesbrough based Fred Greenwell rode well again. He just missed out on a maximum with 11, yet again, but his contribution gave the Golden Eagles a 41–35 win to keep the home fans happy. For Coventry, Meredith and Gooddy both scored 12+1 with Norman Unger next best on four points. Coventry's Bill McGregor was known as 'Wee McGregor' after a character in a series of comic Scottish novels.

June

Jack Kitchen, nephew of Wembley star Bill, starred, this time for Bradford on 13 June, but he had little support from the rest of the Bradford riders. Jack won his first four races, then had to settle for second best to Doug Templeton and Gordon Mitchell in turn in his last two outings. Mitchell left it late, but was ahead at the vital time – at the flag. The man from Hamilton had the crowd on their toes as he chased Jack for most of the race before making his decisive move. Willie Templeton had a new frame in his machine, but didn't settle on this bike. Nevertheless, he did well to score 7+1 despite a heat nine engine failure. Jack 'Red' Monteith had a bit of a red letter day. He scored 7+1.

Jimmy Tannock took another spectacular fall, but steadied himself and collected four points. Doug Templeton was the top Golden Eagle with 11 while Greenwell and Hunter, who scored six and 6+4 respectively, were down on points. However, they gave the crowd their money's worth by winning points by coming from the back. This 48–30 win completed the Golden Eagles' hat trick of wins.

For the Bradford Boomerangs, Kitchen was best with 16 points. However, the next best were Peter Thomson with five points and Stan Holey on four. The Boomerangs lost Roy Swift to a heat two injury which reduced their effectiveness. They also were a man short and used local novice Jimmy Cramb, probably best known in his boyhood as the Ashfield Giants and Motherwell mascot. Jimmy got some rides and scored a couple of points.

The teams representing Golden Eagles and Leicester Hunters were ready to race on 27 June, but the weather played the key card and no one turned a wheel that night.

July

Managed by former Eagle Tommy Miller, who was deputising for Les King, the Leicester Hunters came close to beating the Golden Eagles on 4 July. Leicester had their noses in front going into the last heat, but Mitchell repeated his last heat heroics with Willie Templeton to collect a 5–1 and secure a 40–37 win for the home team. The Hunters were ahead by one point at the end of heat 12, but the bike problems suffered by Doug Templeton and George Hunter in heat 11 had contributed to the Hunters' late match resurgence. Doug's bike spluttered round taking him to the third place that was on offer.

Fred Greenwell top scored for the Golden Eagles with 10 while Willie Templeton was on 8+2 and Gordon Mitchell secured seven points. Cliff Newton was the top Hunter with a full maximum 12 points. His best support came from Australian Noel Conway on 8+1 and Colin Gooddy on 6+2. The Eagles coach Larry Lazarus had a spin in the second half, but was promptly banned by the Control Board as coaches were not meant to ride.

Just like four years previously, it was Ipswich who were the last visitors at The Stadium. This time, on 11 July, the closure would be a bit more final. Yet again, the St Andrews Ambulance members were busy acting as stretcher bearers for the injured riders. The beneficiaries were Jimmy Tannock, Brian Larner and Vic 'Wild Man' Lonsdale.

Hunter failed to shine due to bike problems and troubles at the starting gate. He had to settle for a single point. Doug Templeton and Greenwell were both on 10 points, but Doug had a bonus point. Mitchell continued to show good form and scored 8+1.

Alvin 'Shorty' Schirmer stopped Doug's winning run and he might have scored more than 8+1 had he not fallen in the last heat before remounting to claim the third place on offer. 'Shorty' had an outing or two for Edinburgh in the early 1960s, but did not set the heather on fire. Best for Ipswich was Ronnie Rolfe on 10 while Ken Last scored 8+1.

And that was it for speedway at The Stadium. The venue itself fell into disuse, and was later demolished. The sport made a brief return to the town in 1972. Some of the riders were recruited by the Edinburgh Monarchs in 1960 when they joined the Provincial League. The future of Scottish speedway would be in or around Edinburgh and Glasgow.

7. 1972: The last hurrah

The original stadium had been demolished and, in its place, a 680 yards long trotting track had been laid. Wishing to diversify, the operators, K & K Raceways, looked to the potential of their new stadium for motor sports and decided to introduce stock cars and speedway. The track was fairly close to the adjacent housing, along what was the back straight, while on the home straight a small clubhouse stood in a relatively flat area which did not have much terracing. Long track racing had been a popular sport on the Continent and there were a number of moves to bring it to Britain. The operators of the venue in Motherwell decided to test the water. Three meetings were staged on the trotting track on Sunday 2 January, Sunday 2 April and Sunday 7 May 1972.

The stadium operators also wanted to try their hand at conventional speedway, and, as the centre green of the trotting track was not used for anything else, they constructed a track in the middle of it. The intention was to test the water by running a series of open licence meetings at British League Division Two level and, if it was a success, consider applying for league status. The opening meeting scheduled for Monday 15 May was rained off and the only meeting actually staged took place on Monday 12 June when the Golden Eagles raced and lost to Teesside Tigers 42–33. The Eagles had appeared in a fixture at Barrow on Thursday 28 May, losing 45–33 to the Happy Faces.

Long Track

The opening meeting on 2 January for the Golden Eagle Trophy featured multi- World Champions Barry Briggs and Ivan Mauger with Division One stars Alan Wilkinson, Eric Broadbelt and Glasgow Tigers' Bobby Beaton. The meeting was a standard 20 heat individual event. The riders used standard speedway bikes rather than the specialist long track machines which are fitted with gearboxes. Ivan Mauger won the meeting with an immaculate 15 point maximum. Bobby Beaton took the runner-up spot with 13 ahead of Alan Wilkinson on 12. Barry Briggs suffered an engine failure first time out and scored 11.

The second meeting, on 2 April was for the Duckham's Silver Cup. It again used the standard meeting format and again featured Barry Briggs. However, this time it included Scottish riders Jimmy McMillan, George Hunter and Bert Harkins and riders with stronger Scottish connections such as Reidar Eide and Bernie Persson. Australian rider Garry Middleton, the exciting 'Cas the Gas', who had an interest in the promotion of the meeting, won the event with a full 15 point maximum. Former Edinburgh and Coatbridge Monarchs man, the popular red headed Norwegian Reidar Eide, and George Hunter finished joint second with 13 points each and Glasgow Tigers' Jimmy McMillan was fourth with 11.

The last event was on 7 May. It used a different format. It opened with the Bahnrecord (Track Record) and a Champion of Champions event with six riders a race in a nine heat qualifying event. This was followed by two semi-finals and the final. Jim McMillan became the Champion of Champions from Dane Preben Rosenkilde and Swede Bernie Persson.

Speedway

The opening meeting scheduled for Monday 15 May fell victim of the bad weather in the Clyde Valley and licencing problems. Two further attempts to run this match were also victim of wet weather on 29 May and 5 June respectively.

The first, and what turned out to also be the last, meeting was staged on Monday 12 June when the Golden Eagles, skippered by former Berwick Bandit, Tom Blackwood, faced an almost league strength Teesside Tigers from Middlesbrough. Tim Swales led his team with a 15 point maximum, while twin brother Tony was next best on 10. Mick Moore gave them best backing with eight points.

For the home side, 'Millen the Villain', Jack Millen scored nine with three wins after suffering a couple of engine failures. Alec Nichol added seven points while Harry McLean contributed six. The Tigers defeated the Golden Eagles 42–33.

A Golden Eagles side had raced at Barrow's Holker Street Stadium on Thursday 28 May in a challenge match. Crewe's John Jackson and Dai Evans scored 12 and 10 respectively for the visitors as they went down 45–33 to the Happy Faces who had Mike Watkin and Ian Hindle on 9+1 and Tom Owen on 8+1.

Epilogue

Neither the venture into long track racing, nor the venture into speedway in 1972, was repeated and the second stadium has gone, replaced by a public park.

The Eagles were remembered in the final meeting at Blantyre in 1982. A team billed as The Eagles represented by Bobby Beaton, Jim Beaton, Harry McLean and David Cassells were runners-up in a three-team tournament featuring sides billed as The Cumbrians and Ayr Rebels. A printer's slip up saw the Workington Juniors, the Mothersall Eagles, being programmed as Motherwell Eagles, at Armadale in 2003.

8. The Motherwell riders

The riders in this chapter all rode for the Lanarkshire Eagles between 1950 and 1954. They are arranged in alphabetical order. Their international, individual and Scottish Championship records only cover their time with Motherwell, and are only included where they were involved. Information about birth dates and places with * is confirmed by the rider or official sources.

Guy Allott
Born: 19 September 1922, Penistone, South Yorkshire, England.*

The younger brother of Tommy Allott, Guy joined Tommy in the Sheffield side in 1949. After two seasons at Owlerton he spent 1951 and 1952 at Cradley Heath, moved to Wolverhampton in 1953 then transferred to Motherwell. He spent about half the season in black and white. Surprisingly, he moved to the top flight at Bradford (Odsal) from 1954 to 1956. He started 1957 at Birmingham, then reverted to Bradford. The years 1958 to 1961 saw Guy at Leicester before moving to Sheffield in the Provincial League, where he was a star. A serious injury in 1962 ended his career but the remained connected with speedway, tuning engines for star men.

His short spell at Motherwell started slowly, but he picked up towards the end of his stay. Guy's away form was not great. A non-return in 1954 was probably due to the weakening of the Glasgow Tigers before their closure and the availability of Scottish based riders rather than Guy's future potential being marked down by the Motherwell promotion.

Motherwell Statistics

Season	M	R	Pts	Bon	Tot	CMA	FM	PDM	Notes
1953	13	40	52	6	58	5.80	0	0	NL

Harry Andrews
Born: Scotland.

Harry first rode in junior events at Edinburgh in August 1950 and appeared briefly for the Monarchs in early season matches prior to the commencement of the league campaign the following year. He never rode for the club in an official fixture, but did turn out for Motherwell in a few North Shield fixtures and a National Trophy match at Halifax on 9 May 1951, failing to score from two rides.

Motherwell Statistics

Season	M	R	Pts	Bon	Tot	CMA	FM	PDM	Notes
1951	1	2	0	0	0	0.00	0	0	NT
1951	3	8	3	0	3	1.50	0	0	NS

William Alexander (Bill) Baird
Born: 16 March 1922, Forth, Scotland.

Apart from a spell with Bradford in 1947, Bill raced for Scottish teams. He started at Glasgow in 1946 as a pioneer Tiger, Next, he became a pioneer Edinburgh Monarch in 1948 before his next move, to Ashfield in 1950. His last season was a pioneer Lanarkshire Eagle. Bill has a unique record of having ridden for all four Scottish league teams of the 1940s and early 1950s.

He did not stay long at The Stadium. He retired after being dropped from the team after the National Trophy meeting on 9 May 1951.

Motherwell Statistics

Season	M	R	Pts	Bon	Tot	CMA	FM	PDM	Notes
1951	10	28	17	1	18	2.57	0	0	NS
1951	2	9	0	0	0	0.00	0	0	NT

Stanley (Stan) Bradbury
Born: 18 December 1926, Stockport, Greater Manchester, England.*
Died: 3 June 2021.

A Tiger Stevenson Training School product, Stan eventually forced his way into the Stoke team in 1948 and rode for Potters in second string and reserve berths until moving on to Motherwell in 1951. After a couple of seasons as an Eagle, he moved to Wolverhampton in mid-August 1952 then dropped out of league speedway when Liverpool closed in 1953. He raced in the Manchester area until his move to Canada, calling it a day in1982.

Stan was mostly yo-yo'd between second string, reserve and second half when dropped because of poor form at the tail end of the team. He averaged 5.44 in 1952 and his team spirit is evident as he collected 24 bonus points that year, over a quarter of his total return.

Motherwell Statistics

Season	M	R	Pts	Bon	Tot	CMA	FM	PDM	Notes
1951	29	85	84	15	99	4.66	0	0	NL & NT
1951	7	25	20	2	22	3.52	0	0	NS
1952	27	86	93	24	177	5.44	0	0	NL & NT

Derick Tallentire Close
Born: 13 May 1927, Barnard Castle, County Durham, England.*

Derick Close will be remembered as one of the best riders never to have ridden in top flight speedway in Britain. He started at Middlesbrough in 1946 and spent a brief spell at Newcastle in 1948. He then returned to the Bears before spending two and a half years at Newcastle. During this time, he increased his average to 10.33 prior to transferring to Motherwell at the end of August. In his three and a half seasons at Motherwell he was the top man. He secured 25 full and 12 paid maximums in 100 official fixtures for the Eagles. In 1955 he rode for Leicester and retired at the end of the season.

Derick, who had been in the sights of Scottish rivals Edinburgh, was tempted north to Motherwell in 1951. He moved in as the Eagles top heat leader and held that position for the next two seasons. In 1954, Derick made a slow return from injury and, despite this, his average was only 0.13 below that of Tommy Miller.

But for the horrendous head injuries Derick sustained in a meaningless last heat accident at Harringay in July 1953, who knows how high an average he would have achieved in 1953 and 1954.

The highlight of Derick's career was undoubtedly his appearance in the 1952 World Final at Wembley, He finished with four points which placed him 14th in the World. He was the third Scottish based Division Two man to achieve this honour following in the footsteps of Ken Le Breton (Ashfield 1949) and Jack Young (Edinburgh 1950 and 1951).

There is no doubt Derick was the best rider to appear in the black and white of the Lanarkshire outfit.

Motherwell Statistics

Season	M	R	Pts	Bon	Tot	CMA	FM	PDM	Notes
1951	11	44	103	9	112	10.18	1	2	NL
1952	45	183	473	9	482	10.54	16	5	NL & NT
1953	24	107	263.5	7	270.5	10.11	6	3	NL & NT
1954	20	83	180	10	190	9.16	1	2	NL & NT
1954	8	32	63	5	68	8.50	0	1	NS

Individual Honours: 1951: Did not compete in World Championship as Motherwell rider.1952 World finalist 4 pts, 14th. 1953: Did not compete in World Championship. 1954: Exited Championship at penultimate round.
International Honours: Great Britain: 3 caps, 42+6 pts. Scotland: 5 caps, 69+1 pts.
Scottish Championships: 1952: 11 pts, joint 3rd; 1954: 5 pts.

Cyril Cooper
Born: 25 March 1914, Haslingden, Lancashire, England.*
Died: November 1959.

Fast starting Cyril was an experienced road racer before turning to speedway with Olive Hart as neighbour and mentor. Cyril rode for Wigan in 1947 before moving to Fleetwood for 1948 and 1949. A back injury slowed his progress and in 1950 he joined Coventry. He then moved on loan to Ashfield for 1951 and 1952. Cyril remained close to home at Liverpool in 1953 and when the Stanley Stadium team closed, he came back north to Motherwell. Cooper moved to Ipswich after Motherwell were refused league speedway in 1955, but only stayed for a short time before retiring.

He started like a train at The Stadium and became the second best Eagle albeit from only seven meetings. He was the shot in the arm the Motherwell venture needed. Unfortunately, 1954 saw his form slump after a bright start in the North Shield.

Motherwell Statistics

Season	M	R	Pts	Bon	Tot	CMA	FM	PDM	Notes
1953	7	49	49	2	51	8.50	2	0	NL
1954	21	66	75.5	7	82.5	5.00	0	0	NL & NT
1954	8	22	43	4	47	8.55	0	0	NS

Individual Honours: 1954 Entered the World Championship but did not progress beyond first round.
1954 Division Championship Final: 5 pts.
Scottish Championships: 1954: 2 pts

Joseph Cameron (<u>Joe</u>) Crowther
Born: 27 April 1913, Stanley, County Durham, England.*
Died: 22 February 1991.

Apart from being a fine speedway rider, Joe listed professional footballer and comedian in an opera company as previous occupations. He was a well-loved character on the Scottish speedway scene for many years. He started as a Glasgow Lion in 1939 alongside Will Lowther. Joe stayed as a Tiger until the end of 1950, before moving to Motherwell in 1951 where he stayed for two seasons, He retired after an ill-fated comeback in 1953. Joe had been a regular in 1951, but an injury at Aldershot at the end of May 1952 ended his season and effectively ended his career. The wee man ended his speedway life as team manager at Leicester. Like so many other Eagles, he was on the downslope of his career and age was not on his side.

Motherwell Statistics

Season	M	R	Pts	Bon	Tot	CMA	FM	PDM	Notes
1951	28	103	138	17	155	6.02	1	2	NL & NT
1951	8	32	64	1	65	8.13	1	0	NS
1952	14	47	50	8	58	4.94	0	0	NL & NT
1953	2	6	6	0	6	4.00	0	0	NT

Individual Honours: 1951 Entered the World Championships and second round stage but did not progress.1952 crashed out of the event in the first round. 1953 Did not compete in World Championships.

Clifford William (<u>Bill</u>) Dalton
Born: 8 August 1920, Liverpool, Merseyside, England.*

After learning the basics of the sport on the Army tracks in Germany at the end of the Second World War, Bill joined Belle Vue. He then moved to Tamworth for 1947 to 1949, where he rode well. He was at Sheffield in 1950 before joining Motherwell in May 1951 after Owlerton closed down. Bill had a fair 1951 season at Motherwell then sat out 1952, remaining in South Africa after a winter sojourn there. He came back to Lanarkshire in 1953 when he was in and out of the team. In May he moved to Stoke before retiring.

Bill was one of second string or reserve grade men who staffed many of the Eagles sides who were pushed a bit too hard, expected to perform a great deal better than they did. Bill retired to South Africa,

Motherwell Statistics

Season	M	R	Pts	Bon	Tot	CMA	FM	PDM	Notes
1951	30	106	128	20	148	5.58	0	0	NL
1953	4	4	9	0	9	3.60	0	0	NL & NT

Individual Honours: 1951 Exited World Championships at first round. 1953 Did not compete in Championship while at Motherwell.
International Honours: Scotland: 1 cap, 0 pts.

Robert (Bob) Fletcher
Born: 11 January 1921, Preston, Lancashire, England.*

Bob first rode Army speedway in Germany and appeared at Belle Vue in 1947 before gaining a place at Cradley Heath. In 1948 he moved to Coventry where he stayed to 1951. He was a Belle Vue Ace 1952 to 1954 before dropping down to Edinburgh then moving to Motherwell late that year. Bob retired after one outing at Belle Vue in 1957.

Motherwell Statistics

Season	M	R	Pts	Bon	Tot	CMA	FM	PDM	Notes
1954	5	18	9	5	14	3.11	0	0	NL

John (Johnny) Green
Born: 25 May 1927, Burnley, Lancashire, England.*

A regular figure in the northern speedway scene in the late 1940s and early 1950s, Johnny started out his career at Hull in Division Three. He showed sufficient promise to be given outings by Sheffield at a higher level. Johnny moved to Edinburgh in 1951 and then to Motherwell in mid-September as part of a swap deal involving Keith Gurtner. Green stayed at Motherwell until the end of 1954. He then rode for Leicester in 1955 and 1956. He made a brief comeback in 1961 at Newcastle before retiring. Johnny suffered a fractured skull sustained in a midget car accident at the end of 1953.

Johnny was yet another Eagle who rode well most of the time, but had spells where he had some poor returns. Like his fellow Eagles, Johnny often did not travel too well and his away scores tend to reflect this.

Motherwell Statistics

Season	M	R	Pts	Bon	Tot	CMA	FM	PDM	Notes
1952	8	30	40	1	41	5.47	0	0	NL
1953	38	156	235	27	262	6.72	1	2	NL & NT
1954	21	80	98	10	108	5.40	0	0	NL & NT
1954	7	27	41	6	47	6.96	1	0	NS

Individual Honours: 1953 and 1954 Entered the World Championship, but did not progress beyond first round. 1954 Represented the Eagles in Division Championship at Belle Vue scoring eight points.
Scottish Championships: 1953: 10 pts, joint 3rd.

Keith Frank Gurtner
Born: 21 September 1921, Wagga Wagga, New South Wales, Australia.
Died:

Keith Gurtner rode in Sydney and Brisbane before travelling to Great Britain. He started at Exeter before moving on to Newcastle in May 1948 in a swap deal for Bonnie Waddell. He had a modest average which he upped to 7.77 when, in 1949 he was part of the en bloc Newcastle team move to Ashfield in Glasgow. A dip in average in 1950 saw the man in blue leathers move to Motherwell 1951 where he posted his best season average of 8.30. A fall out in 1952 saw him move to Edinburgh before he settled at Division 1 West Ham for two seasons. He raced regularly in Australia until about 1968.

Keith was signed by Motherwell at the end of the 1950 season and did not appear back in Great Britain until the middle of May. He scored a debut maximum at Leicester. He scored well until the end of the season when he tailed off markedly. 1952 his form was a bit up and down before early September when he moved in a transfer deal to Edinburgh.

It would be fair to say that Keith never hit that consistent run of form that he probably was capable of. When he was good, he was good, then he would have few stinkers.

Motherwell Statistics

Season	M	R	Pts	Bon	Tot	CMA	FM	PDM	Notes
1951	30	120	231	18	249	8.30	4	1	NL & NT
1952	31	122	202	15	217	7.11	1	0	NL & NT

1951: Did not ride in any North Shield meetings.

Individual honours: Never progressed beyond World Championship preliminary round.
International honours: Australia: 3 caps, 33 pts. Scotland: 4 caps, 8 pts.
Overseas: 2 caps, 8 pts.
Scottish Championship: 1951: 11 points, 4th.

Scott Hall
Born: Glasgow, Scotland.

Scott Hall had a few second halves in 1951 and had one team outing at Coventry on 18 August. He had to wait until 1952 for his break into the team. He held down a team spot for all of 1952 and for almost all of 1953, scoring quite modestly. Scott started the 1954 season in a reserve berth. He appeared in most of the North Shield events, the first National Trophy tie and one league match.

The wealth of talent available due to track closures saw him relegated to the second half by mid-May. He was recalled near the end of the season and rode in one completed meeting. He retired at the end of the 1954 season.

Motherwell Statistics

Season	M	R	Pts	Bon	Tot	CMA	FM	PDM	Notes
1951	1	2	1	1	2	4.00	0	0	NL
1952	38	121	84	14	98	3.24	0	0	NL & NT
1953	33	83	79	17	96	4.63	0	0	NL & NT
1954	3	8	5	0	5	2.50	0	0	NL & NT
1954	4	8	9	4	13	6.50	0	0	NS

Individual Honours: Did not compete in World Championship while at Motherwell. 1954 Scottish Junior Champion.
Scottish Championship: 1952: 2 pts.

John (**Larry**) Lazarus
Born: 15 December 1918, Glasgow, Scotland.*
Died: June 2007.

Larry had raced on the sands before the war gained most of his early speedway experience on the R.A.O.C Army tracks in Germany. He rode for Giants in Glasgow from 1949 to 1952 increasing his average each year. He moved to Glasgow rivals the Tigers for 1953 then spent 1954 at Motherwell. With no speedway in Scotland, he spent a brief time at Leicester then two years at Ipswich, retiring a short way into the second season there in 1956.

Small in stature Larry was a resolute character having survived a period of deprivation as a Japanese prisoner of war alongside Howdy Byford best known as for his times at West Ham and Oxford. Larry was a sound middle order team man, 1954 North Shield competition apart, who earned a fair number of bonus points.

Motherwell Statistics

Season	M	R	Pts	Bon	Tot	CMA	FM	PDM	Notes
1954	19	56	76	9	85	6.07	0	1	NL
1954	4	8	19	2	21	10.50	0	0	NS

International Honours: Scotland: 1 cap, 0 pts

Danny Lee
Born: 12 March 1911, London, England.
Died: 20 June 2006

Danny started at West Ham in the mid-1930s, but raced for a few teams at both league and non-league venues throughout England. After the Second World War, Danny rode briefly for Harringay before dropping down to race at Sheffield for two seasons. He then spent three seasons as an Edinburgh Monarch. Leg trailer Danny joined Motherwell at the start of 1951. Diminutive Danny was never a star man, but he was a popular rider nonetheless. He started well at home before injury cut him down in the third meeting at The Stadium. Danny came back late June but after a few poor meetings, he called it a day after a pointless outing at Stoke on 11 July 1951.

Motherwell Statistics

Season	M	R	Pts	Bon	Tot	CMA	FM	PDM	Notes
1951	8	17	9	1	10	2.35	0	0	NL & NT
1951	3	12	16	3	19	6.33	0	0	NS

Bob Lindsay
Born: Troon, Scotland.

Bob, who made an appearance at White City in 1948, was a product of the Bothwell Training Track and had second halves at Edinburgh, Ashfield and Motherwell in 1950. He rode for the Eagles in 1951 and 1952. In 1952 his form was up and down and in 1953 he moved to Edinburgh. After retiring he emigrated to farm in Kenya.

Bob fluctuated between a team and reserve berth and rode in a fair few second halves while seeking another place in the side. He was never a big scorer, but may have improved had he been given more opportunities to show his worth.

Motherwell Statistics

Season	M	R	Pts	Bon	Tot	CMA	FM	PDM	Notes
1951	11	27	15	2	17	2.52	0	0	NL & NT
1951	9	32	12	1	13	1.63	0	0	NS
1952	23	52	32	7	39	3.00	0	0	NL

William Atkinson (Will) Lowther

Born: 11 February 1913, Low Fell, Tyne & Wear, England.*
Died: 1982

Will started out pre-Second World War and became one of the best known speedway partnerships with Joe Crowther at Glasgow in 1939 and then again between 1946 and 1949. He then went home to Newcastle is a swap deal involving Jack Hodgson. He saw out 1949 and 1950 as a Magpie, then Diamond, before signing for Motherwell in 1951. Up to his move to Tyneside he had been a Brough Park specialist, rattling up big scores. He retired at the end of the 1952 season.

Like so many of the Motherwell signings he did not hit the heights in his two year spell, but served as a reasonably consistent second string rider, a far cry from his best days with the Tigers in the immediate post-war boom seasons.

He rode in most of the meetings in his time in Lanarkshire, but he tailed off towards the end of both season after solid showings earlier in each campaign. His tally of 36 bonus points in 1952 was the best by any Eagle

Motherwell Statistics

Season	M	R	Pts	Bon	Tot	CMA	FM	PDM	Notes
1951	30	114	130	18	148	5.19	0	1	NL & NT
1951	10	40	40	4	44	4.40	0	0	NS
1952	46	154	171	36	207	5.38	0	0	NL & NT

Niven McCreadie

Niven was based in Bellshill, Scotland, and began riding in the late 1940s with a few second halves at Edinburgh. Much of his early experience came at the Bothwell training track, not far from his home. He was a familiar figure around the Scottish junior scene for several years.

His only appearances in league racing came in 1952 when he was given three outings by the Eagles, each time as cover for absent team regulars. He rode once for the Eagles in 1950. Niven had a brief flirtation with midget cars in Scotland in 1953.

Motherwell Statistics

Season	M	R	Pts	Bon	Tot	CMA	FM	PDM	Notes
1952	3	6	3	2	5	3.33	0	0	NL

Gordon McGregor, Scott Hall and Derick Close walk the track at Poole before a meeting. (JSC)

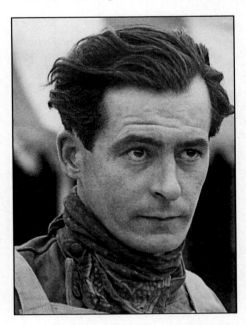

Left: Bill Baird; right: Bob Lindsay. Both riders made a contribution to the Eagles. (JSC)

James Ramsay (<u>Gordon</u>) McGregor

Born: 28 November 1921, Linlithgow, Scotland.*
Died: 29 September 2001.

Known as Gordon McGregor and after some experience on Army tracks he started out at Glasgow White City in May 1947 and by September held down a reserve berth. By the end of 1950 he had upped his average to 7.85 for the Tigers. He joined Motherwell in 1951 and spent four years as an Eagle then moved on to Leicester, Oxford, and Belle Vue between 1955 and 1966. Apart from a spell at Doncaster in 1970 in British League Division Two, he rode a few times between 1967 and his retiral in 1971. Gordon raced in Australia in 1951–52 as an unofficial touring team member.

1951 was his best year as an Eagle. Despite the flamboyant moustache which earned him the nickname of 'The Tash', the dash did not always extend to the track. Gordon never really established himself as the consistently high scorer he was expected to become. His form could be patchy at times to say the least. A move to Leicester in 1954 was thwarted by Ken McKinlay taking the vacant spot in the Midlands.

After some good showings at The Stadium, clearly relishing the opportunity to advance his career, he did not really progress to the heights he maybe should have. Nevertheless, Gordon was an important and valuable Eagle over their four year period in the National League Division Two and a popular racer who spent 25 years in the sport.

Motherwell Statistics

Season	M	R	Pts	Bon	Tot	CMA	FM	PDM	Notes
1951	31	128	257	19	276	8.63	2	1	NL & NT
1951	10	40	97	0	97	9.70	4	0	NS
1952	46	187	348	31	379	8.11	4	5	NL & NT
1953	38	161	298	45	343	8.52	0	5	NL & NT
1954	21	80	118	10	128	6.40	0	1	NL & NT
1954	8	31	38	9	47	6.06	0	0	NS

Individual Honours: 1951 to 1953 inclusive bowed out of the World Championship in the round before the Final. 1954: did not progress beyond round one.
International Honours: Scotland: 5 caps, 29 +11 pts; England: 5 caps, 17+2 pts.
Scottish Championship: 1951: 13 pts, 3rd; 1953: 4 pts.

Thomas Ogilvie (<u>Tommy</u>) Miller

Born: 22 February 1924, High Blantyre, Scotland.
Died: 1975

One of the greatest speedway riders Scotland has ever produced, Tommy Miller burst onto the speedway scene in 1950 after some second halves in 1949. He was a heat leader by mid-season in 1950 and was the top Tiger until the end of 1953. Whilst a Tiger Tommy held the British Second Division Silver Helmet, was Scottish Match Race Champion, was Scottish Champion and had been a tourist to Australia. Tommy was transferred to Motherwell and started the season there in 1954 but, for whatever the real reason was he never settled into the high scoring groove. By early August he had transferred to Coventry scoring a debut maximum against the Eagles. Despite his improvement in the Midlands late 1954 Tommy's form declined and he moved mid-season 1956 to Oxford. He did appear at the practice day at Cowley in 1957 but never appeared in any official fixture and his relative short once stellar career fizzled out.

Motherwell Statistics

Season	M	R	Pts	Bon	Tot	CMA	FM	PDM	Notes
1954	9	39	82	1	83	8.51	2	1	NL & NT
1954	8	32	80	2	82	10.25	1	1	NS

Individual Honours: 1954 Qualified for semi-final round of the World Championship before leaving Motherwell.
International Honours: Scotland: 4 points
Scottish Championship: 1954: 14 pts, winner.

Ronald John Keith (Ron) Phillips
Born: 29 July 1923, Sydney, New South Wales, Australia.

Ron was a junior at the Sydney tracks and made good progress in the 1949–50 season. This attracted Edinburgh's attention and he arrived at the Old Meadowbank Stadium. He initially found life tough and, unable to gain a Monarchs place, he tried out at St Austell. Injuries meant he gained an Edinburgh team place. However, he moved west to Glasgow Ashfield for the 1951 season.

The red headed Australian made huge progress at Saracen Park and doubled his Edinburgh average. The Giants did not compete in league speedway in 1953 and Ron moved to Scottish side number three at Motherwell.

He spent two good seasons at Milton Street then moved south after the Eagles folded. His move to Leicester in 1955 wasn't a success and a crash in August 1956 saw him return home. Ron racing as Ron Smith rode 'down under' until the early 1960s.

He was a popular man in Lanarkshire and was fourth highest scorer in 1953 and third in 1954. Ron had his best two and career zenith years, averaging 7.24 in 1953 and 7.20 in 1954. Once he had The Stadium 'dialled in', he was very good at home for most of his time there. His away form let him down when he should have been capable of capitalising on his experience of racing on most of the tracks when a Giant.

Motherwell Statistics

Season	M	R	Pts	Bon	Tot	CMA	FM	PDM	Notes
1953	38	160	263.5	26	289.5	7.24	1	4	NL & NT
1954	21	83	132.5	17	149.5	7.20	1	2	NL & NT
1954	8	31	61	7	68	8.77	1	1	NS

Individual Honours: 1953 and 1954 Entered the World Championship, but did not progress beyond first round. 1954: Represented the Eagles in Division Championship at Belle Vue scoring five points.
Scottish Championships: 1953: 9 pts; 1954: 10 pts

Jock Pryde
Born: c.1927, Motherwell, Scotland.

Jock appeared in second half events at Edinburgh in 1950. He rode for the Monarchs once in 1950 and three times in 1952 before moving to Motherwell in 1953. He rode once for the Eagles before the arrival of Guy Allott in July and saw out the season in the second half. He went to Australia in the winter of 1954–55 and was popular at the Perth circuit.

Motherwell Statistics

Season	M	R	Pts	Bon	Tot	CMA	FM	PDM	Notes
1953	1	2	2	0	2	4.00	0	0	NL

Malcolm Riddell
Born: Scotland.

A Scottish junior, Malcolm rode briefly for Glasgow in the 1949 season and in Belfast in 1950. He had a very brief two-week spell at Motherwell in 1951,

Motherwell Statistics

Season	M	R	Pts	Bon	Tot	CMA	FM	PDM	Notes
1951	M	9	3	1	4	1.78	0	0	NS

Eric William (<u>Bluey</u>) Scott
Born: 10 July 1929, Auburn, New South Wales, Australia.*

Encouraged by Jack Young, Bluey Scott came to Great Britain with plans to ride for Edinburgh but was given a chance at Motherwell. He raced in Scotland from 1951 to 1954 before moving to Southampton for the start of the 1955 season. Later that year he moved to Ipswich. He stayed in Australia until 1963 when he was turned down by Edinburgh and rode for Long Eaton and Middlesbrough in 1963 and 1964. Bluey spent his last two racing years with Glasgow in 1965 and 1966 and, because his wife was Scottish, stayed for many years before returning to Australia.

The red headed Australian was not the highest scorer at Motherwell, but he was by far the fans' favourite. At an Eagles nostalgia day in Motherwell in the late teens, Bluey was fondly mentioned by veteran Eagles fans, especially the ladies. His never say die, harum-scarum antics as he learned his trade made him a legend. The local press said that his popularity waned as he stayed on and completed more races. In speedway you don't have to the best to be an icon.

Motherwell Statistics

Season	M	R	Pts	Bon	Tot	CMA	FM	PDM	Notes
1951	12	27	28	3	31	4.59	0	0	NL & NT
1951	6	14	3	0	3	0.86	0	0	NS
1952	46	150	135	23	158	4.21	0	0	NL & NT
1953	36	144	122	24	136	3.78	0	0	NL & NT
1954	15	56	69	13	82	5.86	0	1	NL & NT
1954	8	31	44	11	55	7.10	0	1	NS

Individual Honours: World Championship: 1952 to 1954 Only rode in first round.
Scottish Championship: 1954: 9 pts, 7th.

James (<u>Jimmy</u>) Tannock
Born: 17 October 1931, Glasgow, Scotland.
Died: 2 December 2015

Jimmy was one of the most popular characters in Scottish speedway for almost two decades. He started at Ashfield in 1952. He moved to Motherwell for 1953 before being effectively dumped in 1954 after a few second halves. Jimmy came back for a few meetings at Motherwell in 1958. His big break came at Edinburgh in 1960 and he was a reliable if not star second string man in 1964 and 1966. He had few team outings in 1965 and 1967 and retired after a short spell at Coatbridge in 1968.

At Motherwell, Jimmy was a reserve for spells being displaced twice, by Bill Dalton then Guy Allott. Jimmy was 'used' early mid and late season. Clearly, he wasn't valued given the treatment he was handed out in 1954 – placing him on the transfer list was effectively a sacking. How well Jimmy would have improved had he been given the opportunity is not known and his showings in 1958 were not great. Jimmy loved his speedway from both sides of the fence and operated in the motorcycle trade for many years after retiring.

Motherwell Statistics

Season	M	R	Pts	Bon	Tot	CMA	FM	PDM	Notes
1953	32	73	51	13	64	3.50	0	0	NL & NT

Douglas (<u>Doug</u>) Templeton
Born: 18 June 1928, Maybole, Scotland.
Died: 21 December 2019

Doug moved to the shale in 1953 and was a Tiger that year. He started at Glasgow in 1954 only for the venue to close after two meetings. Doug dropped out of the sport until an opportunity arose at Motherwell in early August 1954. He appeared briefly for Ipswich and raced at White City in 1956. Doug was one of the Golden Eagles in 1958. From 1960 to 1967 he skippered Edinburgh Monarchs then moved to Coatbridge. The Fife farmer appeared for Glasgow in 1970 to 1972, Berwick 1972 to 1974 before spending 1975 and 1976 at Coatbridge. Doug was still learning his trade at Motherwell and did not hit any heights.

Motherwell Statistics

Season	M	R	Pts	Bon	Tot	CMA	FM	PDM	Notes
1954	12	25	16	4	20	3.20	0	0	NL

<u>Noel</u> James Watson
Born: c.1923, New South Wales, Australia.
Died: 9 November 1953.

The diminutive Noel was a Sydney bus conductor and started racing in the city around 1947. Recruited by Glasgow Ashfield, he never broke into the team. He was one of the original

Eagles signings in July 1950 and served in the makeshift teams of that short season. He improved with the challenge, showing the Ashfield promotion that they were a bit hasty in not giving him the opportunities he needed in Glasgow.

Noel served his team as a heat leader or second string for the three league seasons he spent at The Stadium without ever hitting the heights. At The Stadium, Noel was a force to be reckoned with. However, he was often less effective on the away tracks. His bonus points record shows he was a good team man. That said, Noel was a popular member of the team and his untimely death in Australia left a big gap in the 1954 Eagles line up.

Motherwell Statistics

Season	M	R	Pts	Bon	Tot	CMA	FM	PDM	Notes
1951	31	128	221	17	238	7.44	1	1	NL & NT
1951	10	40	77	2	79	7.90	0	0	NS
1952	41	166	291	16	307	7.40	2	2	NL & NT
1953	38	148	223	21	244	6.59	2	2	NL & NT

Individual Honours: Noel was in the penultimate round of the World Championship in 1951, in 1952 and 1953 he fell at the International Round hurdle.
International Honours: Australia: 4 caps, 24 pts. Overseas: 1 cap, 4 pts.
Scottish Championship: 1951: 7 pts; 1952; 11 pts, joint 3rd; 1953: 4 pts.

9. The Eagles and the World Championship

The following is a record of how the Eagles fared in the World Championship. One highlight was Derick Close's performance in 1952, a rare occurrence of a Second Division rider reaching the World Final.

1951
First Round
Bill Dalton and Keith Gurtner entered the competition at this stage. Keith raced at Swindon on 2 May scoring a single point, while on the same day Bill raced at Aldershot scoring three points. Neither qualified for the Second Round. Keith wasn't helped by British Rail losing his kit on route between Scotland and Swindon.

Second Round
Joe Crowther, Gordon McGregor and Noel Watson all set out on the road to Wembley. Joe dropped out after scoring 11 points at home on 13 July, but failing to add to his total at Coventry on 21 July. Gordon won the home round with 14 points and added six at Coventry to qualify with 20 points. Noel scored 12 points at The Stadium and added 10 at Stoke on 21 July to qualify.

Third Round
Gordon McGregor rode in the Third Round Meetings at Wembley on 16 August scoring six points and at Birmingham on 18 August scoring four points. Noel Watson scored four at New Cross on the 15 August and a further six points at Wembley on 16 August. Neither gathered sufficient points to qualify for the big night at Wembley.

1952
National Round
Noel Watson, Keith Gurtner and Bluey Scott all started out in the National Round. Noel Watson scored 14 at Ipswich on 29 May to qualify for the next round. Keith Gurtner and Bluey Scott both rode at Aldershot on 31 May scoring eight and one point respectively and neither progressed.

International Round
Noel Watson, Derick Close and Gordon McGregor took part in the International Round. Noel Watson rode at Oxford on 10 July scoring three points and Edinburgh on 19 July scoring five points which was not enough to qualify for the next stage. Derick Close was also at Edinburgh and scored 12 points which added to his 11 at Motherwell on 11 July gave him passage to the Championship Round. Gordon McGregor scored 11 at Stoke on 19 July which added to his two points at Motherwell gave him 13 points, which was just one above the cut off point.

Championship Round
Gordon McGregor raced at Wimbledon on 11 August and scored seven points. He added six points at Belle Vue on 16 August, but the 13 points total was not enough to secure s place at Wembley. Derick Close, on the other hand, scored 12 at Belle Vue and 11 at New Cross on 27 August and his 23 points were enough to take him to the World Final at Wembley.

World Final
On September 18 Derick Close represented England and the Lanarkshire Eagles at Wembley. Derick scored a third place in his opening ride behind Freddie Williams and Ronnie Moore with Arthur Payne, who fell, failing to score. In his second race Derick was last behind Brian

Crutcher, Jeff Lloyd, and Graham Warren. A second place in his third ride was secured when he followed home Dick Bradley but headed Dan Forsberg and Ron How. In unlucky heat 13, Derick was again last, this time he followed home Arthur Forrest, Henry Long and Split Waterman. Derick met up with the Champion elect, Jack Young in his last ride. Bob Oakley won from Jack Young, Derick and Cyril Roger. Derick had gathered four points to end up as 14th best rider in the World and was the third man to represent a Scottish team in the Final.

1953

National Round

Johnny Green, Noel Watson, Ron Phillips and Bluey Scott entered the competition at the National Round stage but only Noel progressed to the next round. Noel scored 12 at Rayleigh on 30 May to make it to the next round, despite being last in a four-man decider at Oxford on 11 June. Johnny managed three and dropped out of the competition. Unfortunately, Ron scored four at Rayleigh on 30 May while Bluey scored one at Oxford on 28 May and both failed to make the cut.

International Round

Noel Watson and Gordon McGregor took part in the International Round. Gordon scored a total of 14 with half at Coventry on 11 July and the other half at Motherwell the previous evening, to make it to the next round. Noel only managed to aggregate seven points which he scored at Stoke on 11 July because he failed to score at Edinburgh on 18 July.

Championship Round

Gordon McGregor rode at Bradford on 22 August scoring a single point and he scored another point at Birmingham on 26 August to aggregate two points. Gordon failed to secure enough points to progress to Wembley.

1954

First Round

Derick Close, Tommy Miller, Gordon McGregor, Ron Phillips, Cyril Cooper, Johnny Green and Bluey Scott all took part in the first round of the World Championship. Derick won the Motherwell round on 9 July with 14 points and scored a further 13 at Edinburgh on 10 July to gather 27 points and a ticket to the semi-final round. Tommy Miller scored 13 at Motherwell and added to the 14 scored when he won the Ipswich round on 1 July, his total of 27 was enough to progress to the next round. Gordon McGregor scored five at Motherwell and added nine at Edinburgh, but his 14 points did not allow further progress. Ron Phillips scored 11 at Motherwell and 10 at Edinburgh, but 21 was not enough to progress. Cyril Cooper scored eight at Motherwell and five at Edinburgh and his 13 was not enough. Johnny Green scored 12 at Motherwell with another 10 at Edinburgh, despite gathering 22 he did not progress either. Finally, Bluey Scott who scored eight at Motherwell and four at Coventry on 10 July to total 12 did not have enough to progress.

Semi-Final Round

Tommy Miller had moved on to Coventry but did not qualify as a Bee. Derick Close scored 10 points at Belle Vue on 14 August, but he only managed to add six at West Ham on 31 July and did not progress to Wembley for a second time.

Appendix 1: Results and scorers

Motherwell 1950

Friday 14 July 1950 Motherwell
Eagles 48 Newcastle Diamonds 36 (Ch)

Motherwell	*Newcastle*
Tommy Bateman 6+3	Son Mitchell 6+1
Gordon McGregor 8	Frank Hodgson 8+1
Don Lawson 4+1	Derek Close 12
Junior Bainbridge 10	Herby King 2
Ernie Brecknell 4	Will Lowther 4
Tommy Miller 11	Wilf Jay 2
Jim Blyth 2+2	Raymond Ridley 0
Don Wilkinson 3+2	Len Nicholson 2

Friday 21 July 1950 Motherwell
The Gala Cup

Jack Young 15
Merv Harding 14
Norman Lindsay 12
Joe Crowther 11
Eddie Lack 10
Clive Gressor 8
Peter Dykes 7
Don Wilkinson 6
Harold Booth 6
Bob Lovell 6
Jim Blyth 5
Len Nicholson 4
Harold Fairhurst 4
Don Lawson 3
Noel Watson 3
Joe Ferguson 2
Raymond Ridley 2
Bob Lindsay 2

Friday 28 July 1950 Motherwell
Eagles 45 North of England Select 39 (Ch)

Motherwell	*North of England*
Frank Young 7+1	Don Wilkinson 3+1
Wilf Jay 6+1	Alan Hunt 12
Norman Lindsay 9	Will Lowther 7
Ernie Brecknell 5+1	Len Nicholson 1+1
Clive Gressor 3+1	Danny Lee 4+1
Junior Bainbridge 9	Derek Close 9+1
Jim Blyth 2	Joe Arthur 3
Noel Watson 4+1	Joe Ferguson 0

Friday 4 August 1950 Motherwell
Eagles 39 The Rest 44 (Ch)

Motherwell	*The Rest*
Jim Blyth 1+1	Son Mitchell 6+1
Gordon McGregor 11	Frank Hodgson 11
Clive Gressor 0	Geoff Godwin 4+2
Noel Watson 1	Larry Lazarus 7
Ernie Brecknell 2	Will Lowther 7
Jack Hodgson 8	Wilf Jay 7
Don Wilkinson 11	Len Nicholson 2+1
Joe Ferguson 5+1	Joe Arthur 0

Friday 11 August 1950 Motherwell
Eagles 33 Cradley Heath Heathens 49 (Ch)

Motherwell	*Cradley Heath*
Ken McKinlay 5+2	Brian Shepherd 8+2
Tommy Miller 5	Alan Hunt 12
Will Lowther 7	Eric Boothroyd 1+1
Jim Blyth 0	Phil Malpass 5
Noel Watson 5+1	Gil Craven 11
George Newton 5	Les Tolley 3+1
Joe Ferguson 1	Frank Young 4+1
Ernie Brecknell 6	Bill Clifton 5+1

Friday 18 August 1950 Motherwell
Eagles 43 Sheffield Tars 41 (Ch)

Motherwell	*Sheffield*
Gil Craven 10+1	Len Williams 10+1
Wilf Jay 7	Jack Gordon 5+1
Son Mitchell 8	Tommy Allott 8
Noel Watson 5	Stuart Hickman 4
Will Lowther 11	Guy Allott 7+1
Don Wilkinson 1	Jack D White 4
Joe Ferguson 0	Johnny Green 2+1
Rusty Wainwright 1+1	Len Howe 1+1

Friday 25 August 1950 Motherwell
Eagles 50 Ashfield Giants Select 34 (Ch)

Motherwell	*Ashfield*
Noel Watson 10+2	Bruce Semmens 11
Will Lowther 10	Bob Lovell 2
Don Lawson 8	Willie Wilson 6
Don Wilkinson 8+2	Geoff Godwin 8+1
Willie Gordon 4+1	Larry Lazarus 6
Ernie Brecknell 5+1	Bob Lindsay 0
Jim Blyth 1	Russell Davis 1
Niven McCreadie 3+1	George Johnstone 0

Friday 1 September 1950 Motherwell
Eagles 37 Glasgow Tigers Select 47 (Ch)

Motherwell	*Glasgow*
Noel Watson 9+1	Peter Dykes 7+1
Will Lowther 5	Joe Crowther 9+1
Don Lawson 3+1	Joe Ferguson 2

97

Don Wilkinson 6
Clive Gressor 2
Ernie Brecknell 7+1

Ken McKinlay 9+1
Gordon McGregor 11
Norman Lindsay 5+3

Jim Blyth 0
Niven McCreadie 5

Gundy Harris 2
Bill Byford 2

Friday 8 September 1950 Motherwell
Eagles 33 Edinburgh Monarchs 51 (Ch)

Motherwell
Noel Watson 4
Will Lowther 8
Ernie Brecknell 8
Tommy Lack 1+1
Ken McKinlay 7
Jim Blyth 1+1
Niven McCreadie 4
Cal Lewins 0

Edinburgh
Harold Booth 11
Harold Fairhurst 4+2
Jock Pryde 1+1
Eddie Lack 11
Bob Mark 9+1
Ron Phillips 10+1
Harry Andrews 2
Billy Buckle 3

Friday 15 September 1950 Motherwell
Eagles 36 Scottish Select 48 (Ch)

Motherwell
Noel Watson 6
Will Lowther 9+2
Stan Beardsall 3
Wilf Jay 4
Son Mitchell 11
Wal Morton 1
Ray Maughan 2
Bill Gordon 0

Scottish Select
Frank Hodgson 7
Peter Dykes 6
Ron Phillips 11+1
Harold Booth 7
Bob Mark 8+1
Alf McIntosh 5
Bill Baird 5
Tom Turnham 2

Friday 22 September 1950 Motherwell
Best Pairs

Will Lowther 11
Noel Watson 14
Total: 25
Ron Phillips 6
Harold Booth 14
Total: 20
Eddie Lack 12
Bob Mark 2
Total: 14
Gordon McGregor 14
Norman Lindsay 8
Total: 22
Wal Morton 2
Wilf Jay 11
Total: 13
Son Mitchell 17
Don Wilkinson 4
Total: 21
Willie Wilson 6
Larry Lazarus 5
Total: 11

Motherwell 1951

Friday 30 March 1951 Motherwell
Eagles 48 Swedish Lions 36 (Ch)

Motherwell
Gordon McGregor 12
Stan Bradbury 2
Merv Harding 9
Danny Lee 3+1
Chum Taylor 6
Noel Watson 11+1
Bill Baird 1+1
Bluey Scott 1
Harold Booth 1

Swedish Lions
Bertil Carlsson 8+1
Stig Pramberg 5+1
Eskil Carlsson 5
Olle Segerstrom 8+1
Sune Karlsson 8
Lennert Carlstrom 1+1
Lennert Eriksson 1
Jan Johnsson 0

Friday 6 April 1951 Motherwell
Eagles 46 Fleetwood Flyers 38 (NS)

Motherwell
Gordon McGregor 12
Stan Bradbury 5+1
Will Lowther 6+1
Danny Lee 7+1
Bob Lindsay 4+1
Noel Watson 8+1
Bill Baird 4
Bluey Scott 0

Fleetwood
Jeff Crawford 2
Norman Hargreaves 2
Angus McGuire 4+1
Don Potter 11
Ted Gibson 3
Alf Parker 11
Ray Harker 5
Tom Turnham 1

Monday 9 April 1951 Newcastle
Newcastle Diamonds 52 Eagles 32 (NS)

Newcastle
Son Mitchell 8
Herby King 5+4
Wilf Jay 8+2
Ernie Brecknell 7+2
Don Wilkinson 5+1
Derick Close 12
Don Lawson 3+1
Barry Pickering 4

Motherwell
Gordon McGregor 9
Stan Bradbury 1
Will Lowther 10
Danny Lee 1
Noel Watson 11
Bob Lindsay 0
Bill Baird 0
Bluey Scott 0

Friday 13 April 1951 Motherwell
Eagles 46 Glasgow Tigers 35 (NS)

Motherwell
Stan Bradbury 6+1
Gordon McGregor 9
Joe Crowther 9
Danny Lee 8+2
Noel Watson 8
Will Lowther 5+1
Bill Baird 0
Bob Lindsay 1

Glasgow
Ken McKinlay 4+2
Alf McIntosh 4
Junior Bainbridge 11
Jack Hodgson 5+2
Norman Lindsay 6
Frank Hodgson 0
Jim Blyth 6
Eric Davis 0

Wednesday 18 April 1951 Glasgow
Glasgow Tigers 51 Eagles 32 (NS)

Glasgow	*Motherwell*
Ken McKinlay 4+1	Stan Bradbury 2
Tommy Miller 12	Gordon McGregor 8
Junior Bainbridge 6	Joe Crowther 8
Jack Hodgson 6+1	Bob Lindsay 2
Norman Lindsay 7	Noel Watson 4
Frank Hodgson 8+1	Will Lowther 8
Alf McIntosh 5	Bill Baird 0
Jim Blyth 2	Bluey Scott 0

Friday 20 April 1951 Motherwell
Eagles 39 Ashfield Giants 45 (NS)

Motherwell	*Ashfield*
Stan Bradbury 4	Merv Harding 10+1
Gordon McGregor 12	Bob Lovell 6
Joe Crowther 7	Bruce Semmens 10
Bob Lindsay 2	Larry Lazarus 4+1
Noel Watson 11	Jackie Gates 6
Will Lowther 1	Willie Wilson 3+3
Bluey Scott 1	Eric Liddell 1
Bill Baird 1+1	Ron Phillips 5+1

Tuesday 24 April 1951 Ashfield
Ashfield Giants 61 Eagles 23 (NS)

Ashfield	*Motherwell*
Merv Harding 11+ 1	Stan Bradbury 1
Bob Lovell 10+2	Gordon McGregor 7
Bruce Semmens 11	Joe Crowther 6+1
Larry Lazarus 7+2	Bob Lindsay 0
Willie Wilson 11+1	Noel Watson 5
Jackie Gates 6	Will Lowther 0
Ron Phillips 3+1	Bill Baird 2
Eric Liddell 2+1	Bluey Scott 2

Friday 27 April 1951 Motherwell
Eagles 42 Newcastle Diamonds 41 (NS)

Motherwell	*Newcastle*
Bluey Scott 0	Son Mitchell 10
Gordon McGregor 12	Herby King 3+3
Joe Crowther 12	Don Lawson 6+2
Bob Lindsay 2	Ernie Brecknell 9+1
Noel Watson 10	Don Wilkinson 5+2
Will Lowther 2+1	Derick Close 9
Malcolm Riddell 2	Mike Tams 1
Bill Baird 2	Ray Maughan 0

Saturday 28 April 1951 Edinburgh
Edinburgh Monarchs 62 Eagles 21 (NS)

Edinburgh	*Motherwell*
Jack Young 12	Bill Baird 1
Eddie Lack 3	Gordon McGregor 5
Don Cuppleditch 12	Joe Crowther 6
Harold Fairhurst 7+3	Bob Lindsay 1
Bob Mark 10+2	Noel Watson 5+1
Dick Campbell 11+1	Will Lowther 3
Harold Booth 4	Harry Andrews 0
Jim Turner 3+1	Malcolm Riddell 0

Wednesday 2 May 1951 Fleetwood
Fleetwood Flyers 39 Eagles 44 (NS)

Fleetwood	*Motherwell*
Norman Hargreaves 7+1	Bill Baird 4
Wilf Jay 4	Gordon McGregor 12
Don Potter 7	Joe Crowther 12
Angus McGuire 1+1	Bob Lindsay 0
Jeff Crawford 8+2	Noel Watson 9
Alf Parker 7+2	Will Lowther 4+1
Ray Pursehouse 1+1	Harry Andrews 2
Ray Harker 4+1	Malcolm Riddell 1+1

Friday 4 May 1951 Motherwell
Eagles 27 Edinburgh Monarchs 57 (NS)

Motherwell	*Edinburgh*
Bill Baird 3	Jack Young 12
Gordon McGregor 11	Eddie Lack 6+3
Joe Crowther 4	Don Cuppleditch 10
Stan Bradbury 1	Harold Fairhurst 7+3
Noel Watson 6	Bob Mark 9+2
Will Lowther 1	Dick Campbell 8
Harry Andrews 1	Harold Booth 3+1
Malcolm Riddell 0	Jim Turner 2

Wednesday 9 May 1951 Halifax
Halifax Dukes 79 Eagles 29 (NT)

Halifax	*Motherwell*
Vic Emms 13+5	Stan Bradbury 1
Al Allison 9+3	G. McGregor 10+1
Ray Johnson 5+1	Joe Crowther 3+1
Arthur Forrest 18	Bill Baird 0
Bill Crosland 12+1	Noel Watson 8
Jack Hughes 12+2	Will Lowther 5+1
Jack Dawson 5+1	Bob Lindsay 2
Dyson Harper 5+1	Harry Andrews 0

Friday 11 May 1951 Motherwell
Eagles 39 Halifax Dukes 69 (NT)

Motherwell	*Halifax*
Bill Dalton 8+1	Vic Emms 15+1
Gordon McGregor 8	Al Allison 7+1
Joe Crowther 2+1	Arthur Forrest 15+1
Bob Lindsay 2	Ray Johnston 5+2
Noel Watson 12+1	Jackie Hughes 9+1
Will Lowther 5	Bill Crosland 8+2
Bill Baird 0	Jack Dawson 5+1
Stan Bradbury 2	Dyson Harper 5+1

Monday 14 May 1951 Leicester
Leicester Hunters 52 Eagles 32 (NLD2)

Leicester	Motherwell
Cyril Page 7+3	Bill Dalton 5
Lionel Benson 8+1	Gordon McGregor 6
Jock Grierson 3+3	Joe Crowther 0
Ron Wilson 7	Keith Gurtner 12
Les Beaumont 7+3	Noel Watson 1
Joe Bowkis 7+1	Will Lowther 5
Harwood Pike 8+1	Stan Bradbury 2
Johnny Carpenter 5	Bob Lindsay 1

Wednesday 16 May 1951 Halifax
Halifax Dukes 60 Eagles 24 (NLD2)

Halifax	Motherwell
Arthur Forrest 9	Bill Dalton 5
Ray Johnson 6	Gordon McGregor 2
Jack Hughes 12	Joe Crowther 2
Bill Crosland 6+2	Keith Gurtner 3
Vic Emms 9+3	Noel Watson 3+2
Al Allison 12	Will Lowther 7
Jack Dawson 2+1	Stan Bradbury 1
Dyson Harper 4+2	Bob Lindsay 1

Friday 18 May 1951 Motherwell
Scottish Best Pairs

Jack Young 15
Eddie Lack 6
Total: 21
Merv Harding: 9
Bruce Semmens: 11
Total: 20
Junior Bainbridge 14
Ken McKinlay 6
Total: 20
Joe Crowther 3
Keith Gurtner 8
Total: 11Gordon McGregor 3
Bill Dalton 6
Total: 9
Noel Watson 0
Will Lowther 5
Total: 5
Stan Bradbury (res) 4

Wednesday 23 May 1951 Glasgow
Glasgow Tigers 57 Eagles 51 (SC)

Glasgow	Motherwell
Junior Bainbridge 12+1	Bill Dalton12+1
Jack Hodgson 7+1	G. McGregor 10+1
Tommy Miller 17	Joe Crowther 7+3
Ken McKinlay 1	Keith Gurtner 9+1
Frank Hodgson 5	Stan Bradbury 1+1
Norman Lindsay 8+1	Will Lowther 7
Alf McIntosh 4+1	Harry Andrews 0
Jim Blyth 3	Bob Lindsay 5

Friday 25 May 1951 Motherwell
Eagles 47 Glasgow Tigers 61 (SC)

Motherwell	Glasgow
Joe Crowther 3+2	J. Bainbridge 15+3
Keith Gurtner 4+1	Jack Hodgson 6+2
Gordon McGregor 13+1	Tommy Miller 15
Bill Dalton 9+1	Ken McKinlay 10
Noel Watson 12	Frank Hodgson 1+1
Will Lowther 2	Norman Lindsay 2
Bob Lindsay 0	Alf McIntosh 10
Stan Bradbury 4	Jim Blyth 2

Friday 1t June 1951 Motherwell
Eagles 34 Liverpool Chads 50 (NLD2)

Motherwell	Liverpool
Bill Dalton 4+1	Len Read 10+1
Gordon McGregor 9	Harry Welch 4+2
Joe Crowther 0	Bill Griffiths 2+1
Keith Gurtner 3	Reg Duval 8+1
Noel Watson 9	George Newton 9+1
Will Lowther 4+1	Peter Robinson 6+2
Bob Lindsay 2+1	Alf Webster 6
Stan Bradbury 3	Tommy Allott 5+1

Wednesday 6 June 1951 Chapelizod Stadium, Dublin
Dublin Eagles 48 Lanarkshire Eagles 24 (Ch)

Dublin	Motherwell
Freddie Williams 10+1	Bill Dalton 6
Ron Mountford 12	Harry Andrews 0
Split Waterman 10+2	Roy Spiller 2+2
Ginger O'Beirne 3+2	Bruce Abernethy 6
Ivor Davies 9+3	Joe Crowther 3+1
Derick Edwards 4	Bob Lindsay 7+1

Friday 8 June 1951 Motherwell
Eagles 47 Walthamstow Wolves 37 (NLD2)

Motherwell	Walthamstow
Noel Watson 9+1	Jim Boyd 5+1
Gordon McGregor 10	Reg Reeves 7+2
Joe Crowther 5+1	Jimmy Grant 3
Keith Gurtner 6	Harry Edwards 11
Bill Dalton 4+2	Benny King 0
Will Lowther 7	Pete Lansdale 8
Stan Bradbury 4+2	Stan Clark 1
Bluey Scott 2	Archie Windmill 2

Friday 15 June 1951 Motherwell
Eagles 65 Ashfield Giants 43 (Lanarkshire Cup)

Motherwell	Ashfield
Noel Watson 12	Merv Harding 11+1
Gordon McGregor 17+1	Larry Lazarus 3
Joe Crowther 4+2	Bruce Semmens 0
Keith Gurtner 14+1	Willie Wilson 10
Bill Dalton 8+2	Cyril Cooper 7+2

Will Lowther 4+1
Bluey Scott 0
Stan Bradbury 6

Jackie Gates 5
Bob Lovell 3+1
Chum Taylor 4+2

Friday 22 June 1951 Motherwell
Eagles 53 Halifax Dukes 31 (NLD2)

Motherwell
Bill Dalton 9+2
Gordon McGregor 7
Noel Watson 10+1
Will Lowther 4+1
Joe Crowther 12
Keith Gurtner 8+2
Stan Bradbury 2
Danny Lee 1

Halifax
Al Allison 4+1
Vic Emms 5
Arthur Forrest 9+1
Jack Dawson 2
Bill Crosland 1+1
Jackie Hughes 6
Dyson Harper 0
Ray Johnston 4

Monday 25 June 1951 Walthamstow
Walthamstow Wolves 50 Eagles 34 (NLD2)

Walthamstow
Jim Boyd 8
Reg Reeves 2
Jimmy Grant 6+2
Harry Edwards 10
Benny King 10+1
Pete Lansdale 7+3
Arch Windmill 6+2
Alby Smith 1

Motherwell
Bill Dalton 2
Gordon McGregor 5
Noel Watson 5
Will Lowther 6+2
Joe Crowther 0
Keith Gurtner 12
Stan Bradbury 3
Danny Lee 1

Tuesday 26 June 1951 Motherwell
Bothwell Bulls 15 Newtongrange Rockets 35
(Junior Challenge) No further information available

Wednesday 27 June 1951 Fleetwood
Fleetwood Flyers 42 Eagles 42 (NLD2)

Fleetwood
Norman Hargreaves 6 +1
Wilf Jay 9
Ray Harker 6+1
Don Potter 6
Alf Parker 4
Jeff Crawford 6+2
Angus McGuire 4+1
Ernie Appleby 2+2

Motherwell
Bill Dalton 8+1
Gordon McGregor 8+1
Noel Watson 8
Will Lowther 4
Joe Crowther 11
Keith Gurtner 3+1
Stan Bradbury 0
Danny Lee 0

Friday 29 June 1951 Motherwell
Eagles 65 Yarmouth Bloaters 19 (NLD2)

Motherwell
Bill Dalton 9+3
Gordon McGregor 12
Noel Watson 9+2
Will Lowther 10
Joe Crowther 8+1
Keith Gurtner 9+3
Stan Bradbury 4+2
Danny Lee 4

Yarmouth
Sid Hipperson 2
Bob Baker 3
Fred Brand 7
Cyril Quick 2+1
Reg Morgan 0
Stan Page 4
Alby Thomas 0
Tip Mills 1

Friday 6 July 1951 Motherwell
Eagles 40 Newcastle Diamonds 44 (NLD2)

Motherwell
Bill Dalton 0
Gordon McGregor 9+1
Noel Watson 11
Will Lowther 1
Joe Crowther 10
Keith Gurtner 5+1
Stan Bradbury 3
Danny Lee 1

Newcastle
Don Wilkinson 7+1
Derick Close 12
Roy Dook 3+1
Jack Chignell 8
Johnny Green 7+1
Son Mitchell 3+1
Peter Orpwood 3+1
Mike Tams 1+1

Saturday 7 July 1951 Edinburgh
Edinburgh Monarchs 36 Eagles 48 (NLD2)

Edinburgh
Harold Booth 2
Jack Young 12
Dick Campbell 7
Bob Mark 7
Eddie Lack 7
Johnny Oram 0
Jackie Campbell 1+1
Jimmy Cox 0

Motherwell
Bill Dalton 5
Gordon McGregor 7+2
Noel Watson 8
Will Lowther 6+1
Joe Crowther 9+2
Keith Gurtner 9+1
Stan Bradbury 2+1
Danny Lee 2

Friday 13 July 1951 Motherwell
World Championship Qualifying Round
Gordon McGregor 14
Noel Watson 12
Don Cuppleditch 11
Joe Crowther 11
George Smith 10
Al Allison 10
Jimmy Squibb 9
Don Hardy 8
Sune Karlsson 8
Bob Jones 7
Will Lowther 7
Bob Baker 5
Bob Fletcher 4
Ron Johnson 2
Peter Moore 1
Ray Moore 1
Bob Lindsay (res) DNR
Keith Gurtner (res) DNR

Saturday 14 July 1951 Stoke
Stoke Potters 37 Eagles 47 (NLD2)

Stoke
Ken Adams 6+1
Brian Pritchett 4+1
Les Jenkins 7+1
Bill Harris 8
Ray Harris 8
Gil Blake 0
Lindsay Mitchell 3
Derek Braithwaite 1

Motherwell
Bill Dalton 2
Gordon McGregor 9+2
Noel Watson 10
Will Lowther 1
Joe Crowther 6
Keith Gurtner 12
Stan Bradbury 7+1
Danny Lee 0

101

Monday 16 July 1951 Motherwell
Eagles 42 America 30 (Challenge)

Motherwell		America	
Bill Dalton	0	Nick Nicolaides	4+1
Gordon McGregor	12	Lloyd Campbell	5+2
Noel Watson	5+2	Johnnie Roccio	4+1
Will Lowther	3	Royal Carroll	4
Joe Crowther	10+2	Johnnie Gibson	1+1
Keith Gurtner	11+1	Don Hawley	2
Stan Bradbury	1+1	Ernie Roccio	10

Friday 20 July 1951 Motherwell
Eagles 37 The Rest 47 (Challenge)

Motherwell		The Rest	
Bill Dalton	0	Bob Mark	11
Gordon McGregor	7+1	Eddie Lack	2
Noel Watson	7	Willie Wilson	9+1
Will Lowther	0	Ken McKinlay	4+1
Joe Crowther	2+2	Merv Harding	11
Keith Gurtner	10	Norman Lindsay	4+1
Stan Bradbury	5	Alf McIntosh	5+1
Bob Lindsay	3+1	Jim Blyth	1

Friday 27 July 1951 Motherwell
Eagles 43 Coventry Bees 41 (NLD2)

Motherwell		Coventry	
Bob Lindsay	1	Bob Fletcher	4+1
Gordon McGregor	11+1	Charlie New	2
Noel Watson	7+1	Derek Tailby	5
Will Lowther	4+1	Les Hewitt	6+3
Joe Crowther	2+1	Johnny Reason	8+1
Keith Gurtner	12	Stan Williams	3+3
Stan Bradbury	1	John Yates	6
Bill Dalton	5+1	Peter Brough	7

Thursday 2 August 1951 Oxford
Oxford Cheetahs 53 Eagles 31 (NLD2)

Oxford		Motherwell	
Bill Kemp	8+4	Bill Dalton	3+1
Harry Saunders	11	Gordon McGregor	5+1
Eric Irons	5+1	Noel Watson	9
Bill Osborne	8	Will Lowther	DNR
Ernie Rawlins	3+1	Joe Crowther	1
Bob McFarlane	8	Keith Gurtner	9
Frank Boyle	6	Stan Bradbury	3
Roger Wise	4+1	Bob Lindsay	1

Friday 3 August 1951 Motherwell
Eagles 46 Norwich Stars 38 (NLD2)

Motherwell		Norwich	
Bill Dalton	5+1	Bob Leverenz	12
Gordon McGregor	8+2	Fred Pawson	7+3
Noel Watson	7+1	Phil Clarke	8
Will Lowther	7+1	Alec Hunter	5+2
Joe Crowther	3	Fred Rogers	2
Keith Gurtner	10	Jack Freeman	3
Stan Bradbury	5	Trevor Davis	0
Bob Lindsay	1+1	Bill Codling	1+1

Friday 10 August 1951 Motherwell
Eagles 55 Stoke Potters 29 (NLD2)

Motherwell		Stoke	
Bill Dalton	3	Ken Adams	5
Gordon McGregor	12	Brian Pritchett	5+2
Noel Watson	9+1	Les Jenkins	1+1
Will Lowther	10+2	Bill Harris	8
Stan Bradbury	2	Gil Blake	5
Keith Gurtner	11+1	Lindsay Mitchell	2
Bluey Scott	6	Ray Harris	1
Bob Lindsay	2	John Fitzpatrick	2

Friday 17 August 1951 Motherwell
Eagles 41 Ashfield Giants 43 (NLD2)

Motherwell		Ashfield	
Bill Dalton	2	Bruce Semmens	12
Gordon McGregor	11	Ron Phillips	6+1
Noel Watson	6	Willie Wilson	3+1
Will Lowther	7+1	Jack Gates	10
Stan Bradbury	2	Merv Harding	5
Keith Gurtner	9	Cyril Cooper	4
Bluey Scott	2+1	Ron Johnson	2+1
Bob Lindsay	2	Bob Lovell	1

Saturday 18 August 1951 Coventry
Coventry Bees 59 Eagles 25 (NLD2)

Coventry		Motherwell	
Bob Fletcher	7+3	Bluey Scott	0
Charlie New	6	Keith Gurtner	10
Les Hewitt	7+1	Noel Watson	2
Derek Tailby	9+2	Stan Bradbury	4
Johnny Reason	7+3	Bill Dalton	4
Stan Williams	12	Will Lowther	3
John Yates	5+1	Bob Lindsay	1
Peter Brough	6	Scott Hall	1+1

Tuesday 21 August 1951 Ashfield
Ashfield Giants 45 Eagles 38 (NLD2)

Ashfield		Motherwell	
Bruce Semmens	3	Bill Dalton	2+1
Cyril Cooper	7	Gordon McGregor	11
Merv Harding	11	Noel Watson	1
Ron Phillips	3+2	Will Lowther	8
Willie Wilson	7+1	Joe Crowther	4+1
Jack Gates	5+1	Keith Gurtner	9+1
Ron Johnson	6	Bluey Scott	1
Bob Lovell	3	Stan Bradbury	2

Friday 24 August 1951 Motherwell
Eagles 46 Glasgow Tigers 38 (LC)

Motherwell		Glasgow	
Bob Dalton	3	Jack Hodgson	5+1
Gordon McGregor	7+1	Tommy Miller	12
Noel Watson	6+1	Ken McKinlay	7
Will Lowther	9+1	Alf McIntosh	3
Joe Crowther	8+1	Frank Hodgson	5+1
Keith Gurtner	9+1	Junior Bainbridge	4
Bluey Scott	0	Norman Lindsay	1+1
Stan Bradbury	3+2	Len Nicholson	1

Monday 27 August 1951 Motherwell
Eagles 43 Leicester Hunters 41 (NLD2)

Motherwell		Leicester	
Bill Dalton	6+1	Cyril Page	1+1
Gordon McGregor	6+2	Len Williams	12
Noel Watson	7	Lionel Benson	10
Will Lowther	5+1	Les Beaumont	7+1
Joe Crowther	7	Harwood Pike	1+1
Keith Gurtner	7+2	Jock Grierson	7
Bluey Scott	3	Vic Pitcher	2
Stan Bradbury	2+1	Laurie Holland	1

Friday 31 August 1951 Motherwell
Eagles 55 Fleetwood Flyers 29 (NLD2)

Motherwell		Fleetwood	
Gordon McGregor	9+2	Wilf Jay	8+1
Will Lowther	4+1	Alf Parker	4+1
Derick Close	8+1	Don Potter	9
Joe Crowther	8	Ray Moore	0
Keith Gurtner	9+1	Jeff Crawford	2
Noel Watson	10+1	Ray Harker	3
Bluey Scott	3	Russ Pursehouse	1
Bill Dalton	4	Angus McGuire	2

Wednesday 5 September 1951 Glasgow
Glasgow Tigers 40 Eagles 44 (NLD2)

Glasgow		Motherwell	
Ken McKinlay	2+1	Gordon McGregor	9+1
Frank Hodgson	5+1	Will Lowther	7+1
Tommy Miller	10	Derick Close	9+1
Norman Lindsay	2+1	Joe Crowther	2
Junior Bainbridge	12	Keith Gurtner	9
Jack Hodgson	5+1	Noel Watson	3
Len Nicholson	4	Stan Bradbury	2+1
Alf McIntosh	0	Bill Dalton	3

Friday 7 September 1951 Motherwell
Eagles 61 Oxford Cheetahs 23 (NLD2)

Motherwell		Oxford	
Gordon McGregor	10+1	Harry Saunders	4
Will Lowther	2+1	Frank Boyle	4
Derick Close	9+3	Roger Wise	3+1
Joe Crowther	10+2	Bill Osborne	4
Keith Gurtner	6+3	Bill Kemp	5+1
Noel Watson	12	Bob McFarlane	3+1
Bluey Scott	6	Eric Irons	0
Bill Dalton	6	Herby King	0

Friday 14 September 1951 Motherwell
Eagles 50 Glasgow Tigers 34 (NLD2)

Motherwell		Glasgow	
Gordon McGregor	7	Jack Hodgson	5+1
Will Lowther	2+1	Ken McKinlay	6+1
Derick Close	11	Frank Hodgson	1
Joe Crowther	2+1	Junior Bainbridge	7
Noel Watson	10+1	Norman Lindsay	0
Keith Gurtner	7+1	Tommy Miller	12
Bluey Scott	3+1	Alf McIntosh	3
Bill Dalton	8+3	Len Nicholson	0

Monday 17 September 1951 Liverpool
Liverpool Chads 41 Eagles 43 (NLD2)

Liverpool		Motherwell	
Bill Griffiths	1+1	Gordon McGregor	10
Len Read	8+1	Will Lowther	2+1
Harry Welch	5	Derick Close	11
Reg Duval	7+1	Bill Dalton	6+1
George Newton	2+1	Noel Watson	3+1
Peter Robinson	7	Keith Gurtner	8
Tommy Allott	11	Bluey Scott	1+1
Buck Whitby	0	Stan Bradbury	2+1

Friday 21 September 1951 Motherwell
Skelly Trophy
Tommy Miller 15
Gordon McGregor 12
Derick Close 12
Bob Mark 12
Ken McKinlay 11
Noel Watson 11
Junior Bainbridge 9
Bill Dalton 6
Joe Crowther 6
Alf McIntosh 5
Will Lowther 5
Stan Bradbury 5
Dick Campbell 5
Danny Lee 2
Bob Lindsay 1
Bluey Scott 1

Monday 24 September 1951 Newcastle
Newcastle Diamonds 28 Eagles 56 (NLD2)

Newcastle		Motherwell	
Peter Orpwood	2+1	Gordon McGregor	11
Son Mitchell	6+1	Will Lowther	0
Mike Tams	1	Derick Close	10+2
Jack Chignell	4	Joe Crowther	10+2

Wal Morton 8
Don Wilkinson 5+1
Roy Dook 0
Norman Johnson 2

Noel Watson 7+2
Keith Gurtner 10
Bill Dalton 1
Stan Bradbury 7+2

Friday 28 September 1951 Motherwell
Eagles 40 Edinburgh Monarchs 42 (NLD2)

Motherwell
Gordon McGregor 8
Will Lowther 0
Derick Close 10+1
Joe Crowther 7+1
Noel Watson 5
Keith Gurtner 4
Bill Dalton 0
Stan Bradbury 6+1

Edinburgh
Harold Fairhurst 6+1
Jack Young 12
Bob Mark 2
Dick Campbell 2+1
Eddie Lack 2+2
Don Cuppleditch 8+1
Johnny Green 8
Jimmy Cox 2

Saturday 29 September 1951 Norwich
Norwich Stars 62 Eagles 22 (NLD2)

Norwich
Bob Leverenz 12
Fred Rogers 8+4
Phil Clarke 9+1
Fred Pawson 5+3
Alec Hunter 9+1
Paddy Mills 9
Jack Freeman 5+1
Bill Codling 5+1

Motherwell
Gordon McGregor 7
Will Lowther 1+1
Derek Close 5
Joe Crowther 1
Noel Watson 6
Keith Gurtner 1
Bill Dalton 0
Stan Bradbury 1

Tuesday 2 October 1951 Great Yarmouth
Yarmouth Bloaters 49 Eagles 35 (NLD2)

Yarmouth
Tip Mills 8+2
Fred Brand 12
Reg Morgan 9
Vic Ridgeon 2+2
Bob Baker 11
Cyril Quick 4+2
Stan Page 3
George Flower 0

Motherwell
Gordon McGregor 8
Will Lowther 0
Derick Close 7+1
Joe Crowther 5+1
Noel Watson 4+1
Keith Gurtner 5
Bill Dalton 1+1
Stan Bradbury 5+1

Friday 5 October 1951 Motherwell
Eagles 43 Cradley Heath 41 (NLD2)

Motherwell
Gordon McGregor 8
Stan Bradbury 1+1
Derick Close 12
Joe Crowther 6
Noel Watson 10
Keith Gurtner 4+1
Bluey Scott 1
Will Lowther 1

Cradley Heath
Phil Malpass 10
Les Tolley 3
Dick Tolley 4+1
Laurie Schofield 8
Guy Allott 9+1
Harry Bastable 4
Don Prettijohn 0
Wilf Willstead 3

Eagles 13 Edinburgh Monarchs 40 (LC)

Motherwell
Gordon McGregor 2
Stan Bradbury 2
Derick Close 1
Joe Crowther 1
Noel Watson 3+1
Keith Gurtner 4+1

Edinburgh
Harold Fairhurst 8+1
Jack Young 5+1
Bob Mark 8+1
Dick Campbell 7+2
Don Cuppleditch 7
Johnny Green 5+2

Friday 12 October 1951 Motherwell
Eagles 42 Glasgow Select 48 (Ch)

Motherwell
Gordon McGregor 4+1
Ken McKinlay 9+1
Derick Close 14
Stan Bradbury 1
Keith Gurtner 12
Joe Crowther 2+2

Glasgow Select
Tommy Miller 14
Ron Phillips 3+1
Bruce Semmens 12
Larry Lazarus 1+1
Willie Wilson 10+2
Junior Bainbridge 8+3

Saturday 19 October 1951 Cradley Heath
Cradley Heath Heathens 41 Eagles 40 (NLD2)

Cradley Heath
Laurie Schofield 7+1
Les Tolley 9+1
Harry Bastable 10
Dick Tolley 4+1
Guy Allott 6+1
Wilf Willstead 0
Dennis Hitchins 2
Don Prettijohn 3+1

Motherwell
Gordon McGregor 4+1
Bill Dalton 8
Derick Close 11
Stan Bradbury 4+1
Keith Gurtner 11
Joe Crowther 2+1
Bluey Scott 0
Danny Lee 0

Motherwell 1952

Tuesday 25 March 1952 Ashfield
Ashfield Reds 18 Ashfield Blues 28
Glasgow Tigers 31 Eagles 19 (4TT)

Ashfield Reds
Eric Liddell 4
Cyril Cooper 7
Dick Howard 2
Bruce Semmens 5

Ashfield Blues
Don Gray 5
Willie Wilson 8
Larry Lazarus 5
Ron Phillips 10

Glasgow
Tommy Miller 12
Ken McKinlay 5
Alf McIntosh 8
Len Nicholson 6

Motherwell
Stan Bradbury 1
Bluey Scott 2
Joe Crowther 7
Gordon McGregor 9

Friday 28 March 1952 Motherwell
Eagles 48 Edinburgh Monarchs 36 (Ch)

Motherwell
Stan Bradbury 6+1
Gordon McGregor 8

Edinburgh
Bob Mark 11
Eddie Lack 1+1

Derick Close 12
Joe Crowther 4+2
Bluey Scott 9+1
Ken McKinlay 6+2
Larry Lazarus 2
Bob Lindsay 1

Jimmy Cox 3+1
Johnny Green 9
Harold Booth 3+1
Harold Fairhurst 6
Jock Pryde 0
Harry Darling 3+1

Friday 4 April 1952 Motherwell
Eagles 50 Liverpool Chads 33 (NLD2)

Motherwell
Stan Bradbury 5+2
Gordon McGregor 11
Derick Close 11
Joe Crowther 5+2
Will Lowther 6+1
Bluey Scott 5
Bob Lindsay 6
Scott Hall 1

Liverpool
George Newton 4
Peter Robinson 9
Tommy Allott 9
Bill Griffiths 3+1
Harry Welch 2+1
Alf Webster 3
Peter Craven 2+1
Buck Whitby 1

Saturday 5 April 1952 Stoke
Stoke Potters 47 Eagles 34 (NLD2)

Stoke
Peter Orpwood 4+1
Ken Adams 12
John Fitzpatrick 6+1
Gil Blake 5+1
Les Jenkins 10
Ron Peace 4
Ray Harris 6
Derek Braithwaite 0

Motherwell
Gordon McGregor 8
Stan Bradbury 3+2
Derick Close 10
Joe Crowther 0
Will Lowther 6+1
Bluey Scott 3+1
Bob Lindsay 1+1
Scott Hall 3

Friday 11 April 1952 Motherwell
Eagles 49 Stoke Potters 35 (NLD2)

Motherwell
Will Lowther 4
Derick Close 8
Bluey Scott 7
Keith Gurtner 10
Gordon McGregor 10+2
Noel Watson 7+1
Stan Bradbury 3
Bob Lindsay 0

Stoke
Peter Orpwood 2+2
Ken Adams 8
John Fitzpatrick 6+1
Gil Blake 3+1
Les Jenkins 6
Ron Peace 3+1
Reg Fearman 4
Ray Harris 3+1

Friday 18 April 1952 Motherwell
Eagles 62 Yarmouth Bloaters 22 (NLD2)

Motherwell
Will Lowther 8+1
Derick Close 12
Bluey Scott 6+2
Keith Gurtner 10+1
Noel Watson 11+1
Gordon McGregor 8+2
Stan Bradbury 3+1
Scott Hall 4+1

Yarmouth
Johnny Chamberlain 1
Stan Page 2
Fred Brand 10
Tip Mills 0
Reg Morgan 0
Terry Courtnell 5
Niven McCreadie 2
Red Monteith 2

Friday 25 April 1952 Motherwell
Eagles 44 Poole Pirates 40 (NLD2)

Motherwell
Will Lowther 2+2
Derick Close 10
Bluey Scott 0
Keith Gurtner 8
Noel Watson 11
Gordon McGregor 5+2
Joe Crowther 8
Scott Hall 0

Poole
Tony Lewis 2
Ken Middleditch 6
Terry Small 9+1
Bill Holden 5+1
Roy Craighead 1+1
Brian Crutcher 10
Jimmy Squibb 4+4
Allan Kidd 3

Friday 2 May 1952 Motherwell
Eagles 50 Coventry Bees 34 (NLD2)

Motherwell
Will Lowther 3
Derick Close 9+1
Joe Crowther 6
Keith Gurtner 8+1
Noel Watson 8+1
Gordon McGregor 10+2
Bluey Scott 4+2
Scott Hall 2

Coventry
Stan Williams 4
Johnny Reason 5
Vic Emms 7+1
Charlie New 8
Les Hewitt 2
Derek Tailby 4+1
John Yates 3
Peter Brough 1+1

Saturday 3 May 1952 Coventry
Coventry Bees 45 Eagles 39 (NLD2)

Coventry
Charlie New 9+1
Vic Emms 4+1
Stan Williams 10
Johnny Reason 6+2
Les Hewitt 0
Derek Tailby 8
John Yates 3+2
Peter Brough 5+2

Motherwell
Will Lowther 4
Derick Close 11
Joe Crowther 0
Keith Gurtner 12
Noel Watson 2
Gordon McGregor 7+2
Stan Bradbury 2+1
Bluey Scott 1

Thursday 8 May 1952 Oxford
Oxford Cheetahs 41 Eagles 43 (NLD2)

Oxford
Jim Gregory 3+2
Bill Osborne 10
Harry Saunders 10
Herby King 3+1
Bill Kemp 0
Ron Wilson 6
Jim Boyd 5
Frank Boyle 4+1

Motherwell
Will Lowther 4+1
Derick Close 11
Joe Crowther 0
Keith Gurtner 9
Noel Watson 8
Gordon McGregor 8
Stan Bradbury 1
Bluey Scott 2

Friday 9 May 1952 Motherwell
Eagles 40 Glasgow Tigers 44 (NLD2)

Motherwell
Will Lowther 5+2
Derick Close 8
Joe Crowther 4

Glasgow
Don Wilkinson 1
Tommy Miller 10
Alf McIntosh 1+1

Keith Gurtner 2
Noel Watson 2
Gordon McGregor 12
Bluey Scott 2
Stan Bradbury 5+1

Junior Bainbridge 9
Ken McKinlay 10+1
Peter Dykes 4+1
Jack Hodgson 5
Frank Hodgson 4

Saturday 10 May 1952 Ashfield
Ashfield Giants 32 Eagles 51 (NLD2)

Ashfield
Bruce Semmens 9
Cyril Cooper 3+2
Willie Wilson 9
Dick Howard 1
Ron Phillips 7
Larry Lazarus 2
Don Gray 0
Jim Blyth 1+1

Motherwell
Will Lowther 7+2
Derick Close 12
Joe Crowther 5+1
Keith Gurtner 9+1
Noel Watson 3
G. McGregor 10+1
Bluey Scott 3+1
Stan Bradbury 2+1

Wednesday 14 May 1952 Glasgow
Glasgow Tigers 43 Eagles 41 (NLD2)

Glasgow
Len Nicholson 1
Tommy Miller 11
Ken McKinlay 7+1
Peter Dykes 9+1
Junior Bainbridge 11
Jack Hodgson 0
Frank Hodgson 2
Don Wilkinson 2+1

Motherwell
Will Lowther 5+2
Derick Close 10
Joe Crowther 5+3
Keith Gurtner 9
Noel Watson 5+1
Gordon McGregor 5
Stan Bradbury 2
Bluey Scott 0

Friday 16 May 1952 Motherwell
Eagles 51 Oxford Cheetahs 33 (NLD2)

Motherwell
Will Lowther 7+1
Derick Close 11+1
Joe Crowther 4
Scott Hall 2
Noel Watson 10+2
Gordon McGregor 11+1
Stan Bradbury 4+1
Bluey Scott 2+1

Oxford
Frank Boyle 5
Bill Osborne 4
Harry Saunders 9
Herby King 3+1
Jim Boyd 3
Jim Gregory 7
Ron Wilson 1
Bill Kemp 1

Friday 23 May 1952 Motherwell
Eagles 61 Coventry Bees 47 (NT)

Motherwell
Will Lowther 2+1
Derick Close 17+1
Joe Crowther 9
Keith Gurtner 1
Noel Watson 6+1
Gordon McGregor 10
Stan Bradbury 9+2
Bluey Scott 7+1

Coventry
Charlie New 12+1
Vic Emms 13
Les Hewitt 3
Derek Tailby 8
John Yates 3+1
Stan Williams 6
John Wright 1
Peter Brough 1

Saturday 24 May 1952 Coventry
Coventry Bees 71 Eagles 36 (NT)

Coventry
Charlie New 12
Vic Emms 17
Stan Williams 12+2
John Yates 6+1
Les Hewitt 9+3
Derek Tailby 5+1
Jack Wright 4+2
Peter Brough 6

Motherwell
Will Lowther 3+1
Derick Close 12
Joe Crowther 0
Stan Bradbury 4+1
Noel Watson 7
Gordon McGregor 8+1
Bluey Scott 1
Scott Hall 1

Monday 26 May 1952 Poole
Poole Pirates 62 Eagles 22 (NLD2)

Poole
Tony Lewis 10
Ken Middleditch 9+3
Terry Small 10+1
Bill Holden 7+2
Roy Craighead 7+3
Brian Crutcher 12
Jimmy Squibb 1
Allan Kidd 6

Motherwell
Will Lowther 2
Derick Close 6
Joe Crowther 3
Bob Lindsay 0
Noel Watson 7
Gordon McGregor 1
Scott Hall 1
Bluey Scott 2+1

Friday 30 May 1952 Motherwell
Eagles 41 Edinburgh Monarchs 40 (NLD2)

Motherwell
Bluey Scott 5+1
Derick Close 10
Noel Watson 4+1
Keith Gurtner 7+1
Will Lowther 4+1
Gordon McGregor 6+1
Joe Crowther 1+1
Stan Bradbury 4

Edinburgh
Dick Campbell 7
Bob Mark 0
Harold Fairhurst 12
Eddie Lack 3
Jimmy Cox 5
Don Cuppleditch 8
Johnny Green 6+1
Jock Scott 0

Saturday 31 May 1952 Ashfield
Glasgow Tigers 50 Eagles 34 (Ch)

Glasgow
Junior Bainbridge 7
Stuart Irvine 0
Ken McKinlay 12
Peter Dykes 7+1
Don Wilkinson 7+2
Tommy Miller 12
Jim Russell 0
Red Monteith 2+1

Motherwell
Scott Hall 4
Derick Close 7
Will Lowther 6
Noel Watson 0
Stan Bradbury 5+2
Gordon McGregor 8+1
Bob Lindsay 2+1
Lindsay Nixon 2+1

Monday 2 June 1952 Leicester
Leicester Hunters 52 Eagles 32 (NLD2)

Leicester
Jock Greirson 9+2
Len Williams 8+1
Les Beaumont 11

Motherwell
Bluey Scott 1
Derick Close 8+1
Stan Bradbury 5+1

Harwood Pike 3+1
Lionel Benson 10
Joe Bowkis 3+1
Alf Parker 5+1
Charlie Barsby 3+2

Keith Gurtner 5
Will Lowther 1
Gordon McGregor 11
Bob Lindsay 0
Scott Hall 1

Tuesday 3 June 1952 Yarmouth
Yarmouth Bloaters 49 Eagles 35 (NLD2)

Yarmouth
Vic Ridgeon 1
Fred Brand 12
Reg Morgan 8+2
Bob Baker 12
Terry Courtnell 5
Stan Page 5+1
Roy Bowers 4+1
Johnny Chamberlain 2

Motherwell
Stan Bradbury 2
Derick Close 9
Bluey Scott 4
Keith Gurtner 7+1
Will Lowther 6+1
Gordon McGregor 6+1
Bob Lindsay 0
Scott Hall 1

Friday 6 June 1952 Motherwell
Eagles 48 Cradley Heath Heathens 36 (NLD2)

Motherwell
Will Lowther 7+1
Gordon McGregor 8+1
Noel Watson 2
Keith Gurtner 9
Stan Bradbury 7+2
Derick Close 12
Bluey Scott 1
Scott Hall 2

Cradley Heath
Phil Malpass 3+1
Les Tolley 4
Dick Shepherd 7
Fred Perkins 3+1
Jim Tolley 9+1
Harry Bastable 5+2
Dick Tolley 2
Wilf Willstead 3+1

Saturday 7 June 1952 Cradley Heath
Cradley Heath Heathens 47 Eagles 37 (NLD2)

Cradley Heath
Phil Malpass 5+1
Les Tolley 4+1
Brian Shepherd 9+1
Fred Perkins 7+2
Jim Tolley 8+1
Harry Bastable 8
Guy Allott 3
Dick Tolley 3+2

Motherwell
Will Lowther 5+3
Gordon McGregor 11
Noel Watson 7
Keith Gurtner 2
Stan Bradbury 0
Derick Close 5+1
Bluey Scott 4+1
Scott Hall 3

Monday 9 June 1952 Motherwell
Eagles 48 Leicester Hunters 36 (NLD2)

Motherwell
Will Lowther 5
Gordon McGregor 12
Noel Watson 8+1
Keith Gurtner 6
Stan Bradbury 4
Derick Close 11+1
Bluey Scott 2+2
Scott Hall 1+1

Leicester
Jock Grierson 7+1
Len Williams 3+1
Les Beaumont 9
Harwood Pike 1+1
Lionel Benson 9+1
Joe Bowkis 5+1
Alf Parker 2
Charlie Barsby 0

Friday 13 June 1952 Motherwell
Eagles 44 Glasgow Tigers 40 (Ch)

Motherwell
Will Lowther 2
Gordon McGregor 11
Noel Watson 7
Stan Bradbury 4+2
Derick Close 7+2
Keith Gurtner 9+1
Bluey Scott 3+1
Scott Hall 1

Glasgow
Junior Bainbridge 5
Alf McIntosh 3+1
Ken McKinlay 8
Peter Dykes 5
Tommy Miller 12
Don Wilkinson 5+1
Frank Hodgson 0
Len Nicholson 1

Saturday 14 June 1952 Edinburgh
Edinburgh Monarchs 46 Eagles 38 (NLD2)

Edinburgh
Johnny Green 3
Bob Mark 12
Eddie Lack 6
Harold Fairhurst 8
Jimmy Cox 6+2
Don Cuppleditch 10
Jock Scott 0
Harry Darling 1

Motherwell
Will Lowther 4+1
Gordon McGregor 8
Bob Lindsay 5+1
Stan Bradbury 7
Derick Close 11
Keith Gurtner 2+1
Bluey Scott 0
Scott Hall 1

Friday 20 June 1952 Motherwell
Eagles 54 Stoke Potters 30 (NLD2)

Motherwell
Will Lowther 3+1
Gordon McGregor 10+1
Keith Gurtner 6+1
Derick Close 12
Stan Bradbury 6+2
Noel Watson 12
Bluey Scott 2+1
Scott Hall 3

Stoke
Ken Adams 8
Derek Braithwaite 1+1
Les Jenkins 3
Reg Fearman 5
Ron Peace 6+1
Ray Harris 6+1
John Fitzpatrick 0
Gil Blake 1+1

Saturday 21 June 1952 Ashfield
Ashfield Giants v Eagles (NLD2) Postponed

Friday 27 June 1952 Motherwell
Eagles 46 Ashfield Giants 61 (SC)

Motherwell
Will Lowther 3
Gordon McGregor 4+1
Keith Gurtner 7
Derick Close 16
Stan Bradbury 1
Noel Watson 8+1
Bluey Scott 6
Scott Hall 1

Ashfield
Larry Lazarus 8
Ron Phillips 5+2
Willie Wilson 13+1
Wilf Jay 4+1
Bruce Semmens 15+1
Cyril Cooper 8+1
Norman Hargreaves 6
Dick Howard 2+1

107

Friday 4 July 1952 Motherwell
Eagles 49 Cradley Heath Heathens 35 (NLD2)

Motherwell	Cradley Heath
Keith Gurtner 8+2	Jim Tolley 4+1
Gordon McGregor 8	Harry Bastable 7+1
Scott Hall 5	Dick Shepherd 6
Derick Close 11+1	Fred Perkins 1+1
Bluey Scott 3	Phil Malpass 6
Noel Watson 10+1	Geoff Bennett 1+1
Will Lowther 2+1	Les Tolley 9
Stan Bradbury 2+2	Wilf Willstead 1+1

Saturday 5 July 1952 Cradley Heath
Cradley Heath Heathens 51 Eagles 33 (NLD2)

Cradley Heath	Motherwell
Jim Tolley 12	Will Lowther 5+1
Harry Bastable 6+1	Gordon McGregor 3
Brian Shepherd 6+2	Stan Bradbury 2+1
Fred Perkins 0	Noel Watson 6
Phil Malpass 9	Keith Gurtner 5+1
Geoff Bennett 5+1	Derick Close 9+1
Les Tolley 10+1	Bluey Scott 2+2
Wilf Willstead 3	Scott Hall 1

Wednesday 9 July 1952 Edinburgh
Edinburgh Monarchs 43 Eagles 41
(Edinburgh Cup first leg)

Edinburgh	Motherwell
Dick Campbell 12	Keith Gurtner 8+1
Bob Mark 5+2	Gordon McGregor 1
Johnny Green 2+1	Bluey Scott 2
Harold Fairhurst 6	Noel Watson 10
Jimmy Cox 4	Will Lowther 5+1
Don Cuppleditch 7+1	Derick Close 10
Harry Darling 3	Stan Bradbury 3
Jock Scott 4	Scott Hall 1+1

Friday 11 July 1952 Motherwell
World Championship Qualifying Round
Tommy Miller 15
Dan Forsberg 12
Derick Close 11
Henry Long 11
Ken Middleditch 11
Geoff Mardon 11
Ernie Roccio 10
Ron Mountford 10
Eric Williams 10
Stig Parmberg 5
Les Hewitt 5
Norman Street 4
Les Beaumont 3
Gordon McGregor 2
Alan Smith 1
Dick Shepherd 1
Dennis Gray (Res) 0

Saturday 12 July 1952 Ashfield
Ashfield Giants 59 Eagles 48 (SC)

Ashfield	Motherwell
Ron Phillips 11+2	Keith Gurtner 11+1
Larry Lazarus 3	Gordon McGregor 6+2
Willie Wilson 9+2	Bluey Scott 5+1
Wilf Jay 14	Noel Watson 6
Bruce Semmens 12+3	Will Lowther 5+1
Cyril Cooper 1+1	Derick Close 12
Norman Hargreaves 4	Stan Bradbury 3
Jim Blyth 5+1	Scott Hall 0

Friday 18 July 1952 Motherwell
Eagles 41 Glasgow Tigers 43 (NLD2)

Motherwell	Glasgow
Keith Gurtner 10+1	Don Wilkinson 3
Gordon McGregor 7+3	Tommy Miller 12
Bluey Scott 4+1	Alf McIntosh 5+1
Noel Watson 9	Junior Bainbridge 10
Stan Bradbury 2+1	Ken McKinlay 8
Derick Close 6	Peter Dykes 2+1
Will Lowther 0	Len Nicholson 2+1
Scott Hall 3+1	Frank Hodgson 1+1

Friday 25 July 1952 Motherwell
Eagles 39 Ashfield Giants 45 (NLD2)

Motherwell	Ashfield
Keith Gurtner 9	Larry Lazarus 2+1
Gordon McGregor 7	Ron Phillips 9
Bluey Scott 3	Bruce Semmens 5+2
Noel Watson 5+1	Cyril Cooper 5+1
Derick Close 12	Willie Wilson 7+1
Scott Hall 1	Wilf Jay 6+1
Will Lowther 1	N. Hargreaves 7+1
Bob Lindsay 1	Jim Blyth 4+1

Saturday 26 July 1952 Edinburgh
Edinburgh Monarchs 45 Eagles 39 (NLD2)

Edinburgh	Motherwell
Bob Mark 7+2	Keith Gurtner 9+1
Dick Campbell 9	Gordon McGregor 5+1
Jock Scott 3	Bluey Scott 2+2
Harold Fairhurst 7+1	Noel Watson 8
Jimmy Cox 1+1	Derick Close 10
Don Cuppleditch 10+1	Scott Hall 2+1
Eric Mason 5+1	Will Lowther 2
Harry Darling 3	Bob Lindsay 1

Friday 1 August 1952 Motherwell
Eagles 42 Edinburgh Monarchs 42 (NLD2)

Motherwell	Edinburgh
Keith Gurtner 6+1	Harold Fairhurst 5+2
Gordon McGregor 4+1	Bob Mark 8

Bluey Scott 1
Noel Watson 11
Scott Hall 2+2
Derick Close 10
Stan Bradbury 3+2
Will Lowther 5

Eric Mason 1+1
Dick Campbell 11
Johnny Green 5+1
Don Cuppleditch 10
Jock Scott 0
Harry Darling 2

Harry Darling 5
Scott Hall 4
Johnny Green 4
Bob Lindsay 3
Wilf Jay 0
Jim Blyth 0

Friday 8 August 1952 Motherwell
Eagles 51 Liverpool Chads 33 (NLD2)

Motherwell
Keith Gurtner 4
Gordon McGregor 10+1
Bluey Scott 4+1
Noel Watson 10+1
Scott Hall 4
Derick Close 12
Stan Bradbury 3+1
Will Lowther 4+1

Liverpool
Reg Duval 6+1
Peter Robinson 7+1
Bill Griffiths 3+2
Don Potter 7
Val Morton 0
Harry Welch 7
Alf Webster 1
Eric Smith 2

Wednesday 20 August 1952 Glasgow
Glasgow Tigers 45 Eagles 39 (NLD2)

Glasgow
Jack Hodgson 2+2
Len Nicholson 7
Ken McKinlay 11+1
Peter Dykes 9+1
Alf McIntosh 6
Don Wilkinson 6+3
Frank Hodgson 4+1
Stuart Irvine 0

Motherwell
Will Lowther 5+2
Gordon McGregor 9
Bluey Scott 3
Noel Watson 9
Derick Close 11
Scott Hall 1
Bob Lindsay 0
Niven McCreadie 1+1

Tuesday 12 August 1952 Yarmouth
Yarmouth Bloaters 62 Eagles 22 (NLD2)

Yarmouth
Reg Morgan 7+4
Fred Brand 9+1
Reg Reeves 10+1
Bob Baker 8+3
Terry Courtnell 7+2
Johnny Chamberlain 11
Stan Page 6
Peter Harris 4+2

Motherwell
Keith Gurtner 2
Gordon McGregor 1
Bluey Scott 1
Noel Watson 3
Scott Hall 1+1
Derick Close 11
Stan Bradbury 2
Will Lowther 1

Friday 22 August 1952 Motherwell
Eagles 54 Oxford Cheetahs 30 (NLD2)

Motherwell
Keith Gurtner 4+1
Gordon McGregor 11+1
Bluey Scott 10
Noel Watson 7
Scott Hall 7+2
Derick Close 11+1
Will Lowther 2
Bob Lindsay 2+1

Oxford
Jim Boyd 6
Frank Boyle 2+1
Bill Kemp 1+1
Ron Wilson 5
Harry Saunders 5+2
Jim Gregory 7
Bill Osborne 2+2
Len Glover 2

Thursday 14 August 1952 Oxford
Oxford Cheetahs 41 Eagles 43 (NLD2)

Oxford
Harry Saunders 6+1
Jim Gregory 6
Jim Boyd 8
Bill Osborne 4+2
Bill Kemp 7+1
Frank Boyle 5+2
Len Glover 1+1
Ron Wilson 4+1

Motherwell
Keith Gurtner 10+1
Gordon McGregor 6+1
Bluey Scott 0
Noel Watson 8
Scott Hall 3
Derick Close 12
Stan Bradbury 1
Will Lowther 3+1

Saturday 23 August 1952 Coventry
Coventry Bees 48 Eagles 30 (NLD2)

Coventry
Vic Emms 6+2
Peter Brough 9+1
Johnny Reason 9
Stan Williams 4+3
Charlie New 4+2
Les Hewitt 9+1
Derek Tailby 5
John Wright 2

Motherwell
Keith Gurtner 2
Gordon McGregor 10
Bluey Scott 6
Noel Watson 3+1
Derick Close 12
Scott Hall 0
Will Lowther 3
Bob Lindsay 0

Friday 15 August 1952 Motherwell
**Scottish Riders Championship
Qualifying Round**
Dick Campbell 14
Don Cuppleditch 13
Bruce Semmens 12
Ron Phillips 11
Keith Gurtner 11
Noel Watson 10
Derick Close 10
Gordon McGregor 9
Will Lowther 6
Bluey Scott 6

Monday 25 August 1952 Liverpool
Liverpool Chads 43 Eagles 41 (NLD2)

Liverpool
Eric Smith 2
Peter Robinson 11
Bill Griffiths 9
Don Potter 4+2
Reg Duval 8+1
Harry Welch 4+1
Jeff Crawford 2+2
Tommy Anderson 3+1

Motherwell
Keith Gurtner 7+1
Gordon McGregor 7
Bluey Scott 2
Noel Watson 9
Derick Close 12
Scott Hall 4+1
Will Lowther 0
Bob Lindsay 0

Friday 29 August 1952 Motherwell
Eagles 55 Yarmouth Bloaters 29 (NLD2)

Motherwell	Yarmouth
Keith Gurtner 4	Fred Brand 6
Gordon McGregor 11+1	Peter Harris 2
Bluey Scott 4+2	Bob Baker 4+1
Noel Watson 11	Johnny Chamberlain 9
Derick Close 12	Terry Courtnell 2
Scott Hall 3+1	Reg Reeves 6
Will Lowther 7	Reg Morgan 0
Bob Lindsay 3	Roy Bowers 0

Friday 5 September 1952 Motherwell
Scotland 56 England 52 (International)

Scotland	England
Derick Close 9	Freddie Williams 13
Noel Watson 5	Eric Williams 2+1
Tommy Miller 16+1	Eddie Rigg 11+2
Don Cuppleditch 4	Arthur Forrest 9+1
Willie Wilson 4	Ken Sharples 4+2
Ken McKinlay 11+1	Brian Crutcher 12
Bob Mark 6+3	Peter Robinson 1
Harold Fairhurst 1+1	Jack Hughes 0
Gordon McGregor DNR	Ken Middleditch DNR

Tuesday 9 September 1952 Ashfield
Ashfield Giants 43 Eagles 41 (NLD2)

Ashfield	Motherwell
Larry Lazarus 10	Gordon McGregor 7+1
Ron Phillips 5+2	Johnny Green 1+1
Bruce Semmens 9	Bluey Scott 6
Norman Hargreaves 3+2	Noel Watson 7
Willie Wilson 10+1	Scott Hall 3
Cyril Cooper 5+1	Derick Close 12
Jim Blyth 0	Will Lowther 4+1
Jimmy Tannock 1+1	Bob Lindsay 1+1

Friday 12 September 1952 Motherwell
Eagles 39 Ashfield Giants 44 (NLD2)

Motherwell	Ashfield
Will Lowther 1	Larry Lazarus 6+1
Gordon McGregor 12	Ron Phillips 7
Bluey Scott 7	Bruce Semmens 11
Noel Watson 1+1	Norman Hargreaves 2
Johnny Green 8	Willie Wilson 6+3
Scott Hall 4+1	Cyril Cooper 9+1
Bob Lindsay 4	Jim Blyth 0
Niven McCreadie 2+1	Jimmy Tannock 3

Saturday 13 September 1952 Stoke
Stoke Potters 50 Eagles 33 (NLD2)

Stoke	Motherwell
Gil Blake 9+1	Johnny Green 2
Ken Adams 4+1	Gordon McGregor 1
Les Jenkins 7+1	Bluey Scott 0
Ron Peace 9+1	Noel Watson 11
Ray Harris 7+1	Derick Close 12
Reg Fearman 8+2	Scott Hall 1
John Fitzpatrick 4+1	Bob Lindsay 1
Fred Siggins 2+1	Will Lowther 5+1

Monday 15 September 1952 Poole
Poole Pirates 60 Eagles 24 (NLD2)

Poole	Motherwell
Tony Lewis 4+1	Johnny Green 3
Ken Middleditch 12	Gordon McGregor 3
Brian Crutcher 7+2	Bluey Scott 2
Jimmy Squibb 7+1	Noel Watson 6
Terry Small 9+3	Scott Hall 3+1
Bill Holden 10	Derick Close 4
Roy Craighead 6	Will Lowther 2+1
Alan Kidd 5+1	Bob Lindsay 1

Friday 19 September 1952 Leicester
Leicester Hunters 48 Eagles 36 (NLD2)

Leicester	Motherwell
Joe Bowkis 6+1	Johnny Green 8
Len Williams 12	Gordon McGregor 6+2
Les Beaumont 10	Bluey Scott 2
Jock Grierson 4+1	Noel Watson 5+1
Alf Parker 3	Derick Close 10
Lionel Benson 9+2	Scott Hall 0
Laurie Holland 1+1	Will Lowther 5+1
Charlie Barsby 3+1	Bob Lindsay 0

Friday 19 September 1952 Motherwell
Novice Championships
Bob Sharp (Tigers) 15
John Paul (Giants) 13
Tammy Woods (Bathgate) 11
Jim Russell (Glasgow) 11
Niven McCreadie (Belshill) 10
Gordon Mitchell (Hamilton) 10
Jock Pryde (Motherwell) 8
Red Monteith (Paisley) 7
Jim Hanson (Manchester) 6
Slim Irvine (Dunlop) 4
Milner Rennie (Edinburgh) 4
Bob Hannah (Dumfries) 3
Vic Conners (Glasgow) 3
Eric Mason (Carlisle) 2
Stuart Irvine (Tigers) 2
Joe Thomson (New Stevenson) 0
Jim Wylie (Glasgow) (res) 1
Lex McCool (Glasgow) (res) 8

Friday 26 September 1952 Motherwell
Eagles 43 Poole Pirates 41 (NLD2)

Motherwell		Poole	
Johnny Green 7		Tony Lewis 5+2	
Gordon McGregor 6+1		Ken Middleditch 9	
Bluey Scott 0		Brian Crutcher 10	
Noel Watson 12		Jimmy Squibb 6+3	
Derick Close 12		Terry Small 7	
Scott Hall 1		Bill Holden 3+3	
Will Lowther 4		Roy Craighead 1+1	
Bob Lindsay 1+1		Alan Kidd 0	

Friday 3 October 1952 Motherwell
Eagles 42 Coventry Bees 42 (NLD2)

Motherwell		Coventry	
Johnny Green 10		Peter Brough 3	
Gordon McGregor 4		Vic Emms 8	
Will Lowther 0		Johnny Reason 10	
Noel Watson 9		Stan Williams 2+1	
Derick Close 12		Les Hewitt 10	
Scott Hall 2		Derek Tailby 4+2	
Bluey Scott 4		Charlie New 5	
Bob Lindsay 1+1		John Wright 0	

Friday 10 October 1952 Motherwell
The Skelly Trophy
Don Cuppleditch 14
Ken McKinlay 14
Derick Close 14
Tommy Miller 12
Gordon McGregor 11
Bruce Semmens 8
Johnny Green 8
Willie Wilson 7
Dick Campbell 7
Bob Mark 7
Will Lowther 6
Larry Lazarus 5
Bob Lindsay 3
Noel Watson 2
Bluey Scott 1
Scott Hall 1

Monday 13 October 1952 Motherwell
Eagles 49 Leicester Hunters 35 (NLD2)

Motherwell		Leicester	
Will Lowther 6+2		Joe Bowkis 4+3	
Gordon McGregor 12		Len Williams 7+1	
Bluey Scott 4+1		Charlie Barsby 6	
Noel Watson 8+1		Jock Grierson 0	
Derick Close 12		Dennis Parker 5	
Scott Hall 3+1		Lionel Benson 5	
Niven McCreadie 0		Harwood Pike 4+1	
Bob Lindsay 4+1		Les Beaumont 4+1	

Monday 20 October 1952 Liverpool
Liverpool Chads 59 Eagles 25 (NLD2)

Liverpool		Motherwell	
Peter Robinson 10		Johnny Green 1	
Alf Webster 7+2		Gordon McGregor 2	
Harry Welch 11		Bluey Scott 1	
Reg Duval 6+3		Noel Watson 3	
Don Potter 11		Derick Close 12	
Bill Griffiths 6+3		Scott Hall 4	
Tommy Anderson 4+1		Will Lowther 2	
Eric Smith 4+2		Bob Lindsay 0	

Motherwell 1953

Friday 27 March 1953 Motherwell
Best Pairs
Tommy Miller 12
Larry Lazarus 8
Total: 20
Ron Phillips 13
Johnny Green 5
Total: 18
Derick Close 10
Scott Hall 4
Total: 14
Gordon McGregor 12
Jimmy Tannock 2
Total: 14
Harold Fairhurst 9
Don Cuppleditch 4
Total: 13
Noel Watson 4
Bluey Scott 6
Total: 10
John Paul (reserve) 0

Friday 3 April 1953 Motherwell
Eagles 53 Coventry Bees 31 (NLD2)

Motherwell		Coventry	
Gordon McGregor 8+2		Vic Emms 3+1	
Noel Watson 12		Charlie New 8	
Ron Phillips 8		Johnny Reason 10	
Johnny Green 2+1		Stan Williams 0	
Derick Close 12		Les Hewitt 4	
Bluey Scott 5+1		Derek Tailby 0	
Scott Hall 4+1		Reg Duval 6	
Jimmy Tannock 2+1		Jack Wright 0	

Monday 6 April 1953 Leicester
Leicester Hunters 43 Eagles 41 (NLD2)

Leicester		Motherwell	
Joe Bowkis 0		Gordon McGregor 11	
Len Williams 10		Noel Watson 4+2	
Jack Mountford 8		Ron Phillips 6+1	
Alf Parker 5+1		Johnny Green 2	

Dennis Parker 9+1
Fred Perkins 1
Charlie Barsby 8
Roy Browning 2+1

Bluey Scott 4+1
Derick Close 11
Scott Hall 1
Jimmy Tannock 2

Friday 10 April 1953 Motherwell
Eagles 39 Edinburgh Monarchs 45 (NLD2)

Motherwell	Edinburgh
Noel Watson 7	Dick Campbell 8
Gordon McGregor 2+1	Bob Mark 7+3
Ron Phillips 9	Don Cuppleditch 8+2
Johnny Green 1	Eddie Lack 8
Bluey Scott 3	Jimmy Cox 3+1
Derick Close 12	Harold Fairhurst 9
Scott Hall 4+1	Jeff Crawford 2
Jimmy Tannock 1+1	Bob Lindsay 0

Saturday 11 April 1953 Coventry
Coventry Bees 43 Eagles 41 (NLD2)

Coventry	Motherwell
Vic Emms 6	Gordon McGregor 9+1
Charlie New 10+1	Noel Watson 5
Johnny Reason 1	Ron Phillips 4+2
Reg Duval 2	Johnny Green 9
Les Hewitt 12	Derick Close 11
Stan Williams 2	Bluey Scott 2+1
Derek Tailby 5+2	Scott Hall 1
Jack Wright 5	Jimmy Tannock 0

Monday 13 April 1953 Poole
Poole Pirates 63 Eagles 21 (NLD2)

Poole	Motherwell
Tony Lewis 6+3	Gordon McGregor 9+1
Ken Middleditch 12	Noel Watson 2
Jimmy Squibb 9+1	Ron Phillips 3
Terry Small 11+1	Johnny Green 3
Brian Crutcher 12	Derick Close 9
Bill Holden 7+3	Bluey Scott 0
Johnny Thomson 3	Scott Hall 0
Allan Kidd 3+1	Jimmy Tannock 0

Friday 17 April 1953 Motherwell
Eagles 56 Stoke Potters 28 (NLD2)

Motherwell	Stoke
Noel Watson 6+3	Ken Adams 9
Gordon McGregor 10+1	Joe Peck 0
Johnny Green 6+2	Don Potter 8
Ron Phillips 9	John Fitzpatrick 0
Bluey Scott 8+3	Les Jenkins 2
Derick Close 12	Alan Hailstone 1
Scott Hall 3	Reg Fearman 7+2
Jimmy Tannock 2+1	Ray Harris 1

Monday 20 April 1953 Wolverhampton
Wolverhampton Wasps 49 Eagles 35 (NLD2)

Wolverhampton	Motherwell
Jim Tolley 9+1	Gordon McGregor 8
Harry Bastable 9+2	Noel Watson 2
Benny King 6	Ron Phillips 4
Brian Shepherd 9+1	Johnny Green 5+1
Eric Irons 6+2	Derick Close 12
Ivor Davies 2	Bluey Scott 3+1
Derek Braithwaite 3 2	Scott Hall 0
Les Tolley 5+1	Jimmy Tannock 1

Tuesday 21 April 1953 Great Yarmouth
Yarmouth Bloaters 61 Eagles 23 (NLD2)

Yarmouth	Motherwell
Fred Brand 12	Gordon McGregor 4
Reg Morgan 8+4	Noel Watson 3
Reg Reeves 7+4	Ron Phillips 4
Bob Baker 10	Johnny Green 0
Terry Courtnell 11	Derick Close 8
Johnny Chamberlain 8+3	Bluey Scott 1
Peter Harris 0	Scott Hall 2
Roy Bowers 5+1	Jimmy Tannock 1+1

Friday 24 April 1953 Motherwell
Eagles 42 Wolverhampton Wasps 40 (NLD2)

Motherwell	Wolverhampton
Noel Watson 4+1	Jim Tolley 6
Gordon McGregor 10	Harry Bastable 4+ 1
Johnny Green 1	Eric Irons 8+2
Ron Phillips 8	Brian Shepherd 6+2
Bluey Scott 4	Benny King 0
Derick Close 10+2	Ivor Davies 6
Scott Hall 3	Derek Braithwaite 4
Jimmy Tannock 2	Les Tolley 6

Friday 1 May 1953 Motherwell
Eagles 49 Poole Pirates 35 (NLD2)

Motherwell	Poole
Noel Watson 6	Tony Lewis 1+1
Gordon McGregor 10+1	Ken Middleditch 7
Johnny Green 6+1	Jimmy Squibb 7
Ron Phillips 10	Terry Small 8+2
Bluey Scott 5+2	Brian Crutcher 6
Derick Close 11+1	Bill Holden 1
Scott Hall 0	Allan Kidd 4+1
Bill Dalton 1	Johnny Thomson 1

Monday 4 May 1953 Motherwell
Eagles 50 Leicester Hunters 33 (NLD2)

Motherwell	Leicester
Noel Watson 6	Charlie Barsby 5+1
Gordon McGregor 7+1	Len Williams 7
Johnny Green 9+3	Fred Perkins 3+1

Ron Phillips 12
Bluey Scott 6+2
Derick Close 6
Scott Hall 0
Bill Dalton 4

Jack Mountford 1
Dennis Parker 1+1
Alf Parker 5+1
Harwood Pike 2+1
Roy Browning 9

Friday 8 May 1953 Motherwell
Eagles 44 Glasgow Tigers 40 (LC)

Motherwell
Noel Watson 6+ 2
Gordon McGregor 10
Johnny Green 4+2
Ron Phillips 10
Bluey Scott 5+2
Derick Close 8+1
Joe Crowther 0
Jimmy Tannock 1

Glasgow
Larry Lazarus 1+1
Tommy Miller 12
Junior Bainbridge 7+1
Alf McIntosh 2
Ken McKinlay 9
Peter Dykes 1
Don Wilkinson 3+1
Bob Sharp 5

Saturday 9 May 1953 Hamilton
Motherwell & District Select 40
Glasgow Select 40 (Ch)

Motherwell
Gordon Mitchell 3
Tammy Woods 10
Joe Crowther 11
Lex McCool 3+1
Slim Irvine 5+1
Jock Pryde 4
Alan Robertson 0
Douglas Craig 4

Glasgow
Arthur Malm 12
Tommy Bryce 6+1
Red Monteith 6
Stan Pennel 1
Douglas Templeton 11
Vic Connors 3+1
Milner Rennie 2+1
Robert Torrance 1

Saturday 9 May 1953 Swindon
Swindon Robins 62 Eagles 46 (NT)

Swindon
Ian Williams 11
Frank Evans 8+1
Bob Jones 10+2
Danny Malone 7+1
Bob Wells 12+1
Ken Wiggins 3+2
Ron Swaine 3
Mick Hard 8+3

Motherwell
Noel Watson 2
G. McGregor 12+2
Johnny Green 5+1
Ron Phillips 2
Bluey Scott 3
Derick Close 18
Bill Dalton 3
Jimmy Tannock 1+1

Wednesday 13 May 1953 Glasgow
Glasgow Tigers 59 Eagles 25 (NLD2)

Glasgow
Larry Lazarus 6
Tommy Miller 12
Ken McKinlay 11
Peter Dykes 7+2
Junior Bainbridge 5+2
Alf McIntosh 11+1
Don Wilkinson 3+1
Bob Sharp 4+1

Motherwell
Noel Watson 0
Gordon McGregor 7
Johnny Green 1
Ron Phillips 8
Bluey Scott 1
Derick Close 5
Joe Crowther 2
Jimmy Tannock 1

Friday 15 May 1953 Motherwell
Eagles 78 Swindon Robins 30 (NT)

Motherwell
Noel Watson 7
Gordon McGregor 17+1
Johnny Green 11+2
Ron Phillips 12+3
Bluey Scott 9+3
Derick Close 16+2
Joe Crowther 4
Jimmy Tannock 2+2

Swindon
Bob Jones 4
Bob Wells 2+1
Ian Williams 7+1
Ken Wiggins 0
Danny Malone 4+1
Frank Evans 0
Mick Hard 4
Ron Swaine 9

Saturday 16 May 1953 Stoke
Stoke Potters 59 Eagles 22 (NLD2)

Stoke
Ken Adams 10+1
John Fitzpatrick 6+3
Don Potter 11
Reg Fearman 4+1
Ron Peace 8+2
Jackie Hughes 12
Les Jenkins 4
Ray Harris 4+2

Motherwell
Noel Watson 7
Gordon McGregor 2+1
Johnny Green 1
Ron Phillips 2
Bluey Scott 0
Derick Close 7
Jimmy Tannock 1
Bill Dalton 1

Monday 18 May 1953 Liverpool
Liverpool Chads 51 Eagles 33 (NLD2)

Liverpool
Peter Robinson 10+1
Harry Welch 7+2
Bill Griffiths 10
Tommy Anderson 7+3
Fred Wills 5
Gil Blake 5+2
Tommy Allott 2+1
Cyril Cooper 5+1

Motherwell
Noel Watson 2
Gordon McGregor 10
Johnny Green 4+1
Ron Phillips 4
Bluey Scott 1
Derick Close 11+1
Jimmy Tannock 1+1
Bill Dalton 0

Friday 22 May 1953 Motherwell
Eagles 48.5 Edinburgh Monarchs 34.5 (NLD2)

Motherwell
Noel Watson 0
Gordon McGregor 11+1
Johnny Green 9+1
Ron Phillips 6+2
Bluey Scott 1
Derick Close 11.5
Scott Hall 6+1
Jimmy Tannock 4+2

Edinburgh
Dick Campbell 5
Bob Mark 3+1
Don Cuppleditch 10.5
Eddie Lack 4+1
Roy Bester 6+2
Harold Fairhurst 4
Wilf Jay 2
Jimmy Cox 0

Monday 25 May 1953 Poole
Poole Pirates 62 Eagles 46 (NT)

Poole
Ken Middleditch 16+1
Tony Lewis 7+3
Jimmy Squibb 6+2

Motherwell
Noel Watson 6
Gordon McGregor 5+1
Johnny Green 3+1

113

Bill Holden 7+1
Alan Kidd 10
Terry Small 8
Johnny Thomson 4+1
Buster Brown 4+1

Ron Phillips 11+1
Bluey Scott 1+1
Derick Close 16
Scott Hall 1
Jimmy Tannock 3

Ron Phillips 11+1
Bluey Scott 4+1
Derick Close 9
Jimmy Tannock 1
Scott Hall 4+1

Reg Reeves 4
Ronnie Genz 4+1
Johnny Chamberlain 7
Roy Bowers 1+1
Terry Courtnell 0

Friday 29 May 1953 Motherwell
Eagles 73 Poole Pirates 35 (NT)

Motherwell
Gordon McGregor 11+3
Noel Watson 11+2
Johnny Green 17+1
Ron Phillips 10
Derick Close 15+1
Bluey Scott 0
Scott Hall 4+1
Jimmy Tannock 5+1

Poole
Ken Middleditch 10+1
Tony Lewis 4
Jimmy Squibb 6+1
Bill Holden 1+1
Terry Small 3+1
Allan Kidd 7+1
Buster Brown 3
Johnny Thomson 1+1

Tuesday 2 June 1953 Motherwell
The Skelly Trophy

Tommy Miller 15
Len Williams 14
Ron Phillips 12
Junior Bainbridge 10
Ken McKinlay 10
Noel Watson 9
Don Cuppleditch 9
Gordon McGregor 9
Johnny Green 8
Bob Mark 7
Bluey Scott 5
Derick Close 4
Roy Bester 3
Dick Campbell 3
Jimmy Tannock 1
Scott Hall 1

Friday 5 June 1953 Motherwell
Eagles 41 Glasgow Tigers 43 (NLD2)

Motherwell
Noel Watson 7+2
Gordon McGregor 8+1
Johnny Green 8+2
Ron Phillips 7
Derick Close 10
Bluey Scott 0
Scott Hall 1+1
Jimmy Tannock 0

Glasgow
Larry Lazarus 4
Tommy Miller 12
Junior Bainbridge 5
Alf McIntosh 3
Ken McKinlay 12
Peter Dykes 3
Bob Sharp 2+1
Don Wilkinson 2+2

Friday 12 June 1953 Motherwell
Eagles 54 Yarmouth Bloaters 30 (NLD2)

Motherwell
Noel Watson 10+1
Gordon McGregor 7+2
Johnny Green 8+1

Yarmouth
Fred Brand 9
Peter Harris 1+1
Bob Baker 4

Saturday 13 June 1953 Edinburgh
Edinburgh Monarchs 53 Eagles 31 (NLD2)

Edinburgh
Dick Campbell 8+3
Bob Mark   9
Don Cuppleditch 11
Eddie Lack 6+1
Roy Bester 6
Harold Fairhurst 9+2
Wilf Jay 3
Jimmy Cox 1+1

Motherwell
Noel Watson 8
Gordon McGregor 1+1
Johnny Green 5
Ron Phillips 6
Derick Close 7
Bluey Scott 3
Scott Hall 0
Jimmy Tannock 1+1

Friday 19 June 1953 Motherwell
Eagles 67 Stoke Potters 17 (NLD2)

Motherwell
Noel Watson 11+1
Gordon McGregor 10+2
Johnny Green 12
Ron Phillips 9+3
Derick Close 12
Bluey Scott 7+3
Jimmy Tannock 3+1
Scott Hall 3+1

Stoke
Ken Adams 0
John Fitzpatrick 2
Don Potter 4
Ray Harris 2
Les Jenkins 2
Jackie Hughes 5
Alan Hailstone 1
Neville Hutton 1

Friday 26 June 1953 Motherwell
Scottish Riders Championship
Qualifying Round
Derick Close 14
Johnny Green 14
Ron Phillips 13
Tommy Miller 12
Dick Campbell 11
Bob Mark 9
Scott Hall 9
Noel Watson 7
Gordon McGregor 6
Bluey Scott 5
Eddie Lack 5
Alf McIntosh 4
Wilf Jay 4
Don Wilkinson 3
Bob Sharp 3
Jimmy Tannock 1

Saturday 27 June 1953 Coventry
Coventry Bees 51 Eagles 57 (QC)

Coventry
Charlie New 11+2
Vic Emms 10+4
Johnny Reason 5

Motherwell
Noel Watson 5+2
Gordon McGregor 16
Johnny Green 12+1

Reg Duval 4
Les Hewitt 5
Peter Brough 2+1
Derek Tailby 8+1
Jack Wright 6+1

Ron Phillips 6
Bluey Scott 4+2
Derick Close 12+1
Scott Hall 0
Jimmy Tannock 2

Ron Phillips 9
Johnny Green 4+2
Bluey Scott 10
Scott Hall 2
Jock Pryde 2

Brian Shepherd 5+2
Ivor Davies 0
Les Tolley 3
Eric Irons 9
Bill Jamieson 0

Friday 3 July 1953 Motherwell
Eagles 63 Harringay Racers 45 (NT)

Motherwell
Noel Watson 6+1
Gordon McGregor 10+3
Johnny Green 11+1
Ron Phillips 16+1
Derick Close 16+1
Bluey Scott 2
Scott Hall 2
Jimmy Tannock 0

Harringay
Split Waterman 14+1
Ron How 5
Ken Walsh 1
Jack Biggs 6
Jeff Lloyd 3+1
Maury Dunn 3+1
Allan Quinn 7
Frank Lawrence 4+1

Saturday 4 July 1953 London
Harringay Racers 85 Eagles 23 (NT)

Harringay
Ron How 12+1
Split Waterman 10+5
Jack Biggs 13+2
Ken Walsh 13+2
Jeff Lloyd 15
Maury Dunn 9+2
Alan Quinn 6
Frank Lawrence 7+2

Motherwell
Noel Watson 6
Gordon McGregor 4+1
Johnny Green 2
Ron Phillips 2
Bluey Scott 1
Derick Close 6
Scott Hall 1
Jimmy Tannock 1

Friday 10 July 1953 Motherwell
World Championship Qualifying Round
Ron Mountford 12
Stig Pramberg 11
Dan Forsberg 11
Graham Warren 10
Ron Clarke 10
Charlie May 9
Don Cuppleditch 9
Merv Neil 8
Billy Bales 8
Gordon McGregor 7
Fred Brand 6
Bill Holden 6
Reg Reeves 6
Fred Wills 2
Harold Fairhurst 2
Jim Boyd 0
Ron Phillips (Res) 3

Friday 17 July 1953 Motherwell
Eagles 50 Wolverhampton Wasps 34 (NLD2)

Motherwell
Noel Watson 10+1
Gordon McGregor 7+4
Jimmy Tannock 6

Wolverhampton
Harry Bastable 3+1
Jim Tolley 10
Derek Braithwaite 4

Tuesday 21 July 1953 Ashfield
Top Four Challenge
Eagles 29 Glasgow Tigers 24
Edinburgh Monarchs 20 Ashfield Giants 11

Ashfield
Ron Phillips 6
Larry Lazarus 0
Willie Wilson 3
Cyril Cooper 2

Glasgow
Tommy Miller 9
Junior Bainbridge 6
Ken McKinlay 9
Peter Dykes 0
Arthur Malm 0

Motherwell
Scott Hall 5
Noel Watson 9
Johnny Green 6
Gordon McGregor 9

Edinburgh
Dick Campbell 5
Bob Mark 3
Don Cuppleditch 9
Harold Fairhurst 3

Friday 24 July 1953 Motherwell
Eagles 43 Glasgow Tigers 41 (NLD2)

Motherwell
Noel Watson 1
Gordon McGregor 10+1
Jimmy Tannock 3
Ron Phillips 2+2
Bluey Scott 7+1
Johnny Green 6+1
Guy Allott 6
Scott Hall 8+1

Glasgow
Bob Sharp 4
Tommy Miller 9
Peter Dykes 8+1
Ken McKinlay 5
Don Wilkinson 8
Larry Lazarus 3+2
Doug Templeton 3
Arthur Malm 1

Tuesday 28 July 1953 Ashfield
Eagles 38 Tigers 22 (Challenge)

Eagles
Noel Watson 6
Gordon McGregor 6+2
Jimmy Tannock 4+2
Ron Phillips 10
Bluey Scott 2+1
Johnny Green 5
Guy Allott 2+1
Scott Hall 3

Tigers
Tommy Miller 9
Larry Lazarus 2
Doug Templeton 3
Peter Dykes 1
Junior Bainbridge 5
Don Wilkinson 1
Arthur Malm DNR
Bob Sharp 0

Friday 31 July 1953 Motherwell
Eagles 55 Poole Pirates 53 (QC)

Motherwell
Noel Watson 18
Gordon McGregor 9+1
Scott Hall 1
Ron Phillips 6+1
Bluey Scott 3

Poole
Tony Lewis 8+1
Ken Middleditch 7+2
Jimmy Squibb 7+1
Bill Holden 5+3
Terry Small 11+1

115

Johnny Green 13+2 Allan Kidd 7+3 Bill Dalton 6+1 Bluey Scott 1

Johnny Green 13+2
Guy Allott 4
Jimmy Tannock 1

Allan Kidd 7+3
Buster Brown 3+2
Johnny Thomson 5

Bill Dalton 6+1
Alf Parker 1+1
Paddy Mills 5+1

Bluey Scott 1
Jimmy Tannock 2
Scott Hall DNR

Saturday 1 August 1953 Edinburgh
Edinburgh Monarchs 55 Eagles 28 (NLD2)

Edinburgh		*Motherwell*	
Dick Campbell 9		Noel Watson 7	
Bob Mark 5+2		Gordon McGregor 6+1	
Don Cuppleditch 11+1		Scott Hall 3	
Eddie Lack 7		Ron Phillips 2	
Roy Bester 8+1		Bluey Scott 5+1	
Harold Fairhurst 10+1		Johnny Green 4	
Jimmy Cox 2		Guy Allott 1	
Wilf Jay 3+1		Jimmy Tannock 0	

Friday 7 August 1953 Motherwell
Scottish Junior Championship

Arthur Malm 13
Gordon Mitchell 12
Jim Russell 12
Stuart Irvine 12
Harry Darling 10
Slim Irvine 9
Tammy Woods 9
Jock Scott 9
Vic Conners 8
Don Adams 7
Milner Rennie 6
Douglas Craig 5
Bill Finnie 3
Jock Pryde 2
Jack Jones 2
Arty Fisher 2
Lex Orr (Res) 1

Friday 7 August 1953 Leicester
Leicester Hunters 46 Eagles 38 (NLD2)

Leicester	*Motherwell*
Ivor Brown 0	Noel Watson 6+3
Len Williams 12	Gordon McGregor 10
Fred Perkins 8+1	Ron Phillips 8
Charlie Barsby 3+2	Scott Hall 1+1
Dennis Parker 9	Johnny Green 10
Reg Fearman 3+1	Bluey Scott 0
Lionel Watling 8+1	Guy Allott 4
Roy Browning 3+1	Jimmy Tannock 0

Saturday 8 August 1953 Stoke
Stoke Potters 46 Eagles 38 (NLD2)

Stoke	*Motherwell*
John Fitzpatrick 6+1	Noel Watson 9
Jack Hughes 7+1	Gordon McGregor 9+1
Don Potter 8	Ron Phillips 3
Ray Harris 7+1	Guy Allott 3+1
Les Jenkins 6+2	Johnny Green 11

Monday 10 August 1953 Poole
Poole Pirates 58 Eagles 26 (NLD2)

Poole	*Motherwell*
Tony Lewis 7+1	Noel Watson 3
Ken Middleditch 10+1	Gordon McGregor 3
Jimmy Squibb 9	Ron Phillips 8
Bill Holden 9+2	Scott Hall 0
Terry Small 12	Johnny Green 9
Allan Kidd 5+1	Bluey Scott 2
Buster Brown 3+2	Guy Allott 0
Johnny Thomson 3+1	Jimmy Tannock 1

Wednesday 12 August 1953 Glasgow
Glasgow Tigers 52.5 Eagles 31.5 (NLD2)

Glasgow	*Motherwell*
Doug Templeton 3+1	Noel Watson 3+1
Tommy Miller 12	Gordon McGregor 10
Ken McKinlay 5+1	Scott Hall 0
Peter Dykes 9.5+1	Ron Phillips 4.5
Junior Bainbridge 11	Johnny Green 8
Don Wilkinson 6+3	Bluey Scott 0
Larry Lazarus 3	Guy Allott 6
Bob Sharp 3	Jimmy Tannock 0

Friday 14 August 1953 Motherwell
Scotland 62 England 46 (Test Match)

Scotland	*England*
Tommy Miller 12	Cyril Roger 6+2
Ken McKinlay 11 3	Bert Roger 6
Don Cuppleditch 11	Eric Williams 6+1
Gordon McGregor 7+2	Eddie Rigg 12+1
Johnny Green 7+1	Ron Mountford 12
Ron Phillips 14	Billy Bales 1
Junior Bainbridge DNR	Jack Hughes 3+2
Dick Campbell DNR	Phil Clarke 0

Friday 21 August 1953 Motherwell
Eagles 43 Poole Pirates 41 (NLD2)

Motherwell	*Poole*
Noel Watson 4+1	Tony Lewis 9
Gordon McGregor 10+1	Ken Middleditch 5+1
Guy Allott 2	Jimmy Squibb 3+1
Ron Phillips 7+1	Bill Holden 9
Bluey Scott 5+2	Terry Small 12
Johnny Green 4	Allan Kidd 0
Scott Hall 5	Buster Brown 0
Cyril Cooper 6	Johnny Thomson 3+1

Saturday 22 August 1953 Edinburgh
Edinburgh Monarchs 8 Eagles 4 (SC)
Abandoned

Edinburgh	Motherwell
Dick Campbell 3	Noel Watson 1
Bob Mark 2+1	Scott Hall 0
Don Cuppleditch 0	Guy Allott 2
Wilf Jay 3	Ron Phillips 1+1
Roy Bester DNR	Bluey Scott DNR
Harold Fairhurst DNR	Johnny Green DNR
John Paul DNR	Cyril Cooper DNR
Harry Darling DNR	Jimmy Tannock DNR

Monday 24 August 1953 Edinburgh
Edinburgh Monarchs 57 Eagles 51 (SC)

Edinburgh	Motherwell
Dick Campbell 10+2	Noel Watson 14
Bob Mark 10	Gordon McGregor 7
Don Cuppleditch 18	Guy Allott 0
Wilf Jay 5+1	Ron Phillips 4+1
Roy Bester 3+2	Bluey Scott 10+2
Harold Fairhurst 9	Johnny Green 5
John Paul 0	Scott Hall 4+2
Harry Darling 2	Cyril Cooper 7+1

Friday 28 August 1953 Motherwell
Glasgow Tigers 61 Edinburgh Monarchs 47 (cc)

Glasgow	Edinburgh
Larry Lazarus 7	Dick Campbell 7+3
Tommy Miller 18	Bob Mark 8
Peter Dykes 1	Don Cuppleditch 14
Ken McKinlay 11	Eddie Lack 1+1
Junior Bainbridge 14+1	Roy Bester 5+1
Don Wilkinson 1	Harold Fairhurst 6+2
Bob Sharp 2	Wilf Jay 3
Doug Templeton 7	Jimmy Cox 3

Friday 28 August 1953 Wolverhampton
Wolverhampton Wasps 48 Eagles 36 (NLD2)

Wolverhampton	Motherwell
Eric Irons 9+1	Noel Watson 2
Jim Tolley 8+2	Gordon McGregor 8+2
Derek Braithwaite 12	Guy Allott 5
Brian Shepherd 4	Ron Phillips 2+1
Ivor Davies 10	Bluey Scott 2
Les Tolley 4+2	Johnny Green 9
Harry Wardropper 0	Cyril Cooper 6+1
Bill Jemison 1	Scott Hall 2+2

Saturday 29 August 1953 Coventry
Coventry Bees 38 Eagles 46 (NLD2)

Coventry	Motherwell
Vic Emms 4+1	Noel Watson 11
Charlie New 7	Gordon McGregor 6+2

Johnny Reason 0	Johnny Green 7+3
Reg Duval 7	Ron Phillips 9+1
Les Hewitt 9+1	Bluey Scott 4
Derek Tailby 3	Cyril Cooper 4+1
Jack Wright 1	Guy Allott 3
Stan Williams 7	Scott Hall 2+1

Tuesday 1 September 1953 Great Yarmouth
Yarmouth Bloaters 61 Eagles 23 (NLD2)

Yarmouth	Motherwell
Fred Brand 12	Noel Watson 2
Roy Bowers 8+4	Gordon McGregor 4
Bob Baker 12	Johnny Green 5
Ronnie Genz 4+1	Ron Phillips 2+2
Arthur Bush 6+2	Bluey Scott 2
Reg Reeves 11+1	Cyril Cooper 1
Terry Courtnell 5+1	Guy Allott 3
Danny Dunton 3	Scott Hall 4

Friday 4 September 1953 Motherwell
Eagles 57 Coventry Bees 27 (NLD2)

Motherwell	Coventry
Noel Watson 11+1	Vic Emms 5
Gordon McGregor 10+2	Jack Wright 0
Johnny Green 6+1	Johnny Reason 7+1
Ron Phillips 7+2	Reg Duval 4
Cyril Cooper 12	Les Hewitt 7
Bluey Scott 1	Derrick Tailby 4+2
Guy Allott 7+2	Stan Williams 0
Scott Hall 3+2	Tommy Anderson 0

Monday 7 September 1953 Motherwell
Eagles 53 Leicester Hunters 30 (NLD2)

Motherwell	Leicester
Noel Watson 4+1	Dennis Parker 3
Gordon McGregor 10+1	Len Williams 10
Johnny Green 8	Charlie Barsby 4
Ron Phillips 10+1	Bill Griffiths 1
Cyril Cooper 8	Lionel Watling 2+2
Guy Allott 7+2	Reg Fearman 6
Jimmy Tannock 3+1	Fred Perkins 0
Scott Hall 3+1	Jack Mountford 4

Friday 11 September 1953 Motherwell
Eagles 50 Edinburgh Monarchs 58 (QC)

Motherwell	Edinburgh
Noel Watson 14	Don Cuppleditch 16
Gordon McGregor 9+2	Eddie Lack 5+1
Johnny Green 7	Bob Mark 8
Ron Phillips 1	Wilf Jay 1
Guy Allott 6+2	Roy Bester 12
Cyril Cooper 4+1	Dick Campbell 11+1
Jimmy Tannock 3+2	Jimmy Cox 3
Scott Hall 6+1	Harry Darling 2

Saturday 12 September 1953 Edinburgh
Edinburgh Monarchs 63 Eagles 45 (QC)

Edinburgh	Motherwell
Don Cuppleditch 17	Noel Watson 5
Eddie Lack 7	Gordon McGregor 10
Bob Mark 7+1	Johnny Green 10+1
Wilf Jay 8	Ron Phillips 7
Roy Bester 6+1	Guy Allott 1+1
Dick Campbell 12+2	Cyril Cooper 3
Jimmy Cox 4	Jimmy Tannock 2+1
Harry Darling 2	Scott Hall 7

Friday 18 September 1953 Motherwell
Eagles 62 Yarmouth Bloaters 32 (NLD2)

Motherwell	Yarmouth
Noel Watson 12	Fred Brand 3
Gordon McGregor 8+4	Arthur Bush 0
Johnny Green 7+2	Bob Baker 1+1
Ron Phillips 11+1	Terry Courtnell 8
Scott Hall 6+2	Ronnie Genz 2
Cyril Cooper 12	Reg Reeves 2
Guy Allott 5+1	Peter Harris 3+1
Jimmy Tannock 1	George White 3

Friday 25 September 1953 Motherwell
Eagles 61 Edinburgh Monarchs 47 (SC)

Motherwell	Edinburgh
Guy Allott 6	Bob Mark 4
Gordon McGregor 7+2	Dick Campbell 12+2
Johnny Green 6+2	Don Cuppleditch 16
Ron Phillips 13	Eddie Lack 2+1
Scott Hall 4+1	Wilf Jay 0
Cyril Cooper 14+1	Roy Bester 10
Bluey Scott 7+1	Jimmy Cox 3
Jimmy Tannock 4+2	Harry Darling 0

Friday 2 October 1953 Motherwell
Eagles 50 Glasgow Tigers 58 (SC)

Motherwell	Glasgow
Guy Allott 9	Larry Lazarus 4
Gordon McGregor 5+3	Tommy Miller 18
Johnny Green 4+1	Ken McKinlay 11+2
Ron Phillips 11	Don Wilkinson 0
Bluey Scott 6+1	Harry Welch 4+1
Cyril Cooper 8+2	J. Bainbridge 15+2
Scott Hall 5	Doug Templeton 5+1
Jimmy Tannock 2+1	Arthur Malm 1

Wednesday 7 October 1953 Glasgow
Glasgow Tigers 65 Eagles 43 (SC)

Glasgow	Motherwell
Larry Lazarus 8	Guy Allott 3+1
Tommy Miller 18	Gordon McGregor 4+3
Ken McKinlay 16+2	Johnny Green 3

Peter Dykes 5+1	Ron Phillips 11+1
Junior Bainbridge 4	Bluey Scott 9
Don Wilkinson 7+3	Cyril Cooper 6+1
Harry Welch 6	Scott Hall 6
Doug Templeton 1	Jimmy Tannock 1+1

Motherwell 1954

Friday 16 April 1954 Motherwell
Eagles 41 Coventry Bees 43 (NS)

Motherwell	Coventry
Gordon McGregor 2+1	Charlie New 12
Tommy Miller 7+1	Johnnie Reason 8
Derick Close 5	Derrek Tailby 2
Bluey Scott 7	Reg Duval 1
Johnny Green 6	Jackie Hughes 1
Ron Phillips 8+1	Vic Emms 7+1
Cyril Cooper 4	Jim Lightfoot 12
Scott Hall 2+1	Peter Brough 0

Saturday 17 April 1954 Edinburgh
Edinburgh Monarchs 43 Eagles 40 (NS)

Edinburgh	Motherwell
Don Cuppleditch 8+2	Gordon McGregor 5
Dick Campbell 11+1	Tommy Miller 8
Bob Mark 10+1	Derick Close 6
Harry Darling 1	Bluey Scott 0
Eddie Lack 8	Johnny Green 9
Jimmy Cox 2	Ron Phillips 5+1
Bert Clark 3+1	Cyril Cooper 4
Jock Scott 0	Scott Hall 3+1

Monday 19 April 1954 Leicester
Leicester Hunters 35 Eagles 49 (NS)

Leicester	Motherwell
Reg Fearman 9	Gordon McGregor 6+1
Don Potter 7+1	Tommy Miller 12
Jack Mountford 0	Derick Close 6+2
Bill Griffiths 3	Bluey Scott 9+3
Charlie Barsby 3+1	Johnny Green 6+1
Jock Grierson 3	Ron Phillips 2
Lionel Watling 6	Cyril Cooper 7
Alf Parker 4+1	Scott Hall 1+1

Friday 23 April 1954 Motherwell
Eagles 58 Glasgow Tigers 25 (NS)

Motherwell	Glasgow
Tommy Miller 12	Ken McKinlay 9
Ron Phillips 10	Larry Lazarus 4
Bluey Scott 7+3	Willie Templeton 1
Johnny Green 3+2	Doug Templeton 1+1
Derick Close 10+1	Bob Sharp 7
Gordon McGregor 6+1	Alf McIntosh 2
Cyril Cooper 6	Vern McWilliams 1

Scott Hall 4+2

Douglas Craig 0

Jock Scott 11
Vic Conners 10
Harry Darling 9
Willie Templeton 8
Arthur Malm 8
Jim Russell 7
Jack Monteith 7
Gordon Mitchell 7
Douglas Craig 4
Bill Finnie 3
Tammy Woods 3
Bob Imrie 1
Joe Ferguson 0
Noble (Bill) McNeil (res) 0

Friday April 30 1954 Motherwell
Eagles 64 Rayleigh Rockets 44 (NT)

Motherwell	Rayleigh
Tommy Miller 13	Gerry Jackson 2
Bluey Scott 4+1	Tom O'Conner 8+3
Johnny Green 5+1	Les McGillivray 10+1
Ron Phillips 10+2	Alby Smith 3
Derick Close 14+2	Peter Clark 7
Gordon McGregor 11+2	Maury McDermott 8
Cyril Cooper 7	Jules Benson 4
Scott Hall 0	Frank Bettis 2+2

Saturday 1 May 1954 Rayleigh
Rayleigh Rockets 65 Eagles 43 (NT)

Rayleigh	Motherwell
Gerry Jackson 12	Tommy Miller 18
Tom O'Conner 9+1	Bluey Scott 6+1
Les McGillivray 8+3	Johnny Green 4
Alby Smith 4+2	Ron Phillips 0
Peter Clark 11+3	Derick Close 8+1
Maury McDermott 11+2	Gordon McGregor 5
Jules Benson 6	Cyril Cooper 0
Frank Bettis 4+2	Scott Hall 2

Friday 7 May 1954 Motherwell
Eagles 55 Ipswich Witches 29 (NS)

Motherwell	Ipswich
Tommy Miller 10	Junior Bainbridge 11
Derick Close 9	Bert Edwards 6
Bluey Scott 5+2	Doug Papworth 1
Gordon McGregor 6+2	Titch Read 2
Cyril Cooper 7+1	Sid Clark 2+1
Ron Phillips 12	Dennis Day 3
Jimmy Tannock 3	John Lawrie 0
Scott Hall 3+1	Len Silver 4

Thursday 13 May 1954 Ipswich
Ipswich Witches 32 Eagles 52 (NS)

Ipswich	Motherwell
Junior Bainbridge 11	Tommy Miller 11
Bert Edwards 8	Derick Close 11
Reg Reeves 0	Bluey Scott 4+1
Tich Read 0	Gordon McGregor 6+3
Sid Clark 6	Johnny Green 4+2
Bob Sharp 5+1	Ron Phillips 7
Dennis Day 1	Cyril Cooper 4+1
Len Silver 1+1	Larry Lazarus 5+1

Friday 14 May 1954 Motherwell
Scottish Junior Championship
Scott Hall 15
Jimmy Tannock 13
Doug Templeton 14

Friday 14 May 1954 Wolverhampton
Wolverhampton Wasps 28 Eagles 56 (NS)

Wolverhampton	Motherwell
Jim Tolley 6	Tommy Miller 12
Les Tolley 7+1	Derick Close 11+1
Eric Irons 5+1	Bluey Scott 5+2
Derek Braithwaite 0	Gordon McGregor 8+2
Henry Serrurier 3	Johnny Green 6+2
Phil Malpass 2	Ron Phillips 7+1
George McPherson 0	Cyril Cooper 6
Vern McWilliams 5	Larry Lazarus 1

Saturday 15 May 1954 Coventry
Coventry Bees 40 Eagles 43 (NS)

Coventry	Motherwell
Charlie New 11	Tommy Miller 10
Vic Emms 9	Derick Close 8
Peter Brough 0	Bluey Scott 3+2
Jackie Hughes 5+2	Gordon McGregor 0
Johnny Reason 7	Johnny Green 2+1
Jack Wright 4	Ron Phillips 8+1
Derek Tailby 1	Cyril Cooper 10
Jim Lightfoot 3	Larry Lazarus 2+1

Monday 17 May 1954 Motherwell
Eagles 66 Leicester Hunters 18 (NS)

Motherwell	Leicester
Tommy Miller 10+1	Ken McKinlay 7
Derick Close 11+1	Reg Fearman 1
Bluey Scott 9+2	Lionel Watling 0
Gordon McGregor 6+2	Charlie Barsby 3
Johnny Green 10+2	Don Potter 2
Ron Phillips 9+3	Jock Grierson 0
Cyril Cooper 5+1	Bill Griffiths 1
Larry Lazarus 6	Dennis Gray 4

119

Friday 21 May 1954 Motherwell
Eagles 64 Wimbledon Dons 44 (Ch)

Motherwell	Wimbledon
Tommy Miller 16	Ronnie Moore 13
Derick Close 4	Geoff Mardon 13
Bluey Scott 6+3	Reg Trott 0
Gordon McGregor 7+2	Cyril Brine 2
Johnny Green 11+1	Barry Briggs 8
Ron Phillips 12+2	Dom Perry 3
Larry Lazarus 4	Bill Longley 5
Cyril Cooper 4	Cyril Maidment 0

Friday 28 May 1954 Motherwell
Eagles versus Wolverhampton Wasps (NT)
Meeting cancelled. Wasps closed down.

Friday 4 June 1954 Motherwell
Eagles 55 Edinburgh Monarchs 29 (NS)

Motherwell	Edinburgh
Tommy Miller 12	Dick Campbell 7
Derick Close 7+2	Don Cuppleditch 7
Bluey Scott 7+1	Bob Mark 1+1
Gordon McGregor 7	Eddie Lack 1
Johnny Green 4	Roy Bester 7+1
Ron Phillips 10+1	Bob Fletcher 4+1
Cyril Cooper 2+1	Alf McIntosh 2+1
Larry Lazarus 6	Jimmy Cox 0

Friday 11 June 1954 Motherwell
Skelly Trophy
Dick Campbell 15
Tommy Miller 14
Derick Close 11
Don Cuppleditch 10
Ron Phillips 10
Junior Bainbridge 8
Cyril Cooper 8
Gordon McGregor 7
Larry Lazarus 7
Bluey Scott 6
Roy Bester 6
Doug Templeton 5
Scott Hall 5
Bob Mark 4
Bob Sharp 3
Johnny Green 2

Friday 18 June 1954 Motherwell
Eagles 62 Rayleigh Rockets 22 (NLD2)

Motherwell	Rayleigh
Tommy Miller 11+1	Peter Clarke 8
Derick Close 12	Gerry Jackson 4
Bluey Scott 7+2	Frank Bettis 2+2
Gordon McGregor 5+2	Eric Ebbs 0
Johnny Green 11	Maurie McDermott 4

Ron Phillips 7+4   Les McGillivray 2
Cyril Cooper 3+1   Jules Benson 2
Larry Lazarus 6   Ken Monk 0

Friday 25 June 1954 Motherwell
Eagles 44 Poole Pirates 40 (NLD2)

Motherwell	Poole
Tommy Miller 7	Ken Middleditch 7+2
Derick Close 10	Terry Small 5+1
Bluey Scott 4+1	Allan Kidd 5+2
Gordon McGregor 0	Bill Holden 8+1
Johnny Green 1	Tony Lewis 5+1
Ron Phillips 12	Jimmy Squibb 6
Cyril Cooper 4+1	Johnny Thomson 4+1
Larry Lazarus 6+2	Vern McWilliams 0

Friday 2 July 1954 Motherwell
Eagles 58 Exeter Falcons 26 (NLD2)

Motherwell	Exeter
Tommy Miller 12	Jack Geran 6+1
Derick Close 11+1	Goog Hoskin 4
Bluey Scott 7+1	Don Hardy 0
Larry Lazarus 4+1	Jack Hart 5+1
Johnny Green 9	Neil Street 7
Ron Phillips 8+2	Johnny Sargent 1
Gordon McGregor 1	Hugh Geddes 3+1
Cyril Cooper 6	Alf Webster 0

Friday 9 July 1954 Motherwell
World Championship Qualifying Round
Derick Close 14
Tommy Miller 13
Dick Campbell 12
Johnny Green 12
Ron Phillips 11
Ron Clarke 9
Bluey Scott 8
Cyril Cooper 8
Charlie New 8
Dick Fisher 6
Bob Fletcher 5
Vic Emms 5
Gordon McGregor 5
Danny Dunton 2
Eddie Lack 0
Cyril Maidment 2

Thursday 15 July 1954 Oxford
Oxford Cheetahs 51 Eagles 33 (NLD2)

Oxford	Motherwell
Peter Robinson 11	Tommy Miller 2
Ronnie Genz 11	Derick Close 11
Bob McFarlane 2+1	Bluey Scott 5+1
Bob Baker 7+4	Gordon McGregor 2
Bob Wells 2+1	Johnny Green 6
Fred Curtis 11	Ron Phillips 4+1

Bill Osborne 3+1
Jim Gregory 4

Larry Lazarus 3
Cyril Cooper 0

Friday 16 July 1954 Bristol
Bristol Bulldogs 59 Eagles 25 (NLD2)

Bristol
Dick Bradley 7+1
Jack Unstead 11
Geoff Pymar9+2
Chris Boss 5+2
Billy Hole 9+1
John Hole 9
Chum Taylor 4+2
Tom Oakley 5+1

Motherwell
Tommy Miller 11
Derick Close 4
Bluey Scott 1
Larry Lazarus 0
Johnny Green 3
Ron Phillips 1
Cyril Cooper 1
Gordon McGregor 4+1

Saturday 17 July 1954 Swindon
Swindon Robins 49 Eagles 17 (NLD2)
Abandoned rain

Swindon
Bob Roger 7+2
Ian Williams 9
George White 7+2
Ron Swaine 7+2
Danny Malone 3+1
Mick Holland 9
Ray Harris 2
Gordon Leigh 5+1

Motherwell
Tommy Miller 1
Derick Close 1
Bluey Scott 3
Larry Lazarus 1
Johnny Green 4+1
Ron Phillips 0
Cyril Cooper 3
Gordon McGregor 4

Monday 19 July 1954 Motherwell
Eagles 50 Bristol Bulldogs 34 (NLD2)

Motherwell
Tommy Miller 7
Derick Close 10
Bluey Scott 8+1
Larry Lazarus 3+1
Johnny Green 3
Ron Phillips 9
Cyril Cooper 6
Gordon McGregor 4+1

Bristol
Dick Bradley 10
Jack Unstead 1
Geoff Pymar 2
Johnny Hole 8
Billy Hole 3
Chris Boss 3
Chum Taylor 4
Henry Serrurier 0

Friday 23 July 1954 Motherwell
Eagles versus Swindon Robins (NLD2)
Rained off

Friday 30 July 1954 Motherwell
Scotland 47 England 61 (Test match)

Scotland
Derick Close 17
Bluey Scott 7+3
Tommy Miller 4
Don Cuppleditch 0
Johnny Green 7
Ron Phillips 5
Cyril Cooper (res) 7
Larry Lazarus (res) 0

England
Eddie Rigg 5+1
Arthur Wright 11
Spit Waterman 14+2
Peter Craven 11+3
Alan Hunt 14+1
Ron Mountford 1
Eric Boothroyd (res) 5
Ron Clarke (res) 0

Saturday 7 August 1954 Coventry
Coventry Bees 57 Eagles 27 (NLD2)

Coventry
Charlie New 12
Tommy Miller 12
Les Tolley 5+2
Vic Emms 5+2
Jim Lightfoot 7+1
Reg Duval 5+1
Jonnie Reason 5+1
Bob Mark 6

Motherwell
Derick Close 9
Ron Phillips 2+1
Bluey Scott 3
Johnny Green 3+1
Gordon McGregor 4+1
Cyril Cooper 4
Larry Lazarus 2+1
Doug Templeton 0

Monday 9 August 1954 Poole
Poole Pirates 51 Eagles 33 (NLD2)

Poole
Ken Middleditch 8.5
Johnny Thomson 4+2
Alan Kidd 6+1
Terry Small 5
Tony Lewis 11+1
Jimmy Squibb 9+1
Vern McWilliams 3+1
Norman Strachan 4.5

Motherwell
Derick Close 9+1
Ron Phillips 7.5
Bluey Scott 3+1
Johnny Green 3+1
Gordon McGregor 3
Cyril Cooper 4.5
Larry Lazarus 3
Doug Templeton 0

Tuesday 10 August 1954 Southampton
Southampton Saints 54 Eagles 30 (NLD2)

Southampton
Brian McKeown 3
Charlie May 8+2
Ernie Brecknell 5+1
John Fitzpatrick 11+1
Ken Adams 4+2
Ernie Rawlins 11+1
Maurie Mattingly 3+1
Merv Hanham 9

Motherwell
Derick Close 6+1
Ron Phillips 3+2
Bluey Scott 6+1
Johnny Green 5+1
Gordon McGregor 6
Cyril Cooper 1
Larry Lazarus 3+1
Doug Templeton 0

Friday 13 August 1954 Motherwell
Eagles 58 Oxford Cheetahs 26 (NLD2)

Motherwell
Derick Close 11+1
Ron Phillips 11+1
Bluey Scott 9+3
Johnny Green 5+1
Cyril Cooper 4
Gordon McGregor 8
Larry Lazarus 6
Doug Templeton 4+2

Oxford
Peter Robinson 5
Ronnie Genz 5+1
Bob McFarlane 0
Bob Baker 4+2
Bill Thatcher 3+1
Fred Curtis 1
Bob Wells 2
Frank Johnson 2

Friday 20 August 1954 Motherwell
Eagles 63 Southampton Saints 21 (NLD2)

Motherwell
Derick Close 9+1
Ron Phillips 10+2
Bluey Scott 0

Southampton
Brian McKeown 7+1
Merv Hanham 2
Ernie Brecknell 4+1

121

Johnny Green 9+1
Cyril Cooper 8+1
Gordon McGregor 11+1
Larry Lazarus 11+1
Doug Templeton 5+2

John Fitzpatrick 2
Ken Adams 2
Ernie Rawlins 3
Maurie Mattingly 0
Gerald Pugh 0

Saturday 21 August 1954 Rayleigh
Rayleigh Rockets 49 Eagles 35 (NLD2)

Rayleigh	*Motherwell*
Gerry Jackson 10+1	Derick Close 10
Les McGillivray 12	Ron Phillips 9
Jules Benson 3	Eric Ebbs 3+2
George Wall 4	Johnny Green 1
Maury McDermott 8	Cyril Cooper 2
Tom O'Conner 6	Gordon McGregor 8
Alby Smith 2+1	Larry Lazarus 1
Ron Howes 4	Doug Templeton 1

Thursday 26 August 1954 Ipswich
Ipswich Witches 55 Eagles 29 (NLD2)

Ipswich	*Motherwell*
Junior Bainbridge 11	Derick Close 9
Bert Edwards 11	Ron Phillips 8
Tich Read 2+1	Bob Fletcher 1
Johnny Chamberlain 5+2	Johnny Green 0
Dick Campbell 12	Cyril Cooper 0
Reg Reeves 4	Gordon McGregor 6
Len Silver 3+1	Larry Lazarus 5+1
Bob Sharp 6	Doug Templeton 0

Friday 27 August 1954 Leicester
Leicester Hunters 54 Eagles 30 (NLD2)

Leicester	*Motherwell*
Ken McKinlay 8+1	Derick Close 9
Roy Bester 12	Ron Phillips 5
Dennis Gray 8+1	Bob Fletcher 3+2
Charlie Barsby 2	Johnny Green 3+1
Jock Grierson 9	Cyril Cooper 0
Len Williams 5	Gordon McGregor 5
Reg Fearman 4+1	Larry Lazarus 3
Bill Griffiths 6	Doug Templeton 2

Monday 30 August 1954 Exeter
Exeter Falcons 57 Eagles 27 (NLD2)

Exeter	*Motherwell*
Jack Geran 5+2	Derick Close 6
Goog Hoskin 11+1	Ron Phillips 6
Jack Hart 11+1	Bob Fletcher 0
Neil Street 9+1	Johnny Green 3+1
Hugh Geddes 8+1	Cyril Cooper 1
Johnny Sargent 8+2	Gordon McGregor 6
Kevin Bock 3	Larry Lazarus 5
Jack Cunningham 2	Doug Templeton 0

Friday 3 September 1954 Motherwell
Eagles 49 Swindon Robins 35 (NLD2)

Motherwell	*Swindon*
Derick Close 12	Bob Roger 1+1
Ron Phillips 8+1	Ian Williams 6+1
Larry Lazarus 3+1	George White 7+1
Johnny Green 6	Mick Holland 4
Cyril Cooper 7+1	Ron Swaine 9
Gordon McGregor 10+1	Danny Malone 3
Bob Fletcher 2+1	Bob Jones 2
Doug Templeton 1	Ray Harris 3

Friday 10 September 1954 Motherwell
Eagles versus Ipswich Witches (NLD2)
Rained off

Monday 13 September 1954 Motherwell
Eagles 23 Leicester Hunters 25 (NLD2)
Abandoned

Motherwell	*Leicester*
Bob Fletcher 2+1	Ken McKinlay 3
Ron Phillips 3	Roy Bester 3
Larry Lazarus 2	Dennis Gray 2
Johnny Green 6	Bill Griffiths 3
Cyril Cooper 6	Jock Grierson 1+1
Gordon McGregor 1	Len Williams 5
Scott Hall 0	Reg Fearman 5
Doug Templeton 3	Bryan Elliot 3+1

Friday 17 September 1954 Motherwell
Eagles 44 Coventry Bees 40 (NLD2)

Motherwell	*Coventry*
Bob Fletcher 3+2	Charlie New 8+1
Ron Phillips 8	Tommy Miller 10
Larry Lazarus 8	Bob Mark 3
Johnny Green 6+1	Vic Emms 6+1
Cyril Cooper 7+1	Johnny Reason 2
Gordon McGregor 8	Jim Lightfoot 7
Scott Hall 3	Reg Duval 1
Doug Templeton 1	Jack Wright 3

Friday 1 October 1954 Motherwell (Rained off)
Eagles versus Ipswich Witches (NLD2)

Friday 8 October 1954 Motherwell
Eagles 45 Ipswich Witches 39 (NLD2)

Motherwell	*Ipswich*
Derick Close 9+1	Junior Bainbridge 4+1
Ron Phillips 7+1	Bert Edwards 10
Larry Lazarus 3	Bob Sharp 2+1
Johnny Green 6+1	Tich Read 3+1
Cyril Cooper 8+1	Dick Campbell 12
Gordon McGregor 7+1	Reg Reeves 4
Bluey Scott 3	J. Chamberlain 4+1
Doug Templeton 2	John Lawrie 0

Motherwell 1958

Friday 16 May 1958 Motherwell
Golden Eagles 50 Belle Vue Babes 27 (Ch)

Motherwell
Doug Templeton 9+2
Willie Templeton 10+2
Red Monteith 6+1
Fred Greenwell 11
Jimmy Tannock 0
Jock Scott 3+2
George Hunter 11+1

Belle Vue
Jack Kitchen 8
Roy Swift 0
Graham Beattie 10
Bob McHugh 0
Tink Maynard 3+1
Derek Jenkins 5
Bert Edwards 1

Friday 30 May 1958 Motherwell
Golden Eagles 41 Coventry Select 35 (Ch)

Motherwell
Doug Templeton 12
Willie Templeton 3
Fred Greenwell 11
Red Monteith 5+3
Jimmy Tannock 3+2
George Hunter 7+1
Gordon Mitchell 0

Coventry
Brian Meredith 11
Bill McGregor 2
Alan Pearce 1
Norman Unger 4
Eric Eadon 3+1
Colin Gooddy 9
Rick France 1+1

Friday 13 June 1958 Motherwell
Golden Eagles 48 Bradford 30 (Ch)

Motherwell
Doug Templeton 11
Jimmy Tannock 4+1
Fred Greenwell 5+1
Red Monteith 7+1
Willie Templeton 7
George Hunter 8+2
Gordon Mitchell 6

Bradford
Jack Kitchen 16
Malcolm Bruce 2
Jimmy Cramb 2
Roy Swift 0
Stan Holey 4
Vic Lonsdale 1
Peter Thomson 5

Friday 27 June 1958 Motherwell
Golden Eagles v Leicester Hunters (Ch)
Rained off

Friday 4 July 1958 Motherwell
Golden Eagles 40 Leicester Hunters 37 (Ch)

Motherwell
Doug Templeton 6
Jimmy Tannock 3+1
Fred Greenwell 10
Red Monteith 2+1
Willie Templeton 8+2
George Hunter 4+1
Gordon Mitchell 7

Leicester
Brian Meredith 7
Mike Lawrence 0
Cliff Newton 12
Jimmy Gleed 1
Noel Conway 8+1
Colin Gooddy 6+2
Tony Eadon 3

Friday 11 July 1958 Motherwell
Golden Eagles 43 Ipswich Witches 34 (Ch)

Motherwell
Doug Templeton 10+1
Gordon Mitchell 8+1
Willie Templeton 7
George Hunter 1
Fred Greenwell 10
Red Monteith 5+2
Jimmy Tannock 2+1

Ipswich
Brian Larner 5+1
Ray Harrison 3
Ken Last 8+1
Shorty Schirmer 8+1
Ronnie Rolfe 9
Bob Sanderson 1+1
Vic Lonsdale 0

Motherwell 1972

2 January 1972 Motherwell Raceway
Long Track 680 yards.
Golden Eagle Trophy

Ivan Mauger 15
Bobby Beaton 13
Alan Wilkinson 12
Barry Briggs 11
Taffy Owen 10
Doug Templeton 9
Don Godden 9
Eric Broadbelt 8
Jim Beaton 7
John Wilson 7
Dave Gifford 5
Ian Paterson 3
George Beaton 2
Bobby Duncan 2
Harry MacLean 2
Allan Emmerson 2
Kenny Omand (Res) 2
Walter Robertson (Res) 1

Sunday 2 April 1972
Motherwell Raceway Long Track
Duckham's Silver Cup

Garry Middleton 15
Reidar Eide 13
George Hunter 13
Jimmy McMillan 11
Martin Ashby 9
Barry Briggs 9
Willie Templeton 7
Bert Harkins 7
John Wilson 6
Douglas Templeton 6
Dave Gifford 6
Roy Trigg 6
Bernie Persson 5
Frank Skinner 2
Harry McLean 2
Derek Allan 2

Sunday 7 May 1972
Motherwell Raceway Long Track
Champion of Champions

George Hunter DNR
Ronnie Moore
Bob Valentine
Oyvind Berg
Ray Wilson
Eric Boocock DNR
Bert Harkins
Julian Wigg
Bernie Persson
Preben Rosenkilde
Garry Middleton
Reidar Eide
Graeme Stapleton
Doug Templeton
Jim Clark
Harry McLean
Jim McMillan
Reserves:
John Wilson
Sandy Cook
Tom Blackwood

Champions of Champions

Ht 1 R. Wilson, Moore, Stapleton, Cook, [McLean, Wigg 80.2
Ht 2 Eide, Valentine, Middleton, D Templeton, Clark, Boocock (ns) 80.8
Ht 3 Rosenkilde, Persson, McMillan, Harkins, [Berg, W Templeton 79.8
Ht 4 McMillan, Stapleton, Clark, J Wilson, Eide, Hunter (ns) 80.0
Ht 5 Rosenkilde, Persson, Valentine, R Wilson, [D Templeton, McLean 81.4
Ht 6 Middleton, Moore, Harkins, W Templeton, Berg, Boocock (ns) 81.4
Ht 7 McMillan, Rosenkilde, Persson, R Wilson, [Clark, Stapleton 79.6
Ht 8 Middleton, Harkins, W Templeton, J.Wilson, [Berg, Valentine 80.4
Ht9 D Templeton, Cook, Moore (et), Blackwood (et), [Wigg, Eide 93.2
SF 1 Rosenkilde, Persson, Clark, D Templeton, Moore (et), Eide (ns) 81.4
SF 2 McMillan, Middleton, Stapleton, Harkins, Cook, W Templeton (ns) 80.0
F McMillan, Rosenkilde, Persson, Stapleton, Clarke, Middleton (f) 81.2

Bahnrekord First Stage
Bob Valentine
Julian Wigg
Prreben Rosenkilde
Graeme Stapleton

Doug Templeton
Jim Clark
Harry McLean
Willie Templeton

Bahnrekord Second Stage
Ray Wilson
Eric Boocock fell
Ronnie Moore
Oyvind Berg
Bernie Persson

Bahnrekord Third Stage
Reidar Eide
Bert Harkins
George Hunter fell
Jimmy McMillan
Garry Middleton

Monday 15 May 1972
Motherwell Raceway Speedway
Golden Eagles v Barrow Bays (Ch)
Rained off

Programmed teams
Motherwell: Malcolm McKay, Harry McLean, Lou Sansom, Tom Blackwood, Kym Amundson, Frank Skinner, Mitch Graham.

Barrow: Mike Watkin, Geoff Lyon, Ian Hindle, Tom Owen, Alan Mackie, Bob Campbell, John Wilson.

Thursday 28 May 1972
Holker Street Stadium, Barrow
Barrow Happy Faces 45 Motherwell 33 (Ch)

Barrow	*Motherwell*
Mike Watkin 9+1	John Jackson 12
John Wilson 7+1	Harry McLean 2
Ian Hindle 9+1	Dai Evans 10
Bob Campbell 6+3	Frank Skinner 2
Tom Owen 8+1	Tom Blackwood 3
Allan Mackie 3	George Wells 0
Geoff Lyon 3+ 1	Alec Nicol 5+2

Friday 29 May 1972
Motherwell Raceway Speedway
Golden Eagles v Barrow Bays (Ch)
Rained off

Programmed teams as per 15 May

Monday 5 June 1972
Motherwell Raceway Speedway
Golden Eagles v Barrow Bays (Ch)
Rained off

Programmed Teams as per 15 May

Monday 12 June 1972
Motherwell Raceway Speedway
Golden Eagles 33 Teeside Tigers 42 (Ch)

Motherwell
Russ Dent 4+1
Harry McLean 6
Jack Millen 9
Frank Skinner 4
Tom Blackwood 2
Alec Nichol 7
Roy Young 1+1

Teeside
Dave Durham 2+2
Tony Swales (Ty) 10
Frank Auffret 4
Mick Moore 8
Pete Reading 0
Tim Swales (Tm) 15
George Wells 2+1

The name Lanarkshire Eagles was revived at
Blantyre's Craighead Park at the end of the 1982
season when they raced against the Cumbrians and
Ayr Rebels in a three team tournament.

Cumbrians
Steve Lawson 9
Jackson Irving 2+2
Des Wilson 5+1
Geoff Powell 4
Bobby Beaton 2

Lanarkshire Eagles
Bobby Beaton 9
Jim Beaton 4+3
Harry McLean 9
David Cassels 2+2

Ayr Rebels
Kenny McKinna 12
Kenny Brailsford 2
Colin Caffrey 11
Tam Bagley 0

In 2003 a printer's slip up saw the Workington Junior
team Mothersall Eagles being programmed as
Motherwell Eagles at Armadale.

Appendix 2: Riders' averages and league tables

Riders Statistics 1951

National League	M	R	P	B	T	CMA
Derick Close	11	44	103	9	112	10.18
Gordon McGregor	29	116	239	18	257	8.86
Keith Gurtner	30	120	238	17	255	8.50
Noel Watson	29	116	201	16	217	7.48
Joe Crowther	26	94	133	15	148	6.29
Bill Dalton	29	101	120	19	139	5.50
Will Lowther	28	99	115	17	132	5.33
Stan Bradbury	27	75	80	15	95	5.07
Bluey Scott	11	27	28	3	31	4.59
Scott Hall	1	2	1	1	2	4.00
Bob Lindsay	8	21	11	2	13	2.48
Danny Lee	8	17	9	1	10	2.35

Maximums: Keith Gurtner 6 (1 Full 2 Paid H, 3 Full A); Derick Close 3 (1 Full 1 Paid H, 1 Paid A); Gordon McGregor 3 (2 Full 1 Paid H); Joe Crowther 3 (1 Full 1 Paid H, 1 Paid A); Noel Watson 2 (1 Full 1 Paid H); Will Lowther 1 Paid H.

North Shield	M	R	P	B	T	CMA
Gordon McGregor	10	40	97	0	97	9.70
Noel Watson	10	40	77	2	79	7.90
Joe Crowther	8	32	64	1	65	8.13
Danny Lee	3	12	16	3	19	6.33
Will Lowther	10	40	40	4	44	4.40
Stan Bradbury	7	25	20	2	22	3.52
Bill Baird	10	28	17	1	18	2.57
Malcolm Riddell	4	9	3	1	4	1.78
Bob Lindsay	9	32	12	1	13	1.63
Harry Andrews	3	8	3	0	3	1.50
Bluey Scott	6	14	3	0	3	0.86

Maximums: Gordon McGregor 4 (3 Full H 1 Full A); Joe Crowther 1 Full Away.

National Trophy	M	R	P	B	T	CMA
Bill Dalton	1	5	8	1	9	7.20
Noel Watson	2	12	20	1	21	7.00
Gordon McGregor	2	12	18	1	19	6.33
Will Lowther	2	10	10	1	11	4.40
Bob Lindsay	2	4	4	0	4	4.00
Joe Crowther	2	9	5	2	7	3.10
Stan Bradbury	2	7	3	0	3	1.71
Harry Andrews	1	2	0	0	0	0.00
Bill Baird	2	9	0	0	0	0.00

Maximums: None

Riders Statistics 1952

National League	M	R	P	B	T	CMA
Derick Close	43	171	444	8	452	10.57
Gordon McGregor	44	176	330	29	359	8.16
Noel Watson	39	156	278	16	294	7.54
Keith Gurtner	30	120	201	15	216	7.20
Johnny Green	7	26	39	0	39	6.00
Will Lowther	44	145	167	33	200	5.52
Stan Bradbury	25	78	82	22	104	5.33
Joe Crowther	12	40	41	7	48	4.80
Bluey Scott	44	142	126	21	147	4.14
Niven McCreadie	3	6	3	2	5	3.33
Scott Hall	37	117	83	14	97	3.32
Bob Lindsay	23	52	32	7	39	3.00

Maximums: Derick Close 20 (9 Full 4 Paid H, 7 Full A); Gordon McGregor 9 (4 Full 5 Paid H); Noel Watson 4 (2 Full 2 Paid H); Keith Gurtner 1 Full A.

National Trophy	M	R	P	B	T	CMA
Derick Close	2	12	29	1	30	10.00
Gordon McGregor	2	11	18	1	19	6.91
Stan Bradbury	2	10	13	3	16	6.40
Joe Crowther	2	7	9	1	10	5.71
Bluey Scott	2	7	8	1	9	5.14
Noel Watson	2	11	13	1	14	5.09
Will Lowther	2	9	5	2	7	3.11
Keith Gurtner	1	2	1	0	1	2.00
Scott Hall	1	3	1	0	1	1.33

Maximums: Derek Close 1 Paid H.

Riders Statistics 1953

National League	M	R	P	B	T	CMA
Derick Close	18	72	175.5	3	178.5	9.91
Cyril Cooper	7	24	49	2	51	8.50
Gordon McGregor	32	128	240	30	270	8.44
Ron Phillips	32	128	210.5	20	230.5	7.20
Noel Watson	32	119	185	18	203	6.82
Johnny Green	32	125	186	21	209	6.69
Guy Allott	13	40	52	6	58	5.80
Scott Hall	29	73	71	16	87	4.77
Bill Dalton	2	5	5	0	5	4.00
Jock Pryde	1	2	2	0	2	4.00
Bluey Scott	30	117	96	19	115	3.93
Jimmy Tannock	26	60	39	9	48	3.20

Maximums: Derick Close 7 (4 Full 2 Paid H, 1 Full A); Gordon McGregor 4 Paid H; Cyril Cooper 2 Full H; Ron Phillips 4 (1 Full 3 Paid H); Noel Watson 3 (2 Full 1 Paid H); Johnny Green 2 (1 Full 1 Paid H);

National Trophy	M	R	P	B	T	CMA
Derick Close	6	35	87	4	91	10.40
Gordon McGregor	6	33	59	11	70	8.48
Johnny Green	6	30	49	6	55	7.33

Ron Phillips	6	32	53	5	58	7.25
Noel Watson	6	30	38	3	41	5.46
Scott Hall	4	10	8	1	9	5.20
Jimmy Tannock	6	13	12	4	16	4.92
Joe Crowther	2	6	6	0	6	4.00
Bill Dalton	1	3	3	0	3	4.00
Bluey Scott	6	27	16	4	20	2.96

Maximums: Derick Close 2 (1 Paid H, 1 Full A); Gordon McGregor 1 Paid H; Ron Phillips 1 Paid H; Johnny Green 1 Paid H.

Riders Statistics 1954

National League*	M	R	P	B	T	CMA
Derick Close	18	71	158	7	165	9.30
Tommy Miller	7	27	51	1	52	7.70
Ron Phillips	19	74	125.5	15	140.5	7.59
Gordon McGregor	19	70	102	8	110	6.29
Larry Lazarus	19	56	76	9	85	6.07
Scott Hall	1	2	3	0	3	6.00
Bluey Scott	13	47	59	11	70	5.96
Johnny Green	19	71	87	10	97	5.46
Eric Ebbs**	1	4	3	2	5	5.00
Cyril Cooper	19	61	69.5	6	75.5	4.95
Doug Templeton	12	25	16	4	20	3.20
Bob Fletcher	5	18	9	5	14	3.11

Maximums: Derick Close 4 (3 Full 1 Paid H); Ron Phillips 3 (1 Full 2 Paid H); Tommy Miller 2 (1 Full 1 Paid H); Gordon McGregor 1 Paid H; Bluey Scott 1 Paid H; Larry Lazarus 1 Paid H.
*Fixtures not completed Home v Leicester not raced; Away at Swindon abandoned but score stands.
** On Loan from Rayleigh.

North Shield	M	R	P	B	T	CMA
Larry Lazarus	4	8	19	2	21	10.50
Tommy Miller	8	32	80	2	82	10.25
Ron Phillips	8	31	61	7	68	8.77
Cyril Cooper	8	22	43	4	47	8.55
Derick Close	8	32	63	5	68	8.50
Bluey Scott	8	31	44	11	55	7.10
Johnny Green	7	27	41	6	47	6.96
Scott Hall	4	8	9	4	13	6.50
Gordon McGregor	8	31	38	9	47	6.06
Jimmy Tannock	1	2	3	0	3	6.00

Maximums: Tommy Miller 2 (1 Full H, 1 Full A); Ron Phillips 2 (1 Full 1 Paid H); Derick Close 1 Paid H; Bluey Scott 1 Paid A; Johnny Green 1 Paid H.

National Trophy	M	R	P	B	T	CMA
Tommy Miller	2	12	31	0	31	10.33
Derick Close	2	12	22	3	25	8.33
Gordon McGregor	2	10	16	2	18	7.20
Cyril Cooper	2	5	7	0	7	5.60
Ron Phillips	2	9	10	2	12	5.33
Bluey Scott	2	9	10	2	12	5.33
Johnny Green	2	9	9	1	10	4.44

| Scott Hall | 2 | 6 | 2 | 0 | 2 | 1.33 |

Maximums: Tommy Miller 1 Full A.

League Tables 1951

National League Division Two

Team	R	W	D	L	F	A	Pts
Norwich	30	24	0	6	1526	990	48
Leicester	30	19	0	11	1350	1169	38
Edinburgh	30	18	0	12	1333	1179	36
Coventry	30	16	3	11	1311	1199	35
Walthamstow	30	17	0	13	1394	1116	34
Halifax	30	17	0	13	1300	1219	34
Motherwell	**30**	**16**	**1**	**13**	**1277**	**1237**	**33**
Ashfield	30	16	0	14	1287	1228	32
Stoke (Hanley)	30	15	0	15	1242	1268	30
White City (Glasgow)	30	14	1	15	1303	1215	29
Yarmouth	30	13	1	16	1158	1355	27
Oxford	30	12	2	16	1183	1330	26
Liverpool	30	12	1	17	1211	1300	25
Fleetwood	30	9	2	19	1049	1453	20
Cradley Heath	30	9	0	21	1138	1372	19
Newcastle	30	7	1	22	1039	1472	15

North Shield

Team	R	W	D	L	F	A	Pts
Edinburgh	10	9	0	1	537	297	18
White City (Glasgow)	10	7	0	3	441	394	14
Newcastle	10	5	0	5	435	404	10
Motherwell	**10**	**4**	**0**	**6**	**352**	**481**	**8**
Ashfield	10	3	0	7	402	434	6
Fleetwood	10	2	0	8	339	500	4

League Table 1952

National League Division Two

Team	R	W	D	L	F	A	Pts
Poole	44	31	1	12	2217	1477	63
Coventry	44	25	5	14	1938	1756	55
Leicester	44	25	2	17	1882	1808	52
Cradley Heath	44	24	0	20	1870	1821	48
White City (Glasgow)	44	23	1	20	1837	1853	47
Edinburgh	44	21	4	19	1926	1763	46
Ashfield	44	19	3	22	1749	1940	41
Motherwell	**44**	**19**	**2**	**23**	**1825**	**1861**	**40**
Yarmouth	44	20	0	24	1812	1883	40
Stoke	44	18	1	25	1774	1916	37
Liverpool	44	16	3	25	1726	1967	35
Oxford	44	11	2	31	1587	2101	24

League Table 1953

National League Division Two

Team	R	W	D	L	F	A	Pts
Coventry	32	19	1	12	1394	1290	39
Poole	32	18	2	12	1492	1192	38
Yarmouth	32	18	0	14	1403	1281	36
White City (Glasgow)	32	16	2	14	1423.5	1262.5	34
Edinburgh	32	15	1	16	1349.5	1333.5	31
Motherwell	**32**	**15**	**0**	**17**	**1313**	**1366**	**30**
Wolverhampton	32	13	1	18	1282	1401	27
Leicester	32	13	1	18	1207	1476	27
Stoke	32	12	2	18	1210	1472	26

League Tables 1954

National League Division Two

Team	R	W	D	L	F	A	Pts
Bristol	20	14	0	6	908.5	769.5	28
Poole	20	12	0	8	896.5	781.5	24
Swindon	20	11	0	9	870	789	22
Leicester	19	11	0	8	829	765	22
Ipswich	20	10	0	10	873	806	20
Exeter	20	10	0	10	851	827	20
Oxford	20	10	0	10	807	868	20
Coventry	20	10	0	10	807	869	20
Southampton	20	9	0	11	800	878	18
Motherwell	**19**	**9**	**0**	**10**	**759**	**819**	**18**
Rayleigh	20	4	0	16	725	854	8

North Shield

Team	R	W	D	L	F	A	Pts
Motherwell	**8**	**6**	**0**	**2**	**401**	**269**	**12**
Coventry	8	5	1	2	365	307	11
Edinburgh	8	3	1	4	307	364	7
Ipswich	8	3	0	5	307	364	6
Leicester	8	2	0	6	298	375	4

Appendix 3: Riders' Other meetings

The following is a rider by rider record of meetings raced by Motherwell based riders as individuals in the period 1950 to 1954. The team in bold type is the one they rode for in the event.

Derick Close

Venue	Event	Date	Scores	Total
White City	**Rest/Scotland** v Scots Australians	12 Sep 1951	1' 2 1 2	6+1
Edinburgh	**Scotland** v England	15 Sep 1951	0 3 0 3 3 3	12
Ashfield	Ken Le Breton Memorial Trophy	6 Oct 1951	3 0 1 2	6
Fleetwood	**Fleetwood** v Stoke	6 May 1952	3 3 3 2'	11+1
Stoke	**Britain** v Overseas	15 May 1952	1' 3 2' 2 1 2'	11+3
White City	**Scotland** v England	28 May 1952	3 2 2 E F 3	10
Coventry	England v **Scotland**	16 Jun 1952	2 X 1 3 3 1	10
Fleetwood	**Fleetwood** v Ashfield	25 Jun 1952	3 0 3 3	9
Fleetwood	**Fleetwood** v Liverpool	2 Jul 1952	3 3 3 2' 3 3	17+1
Oxford	**Britain** v Overseas	3 Jul 1952	3 2' 3 3 2 3	16+1
Sheffield	**Sheffield** v Liverpool	17 Jul 1952	0 2 2 2	6
Edinburgh	World Championship Round	19 Jul 1952	1 3 3 3 2	12
Sheffield	**Sheffield** v Odsal	24 Jul 1952	3 2 3 2	10
Leicester	**Britain** v Overseas	30 Jul 1952	2' 2 2 2 2	12+1
Ashfield	**Scotland** v England	5 Aug 1952	3 3 3 2' 2 2	15+1
Liverpool	England v **Scotland**	11 Aug 1952	2 2 2 3 3 2	14
Fleetwood	August Doubles (with Stan Bradbury 19)	6 Aug 1952	3 1 3 3 2 winners	12
Belle Vue	World Championship Champ Rd.	16 Aug 1952	3 2 3 1 3	12
New Cross	World Championship Champ Rd.	27 Aug 1952	2 3 2 3 1	11
Belle Vue	100 Guineas Trophy	30 Aug 1952	3 3 1 2 1	10
Yarmouth	**Britain** v Overseas	2 Sep 1952	2' 3 3 1' 3 3	15+2
Edinburgh	Scottish Open Riders Final	6 Sep 1952	1 3 2 2 3	11
Wembley	**World Championship Final**	12 Sep 1952	1 0 2 0 1	4
Coventry	All Star Gold Cup Brandonapolis	24 Sep 1952	0 3 3 3 3	12
Belle Vue	100 Guineas Trophy	11 Oct 1952	1 1 2 2 2	8
Ashfield	Ken Le Breton Trophy	14 Oct 1952	E 2 3 1	6
White City	**Scotland** v England	27 May 1953	2 F 3 3 3	11
Edinburgh	Scottish Riders' Champs QR	30 May 1953	2 2 1 2 1	8
Edinburgh	Scottish Riders Champs Final	29 May 1954	2 F 2 0 1	5
Belle Vue	Belle Vue v **Southern Stars**	5 Jun 1954	0 1' 2' 1'	4+3
Coventry	**North** v South	12 Jun 1954	1 1' 2 1'	5+2
Bradford	100 Guinea Trophy	26 Jun 1954	1 1 1 0 F	3
Edinburgh	World Champs QR	10 Jul 1954	3 2 2 3 3	13
Swindon	Parker Trophy	31 Jul 1954	0 3 2 2 3	10

1st in 3 man run off for 4th place in championship decider. Last in decider.

Venue	Event	Date	Scores	Total
Belle Vue	World Championship Semi	14 Aug 1954	3 3 1 2 1	10
Swindon	**Swindon** v Harringay	28 Aug 1954	1' 0 3 2' 3	9+2
West Ham	World Championship Semi	31 Aug 1954	1 2 2 0 1	6
Belle Vue	Best Pairs (with Ron Phillips) 11	11 Sep 1954	2 3 2 F	7
Belle Vue	Second Division Riders Champs	16 Oct 1954	X	0

Cyril Cooper

Venue	Event	Date	Scores	Total
Edinburgh	Scottish Riders Champs	29 May 1954	1 1 0 F 0	2
Edinburgh	World Champs QR	10 Jul 1954	0 0 2 2 1	5
Belle Vue	Supporters' Cup	25 Sep 1954	F E 0 E 0	0
Belle Vue	Second Division Riders Champs	16 Oct 1954	2 2 0 1 0	5

Joe Crowther

Venue	Event	Date	Scores	Total
Stoke	Hanley v **The Scots**	9 Jun 1951	0	0

Track	Event	Date	Scores						Total
Edinburgh	Edinburgh v **Glasgow Select**	19 Jul 1951	2'	3	2'				7+2
Coventry	World Championship Round	21 Jul 1951	0	0	0	0	0		0
Ashfield	Festival Championships	24 Jul 1951	2	0	1	1			4
White City	Festival of Britain Trophy	22 Aug 1951	1	1	0	0	0		2
White City	1952 Tigers v **Ex-Tigers**	26 Mar 1952	1'	1'	2	2			6+2
Aldershot	World Championship Round	31 May 1952	F						0

Bill Dalton

Track	Event	Date	Scores						Total
Coventry	Coventry v **Lancs & Yorks**	2 May 1951	3	2					5
Aldershot	World Championship Round	2 Jun 1951	0	2	0	0	1		3
White City	**Scotland** v England	13 Jun 1951	0	0					0

Bob Fletcher

Track	Event	Date	Scores					Total
Belle Vue	Second Division Riders Champs	16 Oct 1954	2	0	2	1	1	6

Johnny Green

Track	Event	Date	Scores					Total
Rayleigh	World Championship QR 1	30 May 1953	0	E	0	1	2	3
White City	Scottish Riders' Champs QR	17 Jun 1953	1	3	3	1		8
Belle Vue	£500 Gold Cup	11 Jul 1953	3	0	1	2	1	7
Edinburgh	Scottish Riders' Champs Final	25 Jul 1953	0	1	3	1	1	6
Ashfield	**Eagles** v Tigers	28 Jul 1953	3	2				5
Ashfield	Scottish Best Pairs (with Ron Phillips) 18	4 Aug 1952	3	2	1	2 winners		8
Odsal	Northern Riders' Trophy	15 Aug 1953	1	X				1
Coventry	Tournament Topliners Best Pairs*	19 Sep 1953	0	2	0			2
* with Gordon McGregor								
Edinburgh	Scottish Riders' Champs	29 May 1954	2	2	2	2		10
Edinburgh	World Championship QR	10 Jul 1954	2	3	0	0	1	6
Bradford	Casson Trophy	18 Sep 1954	1	1	2	0	1	5
Belle Vue	Second Division Riders Champs	16 Oct 1954	3	2	0	1	2	8

Keith Gurtner

Track	Event	Date	Scores						Total
Brisbane	**Australia** v England	9 Feb 1951							12
Swindon	World Champs Round	2 Jun 1951	0	1	0	0	0		1
Stoke	Hanley v **The Scots**	9 Jun 1951	2	2	2'	2'			8+2
Edinburgh	Best Pairs (with Danny Lee)	30 Jun 1951	3	2	3	3	3		14
Ashfield	**Scotland** v England	3 Jul 1951	3						3
Edinburgh	Scottish Riders' Champs	9 Aug 1951	1	3	2	3	2		11
White City	Festival of Britain Trophy	22 Aug 1951	2	0	3	3	2		10
West Ham	England v **Australia**	28 Aug 1951	0						0
White City	Rest/Scotland v **Scot Australians**	12 Sep 1951	2'	1	2	3			8+1
Ashfield	Ken Le Breton Memorial Trophy	6 Oct 1951	1	3	3	0			7
Brisbane	**Australia** v England	2 Feb 1952	2'	3	3	3	2' 2		15+3
Sydney	**Australia** v England	8 Feb 1952	3	3	3	3	3	3	18
White City	**Scotland** v England	27 May 1952	1	0	1'	2	1	0	5+1
Aldershot	World Championship Round	31 May 1952	3	1	1	2	1		8
Coventry	England v **Scotland**	16 Jun 1952	1	1'	2	0			4+1
Oxford	Britain v **Overseas**	3 Jul 1952	1	0	1	2	0	0	4
Leicester	Britain v **Overseas**	30 Jul 1952	1	0	1	1	0	1	4
Ashfield	**Scotland** v England	5 Aug 1952	0	0					0
Rayleigh	Young England v **Young Overseas**	16 Aug 1952	1	2	2' 1' 0				6+2

Scott Hall

Track	Event	Date	Scores					Total
White City	1952 Tigers v **Ex-Tigers**	26 Mar 1952	1'	0				1+1
Edinburgh	Scottish Riders' Champs QR	30 May 1953	0	0	1	1	0	2
Edinburgh	Scottish Riders' Champs Final	25 Jul 1953	1	F	0	0	1	2
Ashfield	**Eagles** v Tigers	28 Jul 1953	3					3
Edinburgh	Best Pairs	24 Apr 1954	3	1	E	1	0	5

Danny Lee

Venue	Event	Date	Scores						Total
Sheffield	Sheffield v **Division 2 Select**	29 Mar 1951	X	0	0				0
Edinburgh	Best Pairs (with Keith Gurtner)	30 Jun 1951	1	1	2	1	F		5

Bob Lindsay

Venue	Event	Date	Scores			Total
White City	**Scots** v Kiwis	4 Jul 1951	1	0	0	1

Will Lowther

Venue	Event	Date	Scores				Total
White City	1952 Tigers v **Ex-Tigers**	26 Mar 1952	1'	3	2	0	6+1

Gordon McGregor

Venue	Event	Date	Scores						Total
Stoke	Hanley v **The Scots**	9 Jun 1951	3	0	3	3			9
White City	**Scotland** v England	13 Jun 1951	2'	0	0	0	0		2+1
Edinburgh	Best Pairs (with N. Watson)	30 Jun 1951	0	0	0	2	2		4
White City	**Scots** v Kiwis	3 Jul 1951	3	3	3	2			11
Coventry	World Championship Round	22 Jul 1951	2	0	0	2	2		6
Ashfield	Festival Championships	24 Jul 1951	1	2	3	0			6
Odsal	Best Pairs (with K. McKinlay)	4 Aug 1951	2	3	1	1	0		7
Edinburgh	Scottish Riders' Championship Final	9 Aug 1951	2	2	3	3	3		13
Wembley	World Championship Round	16 Aug 1951	2	2	1	0	1		6
Birmingham	World Championship Round	18 Aug 1951	2	2	0	0	0		4
White City	Festival of Britain Trophy	22 Aug 1951	3	3	1	3	3		13
White City	**Rest of Scotland** v Scots Australians	12 Sep 1951	2'	2'	2	1			7+2
Edinburgh	**Scotland** v England	15 Sep 1951	1	0					1
Ashfield	Ken Le Breton Memorial Trophy	6 Oct 1951	0	0	0	3			3
Sydney Sports	New South Wales v **England**	Dec 1951							0
Sydney Show	Australia v **England** 1st Test	5 Jan 1952	1						1
Sydney Sports	Australia v **England** 2nd Test	11 Jan 1952	1	2'	1	1	1		6+1
Sydney Show	Australia v **England** 3rd Test	19 Jan 1952	0	1'	0	0	1		2+1
Sydney	Best Pairs (with Arthur Payne)	26 Jan 1952	Winner						
Brisbane	Australia v **England** 4th Test	2 Feb 1952	1	1					2
Sydney	Australia v **England 5th** Test	8 Feb 1952	3	2	1	0			6
White City	1952 Tigers v **Ex-Tigers**	26 Mar 1952	2	2	2	3			9
Stoke	World Championship Round	19 Jul 1952	2	3	2	3	1		11
Wimbledon	World Championship Champ Rd	11 Aug 1952	2	0	2	2	1		7
Belle Vue	World Championship Champ Rd.	16 Aug 1952	1	2	1	2	0		6
Belle Vue	E O Spence Memorial Trophy	4 Oct 1952	1	3	2	2	0		8
Ashfield	Ken Le Breton Trophy	14 Oct 1952	2	2	3	3			10
White City	**Scotland** v England	27 May 1953	2'	2'	0	2'			6+3
Ashfield	2nd Division Event	9 Jun 1953	2	2	2	3			9
Ashfield	Wasps v **McGregor's Clan**	16 Jun 1953	3	3	3	3			12
White City	Scottish Riders' Champs QR	17 Jun 1953	3	3	3	1	3		13
Ashfield	**Scottish Stars** v Dominions	23 Jun 1953	2	1	3	1	1'		8+1
Ashfield	Red Devils v **Dandies**	7 Jul 1953	3	3	3	3			12
Coventry	World Championship QR 2	11 Jul 1953	2	3	E	0	2		7
Wolverhampton	England v **Scotland**	14 Jul 1953	2'	1	1	0	1	0	5+1
White City	**The Scots** v New Zealand	22 Jul 1953	0	3	1	1	0		4
Edinburgh	Scottish Riders' Champs Final	25 Jul 1953	2	0	1	0	1		4
Ashfield	Scottish Best Pairs (with Noel Watson)	4 Aug 1953	2	1	2	2			7
Bradford	World Championship QR 3	22 Aug 1953	0	0	0	1	0		1
Birmingham	World Championship QR 3	26 Aug 1953	0	0	1	0	0		1
Coventry	Tournament Topliners Best Pairs*	19 Sep 1953	2	1'	1				4+1
Edinburgh	**Scotland** v England	22 Sep 1953	2'	F	1'	3	2'	1'	9+4
Ashfield	Ken Le Breton Trophy	29 Sep 1953	3	F	3	1			7
Belle Vue	Belle Vue v **Scotland**	10 Oct 1953	3	0	1				4
Edinburgh	Scottish Riders Champs	29 May 1954	3	1	0	1	1		6
Edinburgh	World Championship QR	10 Jul 1954	3	2	2	2	0		9

* with Johnny Green

133

Tommy Miller

Wimbledon	Wimbledon v Division II Stars	5 Apr 1954	3	1	2	0			6
Edinburgh	Best Pairs	24 Apr 1954	2	3	3	F	3		11
Edinburgh	Scottish Riders Championship	29 May 1954	3	2	3	3	3		14
Ipswich	Revett Cup	3 Jun 1954	3	3	2	0	2		10
Belle Vue	Belle Vue v **Southern Stars**	5 Jun 1954	2	3	1'	3			9+1
Coventry	**North** v South	12 Jun 1954	0	1'	1	0			2+1
Harringay	Television Trophy (Scotland)	14 Jun 1954	1	1	0	0			2
Bradford	100 Guinea Trophy	26 Jun 1954	2	2	0	2	0		6
Ipswich	World Championship QR	1 Jul 1954	3	3	2	3	3		14

Gordon Mitchell

Edinburgh	Best Pairs	24 Apr 1954	2	2	1	0	0		5

Ron Phillips

Rayleigh	World Championship QR 1	30 May 1953	0	1	2	1	0		4
Ashfield	2nd Division Event	9 Jun 1953	3	3	3	1			10
White City	Scottish Riders' Champs QR	11 Jun 1953	2	1	2	1	2		8
Ashfield	**Wasps** v Clan	16 Jun 1953	3	3	2	3			11
Ashfield	Scottish Stars v **Dominions**	23 Jun 1953	2	2	1	F	3		8
Ashfield	**Red Devils** v Campbell's Dandies	7 Jul 1953	2	3	2	2			9
Edinburgh	Scottish Riders' Champs Final	25 Jul 1953	0	3	2	2	2		9
Scottish Best Pairs	(with Johnny Green) 18 winners	4 Aug 1953	1	3	3	3			10
Ashfield	Ken Le Breton Trophy	29 Sep 1953	2	2	3	2			9
Edinburgh	Scottish Riders Championship	29 May 1954	0	3	2	2	3		10
Edinburgh	World Champs QR	10 Jul 1954	2	1	2	1	2		8
Belle Vue	Best Pairs (with Derick Close) 11	11 Sep 1954	1	0	1	2			4
Bradford	Casson Trophy	18 Sep 1954	0	2	1	2	1		6
Belle Vue	Supporters' Trophy	24 Sep 1954	0	0	0	1	0		1
Belle Vue (Res)	Second Division Riders Champs	16 Oct 1954	2	0	3				5

Bluey Scott

Aldershot	World Championship Round	31 May 1952	1	0	0	0	F		1
Oxford	World Championship Round	28 May 1953	0	F	1	0	0		1
Edinburgh	Scottish Riders' Championship QR	30 May 1953	0	1	0	3	0		4
Belle Vue	Belle Vue v **Southern Stars**	5 Jun 1954	1	0					1
Edinburgh	Scottish Riders' Championship	28 May 1954	1	F	2	3	3		9
Coventry	World Championship QR	10 Jul 1954	2	0	1	1	0		4

Jimmy Tannock

Edinburgh	Scottish Riders' Championship QR	30 May 1953	1	1	0	1	0		3
Ashfield	**Scottish Stars** v Dominions	23 Jun 1953	DNR						
Ashfield	Ken Le Breton Trophy	29 Sep 1953	1	1	0	1			3

Noel Watson

Newcastle	Newcastle v **Frank Hodgson's Select**	11 Sep 1950	2	0	0	1		3
Paramatta	Trial Meeting Probables v Possibles	15 Nov 1950						9
Sydney	**Overseas** v Royale v Sports Ground	18 Nov 1950						9
Sydney	Individual	25 Nov 1950	No Points					
Sydney Sp.	Individual	1 Dec 1950	No Points					
Sydney	Individual	2 Dec 1950	No Points					
Parramatta	**Parramatta** v Overseas	6 Dec 1950						8
Paramatta	**Parramatta** v Newcastle	13 Dec 1950						6
Sydney	**Australia** v England 1st[t] Test	16 Dec 1950	0					0
Paramatta	**Parramatta** v Bathurst	20 Dec 1950						7
Sydney Sp.	New South Wales Champs	22 Dec 1950						5
Parramatta	Individual	26 Dec 1950	No Points					
Parramatta	Best Pairs (with Don Lawson) winners 15	3 Jan 1951						
Sydney	Australian Three Lap Championship	6 Jan 1951						2

Venue	Event	Date						Total
Sydney	Australian Four Lap Championship	12 Jan 1951						0
Sydney Sp.	Sports Ground v **Royale**	3 Feb 1951						5
Paramatta	**Parramatta** v Newcastle (night)	3 Feb 1951						6
Sydney Sp.	Spartans v **Lions**	Feb 1951						7
Stoke	Hanley v **The Scots**	9 Jun 1951	0	0	0			0
Edinburgh	Best Pairs (with G. McGregor)	30 Jun 1951	2	3	2	1	0	8
Stoke	World Championship Round	21 Jul 1951	2	3	3	0	2	10
Edinburgh	Scottish Riders' Champs	9 Aug 1951	2	1	2	1	1	7
New Cross	World Championship Round	15 Aug 1951	0	X	1	2	1	4
Wembley	World Championship Round	16 Aug 1951	0	1	3	2	0	6
White City	Rest/Scotland v **Scots Australians**	12 Sep 1951	0	0	2	2		4
Ashfield	Ken Le Breton Trophy	6 Oct 1951	2	3	3	X		7
Sydney Sports	Home v **Overseas**	11.1951						4
Sydney Show	Open	11.1951						
Sydney Show	**Australia** v England 1st Test	5 Jan 1952	1	1' 2'		1' 2'		7+4
Sydney Sports	**Australia** v England 2nd Test	11 Jan 1952	1					1
Sydney Show	**Australia** v England 3rd Test	19 Jan 1952	0	0		3	3 2'	8+1
Sydney Sports	**Australia** v England	8 Feb 1952	X	1' 0	3	3 1		8+1
Ipswich	World Championship Round	29 May 1952	2	3	3	3	3	14
Stoke	Britain v **Overseas**	15 May 1952	0	0	0	0	0 1	1
Oxford	World Championship Round	10 Jul 1952	2	0	1	0	0	3
Edinburgh	World Championship Round	19 Jul 1952	1	2	1	0	1	5
Leicester	Britain v **Overseas**	30 Jul 1952	3	1' 0				4+1
Rayleigh	Young England v **Young Overseas**	16 Aug 1952	2'	2	3	1		8+1
Belle Vue	100 Guineas Trophy	30 Aug 1952	1	2	3	0	3	9*
Edinburgh	Scottish Open Riders Final	6 Sep 1952	3	2	3	ef	3	11
Belle Vue	100 Guineas Trophy	11 Oct 1952	1	3	0	1	0	5
Ashfield	Ken Le Breton Trophy	14 Oct 1952	1	3	2	2		8
Rayleigh	World Championship Qualifier	30 May 1953	3	3	2	3	1	12
Oxford	World Championship Round Decider (SH)	11 Jun 1953	4th place in run off					
Ashfield	Wasps v **Clan**	16 Jun 1953	2	3	2	3		10
White City	Scottish Riders' Championship QR	17 Jun 1953	0	0	0	2	2	4
Ashfield	Scottish Stars v **Dominions**	23 Jun 1953	3	0	2	2	1	8
Stoke	World Championships QR 2	11 Jul 1953	2	1	3	0	1	7
Edinburgh	World Championship QR 2	18 Jul 1953	0	0	0	0	0	0
Edinburgh	Scottish Riders' Championship Final	25 Jul 1953	0	2	N	2	N	4
Ashfield	Scottish Best Pairs (with Gordon McGregor)	4 Aug 1953	3	2	0	1		6

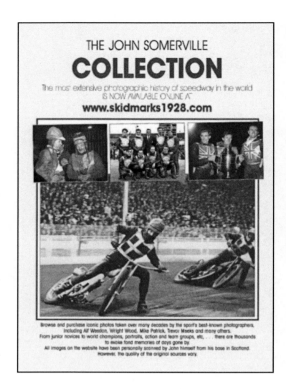

My Crazy Speedway World by Bert Harkins

"Here we are folks, after many months of being stuck to my computer keyboard, I finally finished my autobiography having bashed out every word, dot and comma along the way. It covers my early days growing up in Glasgow, to cycle speedway, road racing, speedway and life after I had hung up my white boots and tartan leathers. This is the story of a wandering Speedway Scotsman and I hope that you enjoy it."

Bert Harkins

Published in February 2018. Now available @ £16.95

Order direct from the publishers: London League Publications Ltd, for just £16.50 post free in the UK. Visit www.llpshop.co.uk for credit card orders or write to (cheques payable to London League Publications Ltd): PO Box 65784, London NW2 9NS. Also available on Amazon, AbeBooks, EBay and as an E-Book on Amazon for Kindle.
Or order from any bookshop. ISBN: 9781909885165. 252 pages with lots of photos.

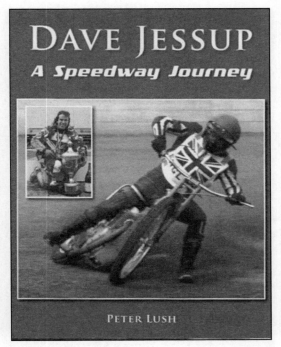

When the Lions Roared: From 1929 to 1956, the Wembley Lions were the glamour team in British speedway. They won 10 League Championships, the National Trophy four times and the London Cup on nine occasions. Three Wembley riders won the World Championship: Lionel Van Praag, Tommy Price and Freddie Williams. This book covers from 1929 to 1971, but looks in more detail at the post-war period. With a foreword by former Wembley captain Bert Harkins, this is a book for every speedway fan.

Published in 2016 @ £14.95. Order direct from the publishers: London League Publications Ltd, for just £14.50 post free in the UK. Visit www.llpshop.co.uk for credit card orders or write to (cheques payable to London League Publications Ltd): PO Box 65784, London NW2 9NS. Also available on Amazon and Abe Books, and as an E-Book on Amazon for Kindle. 264 page paperback. ISBN: 9781909885110

Dave Jessup - A Speedway Journey

Dave Jessup was one of the top British speedway riders in the 1970s and 1980s. His achievements in the sport include: Winning the World Team Cup five times; Winning the World Best Pairs; Runner-up in the 1980 World Championship Final; British Champion in 1980; Over 100 appearances for England; Team manager for England, including two World Team Cup Finals.

When he retired from speedway, he was able to develop his participation in golf. For three years he played for the senior England Amateur team, making him a dual-sports international.

Based on extensive research and interviews, this well-illustrated, authorised biography will be of interest to all speedway fans.

Published in 2020 @ £14.95. Order direct from the publishers: London League Publications Ltd, for just £14.50 post free in the UK. Visit www.llpshop.co.uk for credit card orders or write to (cheques payable to London League Publications Ltd): PO Box 65784, London NW2 9NS. Also available on Amazon, AbeBooks, EBay +and as an E-Book on Amazon for Kindle. 200 page paperback. ISBN: 9781909885240.

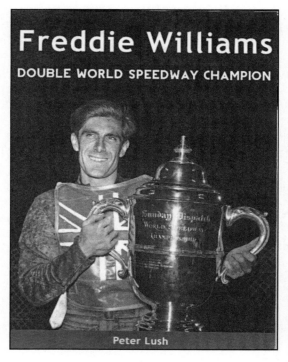

Freddie Williams was the first British speedway rider to win the World Championship twice. He won the title at Wembley in 1950, aged just 24 and was the youngest ever World Champion at that time. He was in only his third season as a member of the Wembley Lions team. He was runner-up to Jack Young in 1952 before again winning the title in 1953.

His achievement was equalled by Peter Craven in 1962, but not surpassed until Tai Woffinden won his third title in 2018.

This authorised biography covers Freddie's life from his early days in Port Talbot, where he developed his skills riding grass track races. He signed for the Wembley Lions in 1946, and stayed with them for the rest of his career. He became a key member of the team that dominated the sport until 1954 and retired as a rider in 1956. With Wembley, he won the National League five times, the National Trophy twice and the London Cup five times. He rode for England 39 times.

He became manager of the Wembley Lions when the team returned to league racing in 1970 and 1971. He was President of the Veteran Speedway Riders Association in 1981, and became a member of the Welsh Sports Hall of Fame in 1998. He presented the trophies at the Speedway Grand Prix in Cardiff in August 2012 and did much else to support the sport. He died in January 2013 at the age of 86. The book also covers the sporting careers of his brothers Eric and Ian Williams, who were both distinguished speedway riders in their own right, and of Freddie's wife Pat, their children and grandchildren. A book that every speedway fan will enjoy!

Published in March 2019 @ £13.95. ISBN: 9781909885219
160 page paperback illustrated with over 100 photos.
Order direct from the publishers: London League Publications Ltd, for just £13.50 post free in the UK. Visit www.llpshop.co.uk for credit card orders or write to (cheques payable to London League Publications Ltd): PO Box 65784, London NW2 9NS. Also available on Amazon, AbeBooks, EBay and as an E-Book on Amazon for Kindle.

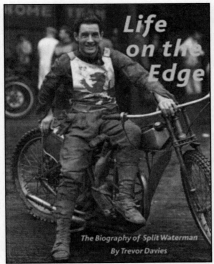

The Biography of Split Waterman
By Trevor Davies

Split Waterman was one of the stars of Speedway's boom period of the 1940s and early 1950s. His success on the track, film star good looks and charismatic personality made him a household name in the national press.

Having watched Speedway before the Second World War, Squire Francis Waterman – soon to become known as 'Split' – was injured in action and then posted to the Royal Electrical Mechanical Engineering (REME) base at Pozzuoli near Naples. It was here that Corporal Waterman began to develop his speedway talent on the rough and ready Army track at the Vomero Stadium.

After the War, many Armed Forces motorcyclists sought fame and fortune in Speedway. Split was one of the most successful. His 15 year racing career began with the famous Wembley Lions. After developing his skills in 1947, he was selected for England, beat many of the top stars including the legendary Vic Duggan and reached the British Riders Championship Final in 1948.

In 1950 he joined the Harringay Racers for a then record transfer fee. In the early 1950s he was twice runner-up in the World Championship Final, and ended Jack Parker's domination of the Golden Helmet match race series. He also regularly represented England. After Harringay closed in 1954, he rode for West Ham for a year, then returned to Wembley. In 1957, he joined Southampton, then rode for Wimbledon, New Cross, Ipswich and Belle Vue before retiring in 1962.

This authorised biography offers an insight into the real Split Waterman, on-and-off the track. It includes memories from riders who rode with and against him, speedway officials and supporters. It also outlines the facts regarding his brushes with the law. When he died in October 2019, his passing was recognised with full page obituaries in *The Times* and the *Daily Telegraph*, newspapers which usually barely mention Speedway.   This well illustrated book will be of interest to all speedway fans. The author, Trevor Davies, wrote a groundbreaking history of speedway in the Armed Forces during and after the Second World War and worked as a journalist for the *Speedway Star*.

Published in April 2021 @ £14.95. ISBN: 9781909885257
Book details: 144 page paperback illustrated with over 50 photos.
It is available to order from the publisher at www.llpshop.co.uk , on Amazon, AbeBooks and EBay, and can be ordered from any bookshop. An E-Book for Kindle users is also available on Amazon.
The book can be ordered from the London League Publications Ltd website, www.llpshop.co.uk for £14.50 post free in the UK.

Fascinating story of the sport's early days in Glasgow by Jim Henry.
Currently only available as an E-Book for Kindle @ £4.95.